What I Learned from My Cat

Chicken Soup for the Soul: What I Learned from My Cat
101 Tales of Our Favorite Felines
Amy Newmark

Published by Chicken Soup for the Soul, LLC www.chickensoup.com
Copyright ©2025 by Chicken Soup for the Soul, LLC. All Rights Reserved.

No part of this publication may be reproduced, stored in a retrieval system or transmitted in any form or by any means, electronic, mechanical, photocopying, recording or otherwise, without the written permission of the publisher.

CSS, Chicken Soup for the Soul, and its Logo and Marks are trademarks of Chicken Soup for the Soul, LLC.

The publisher gratefully acknowledges the many individuals who granted Chicken Soup for the Soul permission to reprint the cited material.

Front cover courtesy of iStockphoto.com (©pwollinga)
Back cover and interior image created by Daniel Zaccari using Adobe Firefly from the prompt "profile of woman and cat facing each other with green field background"

Photo of Amy Newmark courtesy of Susan Morrow at SwickPix

Cover and Interior by Daniel Zaccari

Publisher's Cataloging-in-Publication Data

Names: Newmark, Amy, editor.
Title: Chicken soup for the soul : what I learned from my cat , 101 tales of our favorite felines / Amy Newmark.
Description: Cos Cob, CT: Chicken Soup for the Soul, LLC, 2025.
Identifiers: LCCN: 2025931929 | ISBN: 978-1-61159-121-7 (print) | 978-1-61159-355-6 (ebook)
Subjects: LCSH Cats--Anecdotes. | Cat owners--Anecdotes. | Human-animal relationships--Anecdotes. | Humor. | BISAC PETS / Essays & Narratives | PETS / Cats / General | HUMOR / Topic / Animals
Classification: LCC SF445.5 .C552 2025 | DDC 636.8--dc23

Library of Congress Control Number: 2025931929

PRINTED IN THE UNITED STATES OF AMERICA
on acid∞free paper

30 29 28 27 26 25   01 02 03 04 05 06 07 08 09 10 11

What I Learned from My Cat

101 Tales of Our Favorite Felines

Amy Newmark

Chicken Soup for the Soul, LLC
Cos Cob, CT

Changing your world one story at a time®
www.chickensoup.com

Table of Contents

❶
~Cats and Comedy~

1. Are You Sure You Want a Dog? *Victoria Lorrekovich-Miller* 1
2. Snickers, *Monica Lawson* 3
3. Walking Your Cat Can Be a Drag, *Rachel Remick* 5
4. The Invisible Force Field, *Pamela Dunaj* 8
5. Crotchety Cat, *Leslie C. Schneider* 10
6. Baby's First Tooth, *Kristi Adams* 13
7. Home Remedy, *Laura McKenzie* 16
8. A Battle of Wills, *Manley Fisher* 19
9. Chance the Darkness, *Alexes Lester* 22

❷
~Clever Cats~

10. Feline to the Rescue, *Rita Durrett* 27
11. A Bitter Pill, *Donna L. Roberts* 30
12. And the Rains Came, *Leslie C. Schneider* 32
13. A Girl Named Joseph, *Leeann Lynton* 35
14. The Signal, *Robert Grayson* 39
15. Dr. Callie, *Mary Grant Dempsey* 43
16. Herding Cats, *Sheila Hollihan-Elliot* 44
17. The Power of the Purr, *Lynn Hendricks* 47
18. Cat-a-combs, *Timothy Nipko* 50
19. Neighborhood Visitor, *Heather Hartmann* 52

❸
~Saving Kitty~

20. The Power of the Purr, *Chip Kirkpatrick* 56
21. Meow Loudly, *Charlotte Louise Nystrom* 60
22. Fostering Joy, *Audrey Wick* 63
23. Patched Up, *Marsha Porter* 65
24. How I Made Three Cats Happy, *Helen Krasner* 68
25. Unexpected Blessings, *Laurie Heard* 72
26. Urgent Care, *James R. Coffey* 75
27. Can't Judge a Cat by His Cover, *Rosie Sorenson* 78
28. Fearsome Feral to Pampered Pet, *Joan Friday McKechnie* 82
29. Rehoming Tom and Jerry, *Helen Krasner* 86

❹
~What a Character~

30. Hidden Treasures, *Robert Grayson* 91
31. The Cat with Six Names, *Ramona Scarborough* 94
32. As Cunning as a Fox, *Karen Storey* 98
33. Tail or No Tail, *Jill Haymaker* 101
34. Taming the Tank, *Tracy Crump* 104
35. Never Name a Cat After a Natural Disaster,
    Barbara A. Besteni 107
36. The Cat Who Wouldn't Squeak, *Eva Carter* 111
37. A Spa Day, *Irene Maran* 115
38. Barry on Board, *Laird Long* 117
39. Wait for Me! *Brenda Leppington* 121

❺
~Changed by the Cat~

40. Respect, *Judy Kellersberger* 125
41. The Twinkie Effect, *Laurie Spilovoy Cover* 127
42. Life Lessons from My Cat, *Betsy S. Franz* 130

Table of Contents

43. A Senior Cat and the Value of Memories,
    Lindsay Detwiler 133
44. A Cat's Love Throughout the Years, *Liz Palmer* 136
45. Cute Kitties and Barbie Dolls, *Jessica Lorin Wood* 139
46. Belle, *John Danko* 142
47. Two Lives — One Kitten, *Susan Traugh* 145
48. A Scrap of Forgiveness, *Glenda Ferguson* 149
49. My Furry Assistant, *Julia Gousseva* 152

❻
~Quirky Cats~

50. Chloe and the Beanie Babies, *Carol Gentry Allen* 156
51. Trading Stuff, *Candace Sams* 158
52. Kitty Didn't Attack People, *Elton A. Dean* 161
53. A Hairy Problem, *Ellen Fannon* 163
54. Matching Agendas, *Heather Harshman* 165
55. Kat in Wonderland, *Kathleen Gerard* 169
56. Shadow, *Roger A. Wilber* 173
57. George and His Hairy Snake, *Janet Wells* 176
58. Adventures in Cat Food, *Dorenda Crager Watson* 180
59. If He Only Had a Thumb, *Billie Holladay Skelley* 182

❼
~Learning to Love the Cat~

60. The Gentleman Cat, *Annette M. Clayton* 187
61. I'm a Dog Person, *Rebecca Ruballos* 190
62. Feeling Fine Feline, *Laurel L. Shannon* 193
63. The Feral Cat and the Family Dog, *Kendra Phillips* 196
64. Petal's Budding Romance, *Jill Berni* 200
65. Mimi Made Me a Cat Lady, *Mary F. Oves* 203
66. The Cat Plan, *Gwen Swick* 206
67. There's a Problem, *Marie-Lynn Hammond* 209
68. Living in Harmony, *Jodi M. Webb* 213

69. Sometimes the Best Revenge Is Living, *T. Jensen Lacey* 216
70. A Cat Hater's Tale, *Diana Derringer* 220

❽
~Meant to Be~

71. Samantha, *Pamela K. Knudsen* 224
72. Unexpected Love, *Amber Curtis* 228
73. The Story of Poppy, *Artie DeMonte* 230
74. Formula for the Perfect Number of Cats,
    Mandy Shunnarah 233
75. A Cat Named Zubenelgenubi, *Louise Butler* 237
76. Going Through Hell? Keep Going! *Jon M. Ketcham* 241
77. Eight Lives to Go, *Angie Blackledge* 243
78. He'll Stand on Your Shoulders, *Chip Kirkpatrick* 246
79. Lucky Break, *Christine Grecsek* 250
80. The Cat Who Adopted Us, *Jeffree Wyn Itrich* 253
81. A Perfect Match, *Wendy Joyce Patterson* 257

❾
~My Very Good, Very Bad Cat~

82. My Betrayal, *Elizabeth Brown* 260
83. The Jumper, *Victoria Lorrekovich-Miller* 262
84. Klepto-Kitty, *Barb Miller* 266
85. Norman Bates, *S.R. Karfelt* 268
86. The Bandit and the Burglar, *Sandy Wright* 272
87. Our Last Cat, and That's Final, *Garrett Bauman* 274
88. Tempting Fate, *Thomas Canfield* 278
89. The Reign of King Louis, *Dave Bachmann* 281

~Opening Hearts~

90. Remembering Sir Lancelot, *Christina Ryan Claypool* 285
91. Baby Steps, *Diane Stark* 288
92. Neighborhood Glue, *Melissa Hart* 292
93. Becoming a Cat Person, *Carissa Ann Lynch* 296
94. One More Surprise, *Mary DeVries* 300
95. Puffy, *Marie-Eve Bernier* 303
96. Baby Nurse, *Rebecca Fischer-Smith* 306
97. Mom's Farewell Wish, *Kay L. Campbell* 310
98. Foster Fail, *Deb Stark* 313
99. The Kitten Who Never Grew, *Marie-Lynn Hammond* 316
100. She'll Wait for Me, *Nancy C. Anderson* 320
101. I Know She Loves Me, *Stephanie Luevano-Powell* 324

Meet Our Contributors 326
Meet Amy Newmark 337
Thank You 339

Chapter 1

Cats and Comedy

Are You Sure You Want a Dog?

> Cats are something else. Once they accept
> you into their life, it's forever.
> ~André Brink

I grabbed the next application and called out a name. A petite woman in her early forties raised her hand. I approached her and introduced myself as the adoption counselor who would help her find her new companion.

We sat at a table, and I glanced down at the questionnaire.

"Okay, let's get started," I said. "I see that you're looking for a puppy today at the shelter."

"Yes, but one that is potty-trained."

"Okay, we can't guarantee that in a puppy. Perhaps an older dog would be better."

"No, I'd like a puppy. One that's not too big, though. Or too small."

"Okay."

"Also, I want a dog that won't bark at people or other animals or when the doorbell rings."

"I see."

"I don't want a dog who pulls on a leash. Better yet, I'd like a dog that doesn't really like to go for walks. Do you have some of those?"

"I'm pretty sure most of our dogs would enjoy going for walks."

"Also, I can't stand a dog that drools, so it should have tight lips."

Cats and Comedy |

I also don't want a bad-smelling dog because that's just gross. And absolutely no begging at the table."

"Well, a smelly dog can be bathed. A beggar can be trained. But drooling? That's probably not something you can fix. Is there anything else I should know before I make a recommendation?"

"Uh, let's see. I'd like a nice dog but not one that is overly needy. Sometimes, I like my own space."

"Is that it?"

"I think so," she said.

"Well, you are in luck. I have the perfect girl for you. Her name is Lucy. Follow me."

When we entered the small room, the woman looked at me with confusion on her face. "I don't understand. That's a cat."

"Yes, it turns out that your perfect dog is actually a cat," I said to her.

It took a moment for this to sink in, but after we talked some more, she agreed that Lucy did check all her boxes.

So, Lucy found her forever home that evening, and her new owner found her perfect dog—who just happened to be a cat!

— Victoria Lorrekovich-Miller —

Snickers

Laughter is a tranquilizer with no side effects.
~Arnold Glasow

I called my husband after I left work to confirm that he had picked up our cat Snickers from the veterinarian's office. It was nothing serious, just a regular check-up for our elderly fur-buddy.

When I walked into the house through the mudroom door, I fully expected Snickers to be pacing back and forth beside his empty food dish.

"Eldon, where's Snickers?" I asked.

"He's under our bed, hiding there since I let him out of the crate," Eldon explained.

"Hmmm," I muttered. "Strange. He never goes under our bed."

I knelt down at the foot of the bed, pulled up the quilt, and peered into the dark space. Snickers stared back at me.

I scooted him toward me, stood up, and faced my gentle, giant kitty. I stared at the gentle giant's face inches from mine.

"Eldon, this is not Snickers!"

He stood beside us and took the cat from my arms.

"This is not Snickers," he shouted, staring into the cat's eyes.

A quick call to the veterinarian's office confirmed that they had given us a Snickers look-alike.

We returned the sweet imposter to the vet's office and traded him for our actual gentle giant.

Just as we were about to walk out the door with the real Snickers, the vet reached out her hand and handed each of us a small gift. We got to the car and unwrapped them. We laughed all the way home while enjoying our mini Snickers bars.

— Monica Lawson —

Walking Your Cat Can Be a Drag

Against the assault of laughter, nothing can stand.
~Mark Twain

A few years ago, my roommate Lisa and I rescued two cats and named them Gish and Blackie. Although I was fully invested in my new status as a cat mommy, as a former "dog person" I shared my disappointment with Lisa that cats couldn't be taught commands such as "sit" and "stay" and perform tricks like "give me a paw" and "roll over." I also liked the bonding and the exercise that you get from taking a dog for a long walk and regretted that I'd never be able to do that with our cats.

"Not true," Lisa said, assuring me that cats could absolutely be trained to perform tricks. And, she added, "I once saw a man walking a cat on a leash through my neighborhood when I was a kid." After witnessing that, she told me, she'd always dreamed of one day owning a cat that she could walk. After our conversation, she became determined to make Blackie and Gish those cats.

She went out and bought the necessary accessories: cute leashes and tiny harnesses. But when she draped one over Blackie's head, slid his little feet through the loops, and clicked the fastener, he promptly stiffened and fell over onto his side like a fainting goat.

Undaunted, Lisa said, "He always follows Gish's lead. If he sees her with the harness on, then he'll feel better about it."

Gish, however, had witnessed Blackie's bondage and was hiding under Lisa's bed. When even her favorite cat toy on a stick failed to lure her out, the walking plan was shelved for the evening, with Lisa believing it was just a temporary setback. She was determined to get those cats outside, walking on leashes.

"Maybe they don't like the feeling of the harnesses against their skin," Lisa reasoned. She bought them little sweaters to wear underneath the harnesses.

The following day, we each held a cat while Lisa slipped on their sweaters and harnesses. Blackie flopped onto his side again, and Gish froze in shock.

Lisa got the idea to sprinkle treats along the carpet. Eventually, the cats became reanimated and gobbled them up. She did this for a week, progressing to attaching the leashes and giving them a little tug, coaxing the cats to walk toward the treats. That resulted in both cats falling over in protest.

Lisa persisted, and within another week, the cats were walking in a straight line to and from the treats while Lisa held their leashes.

"I think they're ready," she announced. We put on their little sweaters and harnesses, leashed them up, and opened the door. Lisa dropped some treats, and Gish stepped tentatively onto the porch and ate one. Soon, Blackie followed her out, and we were dropping treats down the short flight of stairs and onto the path that led to the sidewalk. They were moving slowly, but the cats were indeed walking on leashes.

"Let's just go to the end of the block and back," Lisa said. "I don't want to get overly confident on our first day."

We walked slowly, glancing back at the cats every now and then, noticing that, each time we did, they would stop moving.

"I think we're making them self-conscious," Lisa said.

"Right," I agreed. "Cats are independent."

We decided to stop checking on them and made it halfway down the block with nary a tug in protest. There was a child walking with her mother across the street, and she stopped to point.

"Mommy!" she exclaimed. "What is that lady doing to that cat?"

Quite pleased with herself, Lisa smiled and waved at the two of them. I turned around to marvel at her impressive display of cat training and immediately grabbed Lisa by the arm, stopping her.

"Uh, Leese?"

She turned as well and gasped.

Both cats were on their sides, purring contentedly, with bits of sweater fabric in their wake. We'd apparently dragged them the entire way down the sidewalk, their sweaters providing them with a nice cushion for their ride.

—Rachel Remick—

The Invisible Force Field

Cats seem to go on the principle that it never does any harm to ask for what you want.
~Joseph Wood Krutch

I was relaxing on my bed, watching an interesting documentary about black crows. The TV was about two feet away from the foot of my bed. Jake, my muscular, twenty-five-pound cat, hopped onto the bed to watch the crows with me.

At first, he sat upright, with his head cocked in curiosity. But when the camera zoomed in on two of the crows, Jake dropped onto his belly, assuming his lethal predator hunting mode: His ears were folded back and his tail was twitching as he locked onto his enemies with a laser-like focus. How dare those crows openly strut about in front of him!

Suddenly, both crows turned, faced the camera, and began loudly squawking directly at Jake. The audacity! Jake leapt from the foot of the bed, launching himself like a missile directly at the TV screen. The mighty warrior wasn't deterred when his head bounced off the screen and he tumbled to the floor. He merely hopped back onto the foot of the bed and returned to attack mode. After all, the offending crows were still there, squawking even louder. It was abundantly clear they were taunting him, the fierce warrior.

However, before launching his second attack, Jake solicited my assistance. This time, while in hunt mode — flat on his belly, ears flat against his head, tail snapping — he turned his head and meowed at me repeatedly, as if he was imploring me to notice: "Look, the crows are still right there! But there's an invisible force field protecting them that I cannot penetrate — but you, as a human, can!"

The two crows continued to cruelly mock his valiant efforts, squawking even louder. Jake decided that the situation was too dire to wait another moment. He would bravely lead the second charge without human assistance. Compelled by the crisis at hand, he launched himself directly at the offending, audacious crows again, bravely risking life and limb to penetrate the invisible force field. Again, like in a cartoon, his head bounced off the TV screen, and he tumbled to the floor in defeat a second time.

I admired the great warrior spirit that he displayed despite his repeated defeats. So, I gave him a toy mouse infused with catnip to distract him from the offending crows and reward his valiant efforts. Happily, he launched several successful toy mouse attacks, and his wounded warrior spirit was fully restored.

— Pamela Dunaj —

Crotchety Cat

Each cat is a singular being — a pulsing centre of the universe — with this colour eyes, this length and density of fur, this palate of preferences, habits and dispositions. Each with his own idiosyncrasies.
~David Wood

Bean was alone in a huge cage, the last kitten of her litter. She dashed from corner to corner, stopping on each perch and imploring us with the sweetest little meow we'd ever heard. It was so sweet that, in my besotted state, I was able to instantly translate it into English: "Oh, please take me home. You won't be sorry. Honest."

I was ready to fold, but Bill was with me and he usually keeps me sensible. We already had two cats, a dog, two sons, and an aquarium filled with tropical fish. So, plenty of pets.

Then, I heard a defeated sigh beside me. "Oh, go ahead."

I brightened. "Really?"

"I guess."

We called her Bonanza Jellybean after the character in a book I'd just read and because of her jellybean colors. Bean, for short.

At first, the kids and the other pets loved her, but it didn't take long for us to realize that those saccharine meows had been a ploy. Under that saintly exterior lurked a very black heart, and she displayed her disgust for mankind without playing favorites. She scratched, she bit, and she made demonic sounds. No one was safe.

Cats and Comedy

Still, she was so pretty that people chose to ignore the crazy look in her eyes, even when she was a full-grown twelve pounds.

"Don't touch her!" I'd cry.

"It's okay," they'd unfailingly say. "I'm a cat person."

Then there would be blood.

But as our lawyer friend observed as he held his maimed hand under the faucet, without a legal leg to stand on, "I can't say you didn't warn me."

We seldom left town because only one place would board her, and only because I was friends with the owner. As I'd carry Bean in, the staff would start singing the Elton John song, "The B*tch Is Back."

When we arrived to pick her up, her litter box was invariably full, her food bowl empty, and the staff was wearing leather gauntlets.

It was a tumultuous kitten-hood. She was so mean that we'd begun to believe she might actually be crazy, and we discussed giving her to a farmer we knew who kept cats in his barn to control rodents. Maybe killing tiny, furry creatures all day would cheer her up.

Before we could move forward with that plan, though, she changed. She left her cat bed and decided to sleep with Bill and me. One of us always had at least one weeping scratch — she didn't like it when we turned over — but we weren't about to tell her no. After all, this might be the beginning of a truce of sorts.

In those days, Bill snored — and I mean snored. One night, he'd just dozed off, and I lay there trying to get to sleep before the din began. If I could fall asleep fast enough, I'd manage a few hours before his snoring woke me, but he began immediately.

Bean had been snoozing in a furrow of covers between us when she heard him, and I saw her head pop up with interest. I grabbed the water sprayer I kept on my nightstand for a Bean emergency.

On Bill's next noisy inhale, she jumped to her feet. I put my finger on the sprayer trigger. On his exhale, she hurried up the bed to look into his face, her expression fierce but fascinated. I pointed the sprayer in her direction.

Then, she started imitating him with loud, accurate snoring sounds. It was so cute! I think I even said, "Awww."

But things soon became ridiculous, for as soon as Bean began her imitation, the noise roused Bill, and he stopped snoring. Bean became quiet again and waited, studying Bill's face with excitement.

In the silence, Bill fell deeply asleep again, and his snoring resumed. Bean chimed in again, and Bill roused again and stopped snoring. So, Bean stopped, too.

This game of copycat continued for a good three minutes. By that time, I was laughing hard and had awakened Bill. I told him what happened, and after we'd laughed together, he turned onto his side. Bean retreated to the furrow in the covers, and the rest of the night was peaceful.

Although Bean slept between us for the rest of her life, the incident of synchronized snoring was never repeated. But Bean had found her people, and though she continued to lose her temper, she never hurt us again.

She saved her hostility for the rest of the world, though. That didn't change.

— Leslie C. Schneider —

Baby's First Tooth

A teething baby is so much fun. Said no one ever!
~Author Unknown

"Ow, you little stinker!" Our rambunctious four-month-old kitten had given me another chomp, this time launching a sneak attack from behind and sinking his needle-sharp teeth right into my calf.

We were perplexed. Our kitten Tiki was a ball of energy from day one, but he hadn't been a biter until recently. He began biting the corners of my paperback books and chewing on my socks and shoes, but, most unnerving, he was now chomping on electrical cords. We found some bitter spray and coated every cord we could find, so he had now resorted to biting us.

A consult with our veterinarian provided the answer: Tiki was teething! Our doctor explained that, just like human babies, kittens go through a teething stage. The thought hadn't crossed our minds, as my husband and I had never raised a kitten, nor a child, before. The doctor recommended a frozen washcloth for him to chew on and even to peruse the teething toys in the baby section. "Look for something that he can get his teeth around and really chew," she helpfully offered.

And so, there I was, staring at an endless display of teething options: rattles, necklaces, bracelets, and soft cloth books. It was overwhelming. I had just picked up a soft, beaded bracelet when a woman cornered me. She was wearing an infant in a carrier and pushing an overflowing shopping cart.

She wanted to chat.

"Always something to buy, right?" she began.

I nodded and avoided eye contact, hoping she'd take the hint and move on. I continued scanning the shelves, pondering the merits of a silicone ring filled with some kind of liquid that squished between my fingers. Something told me that Tiki's little fangs would pierce right through it, so I put it back.

"Those water teethers are really great," the chatterbox offered. "My oldest liked those a lot, but we'll have to see what little sister here likes," she said, patting the infant snuggled into her chest. "How was your birthing experience? Did you deliver here?"

I started to explain that I was actually looking at teethers for a kitten with growing anger-management issues, but she proceeded to answer her own questions.

"I did, and let me tell you, I'll pick a natural birth over a C-section any day of the week," she said. Then, she proceeded to enlighten me with medical details that I absolutely could have done without.

"What kind of diapers do you like best to handle blow-outs?" she asked.

"Uh…," I stammered, trying to stifle laughter. I could take one guess at what a blow-out was before she launched into another line of conversation.

"And baby monitors," she said, shaking her head. "What a nightmare that has been, let me tell you."

"Speaking of nightmares…," I wanted to say, but I kept mum, trying to quickly settle on something that our grouchy feline could chew on so I could make my getaway.

I finally landed on two nubby bracelets and a pineapple-shaped silicone ring when she reverted to teething.

"So, your little one is teething, huh?" she said, pausing briefly to come up for some air.

I'd had enough of this motormouth and decided to have some fun.

"Oh, yeah, he's teething something awful," I said. "And biting everything in sight."

Cats and Comedy

Her eyes gleamed. She was going to take the bait. Hook, line, and sinker.

Sensing she'd found a maternal comrade-in-arms, I waited to launch my attack, as she relayed several stories about her teething adventures before she finally turned the conversation back to me.

"So, how old is your little one? What have you tried?"

"Oh, he's just about four months old," I said.

She cast me a knowing glance. "A bit early, but yeah, it happens. My Oliver, his teeth started breaking through, oh, I'd have to say six months maybe, but he was so fussy. How many teeth does your little one have now?"

"Well, our little stinker has a full set," I grinned. "And he's chomping everything in sight and leaving bite holes in my books, but he really likes biting me in particular. And, let me tell you, his teeth are sharp!"

My plan had worked. I had nearly shocked her into silence.

"I… did you say he has a full set? Of teeth?" she finally said, completely baffled.

"Oh, yeah," I nodded. "And he knows how to use them."

"What does your doctor say about all this?" she asked, looking at me in astonishment.

"She told me to wash out the bites with peroxide and get ointment on them right away. And that I needed to really get something for him to start teething on," I said with a smirk. "So, here I am!"

"He draws blood?" she stammered.

"Let's just say Dracula would beam with pride at his little fangs," I smirked. "I should probably get going. He's with his PePaw right now, and I know he has to be getting fussy."

She reached over and clutched my forearm. "Bless your heart, honey! I'll sure be praying for you!"

— Kristi Adams —

Home Remedy

To a cat, "No" means "Not while I'm looking."
~Author Unknown

When we moved into our new house, it had just been recarpeted. "Oatmeal" was the name of the whitish-colored, woven carpet, highlighted with bits of pale gray and tan tones. It was fresh, clean, and beautiful. The operational word here is "was." Soon after we moved into the house, the dining room began to smell of cat urine. Then, we saw one of our two Siamese cats using our dining room as her personal litter box. Our gorgeous carpet was soon covered with yellow stains. What in the world could have possessed our sweet kitties to behave this way?

After some investigation, we found that the previous owners had indoor cats, and their felines must have started this egregious habit. When they had the new carpet installed, they must have kept the same old carpet pad underneath it. The scent of cat urine communicated to our kitties that this was an acceptable place to use as a restroom, and they were probably marking their territory by covering up the old scent.

We knew we would have to retrain our kitties and scrub the carpet until no scent could be detected. But no matter what kind of cleaner or deterrent we used, the cats always made another fresh spot. I stood guard with a spray bottle of water and did everything I could to discourage our cats from using our beautiful dining room as their personal latrine, but nothing worked.

Cats and Comedy

It would be Thanksgiving in a few weeks, and we had invited the extended family to come and see our new home. And, of course, a lovely Thanksgiving meal would be served in the dining room: the room that smelled like ammonia 24/7. My husband suggested that maybe we should cancel our Thanksgiving plans. I couldn't imagine my mother-in-law, as nice as she was, not pointing out the smell.

Somewhere, I read that cayenne pepper would do the trick. I could just sprinkle an abundance of the stuff around, and our fur babies would get a whiff and head for the hills... or litter box. Then, the pepper could be vacuumed up, and my carpet (and sanity) would be restored, just in time for Thanksgiving.

I went to the market and selected an especially large container of cayenne pepper and brought it home with high hopes. I decided to surprise my husband, so that night after he went to bed, I sprinkled the spice all around the dining room. The pungent aroma smelled slightly smoky and almost sweet. "That ought to do it," I said to myself and went to bed feeling proud.

The next day, I woke early and snuck downstairs to take a look at the pepper zone. To my dismay, both kitties were walking around on the cayenne dust, and one was finishing her morning potty in one of the usual spots. As I yelled to her, she ran off, tracking little, spicy footprints around as well as dribbles of kitty wetness. By now, my husband was awake and came to watch what was going on. He turned and looked at me as though I was the offending feline.

After my "reasonable" explanation on why there was wet and spicy cayenne pepper all over the dining room carpet (and also tracked into the living room), my husband looked like he wanted to commit a capital crime.

Within a few days, we booked a professional carpet cleaner and pet-stain expert. He was able to clean the carpet and pad, and he used his industrial-strength pet deterrent to convey the message to our cats to stay out of the dining room. Of course, there was a hefty bill with an extra cleaning fee to get the red-orange cayenne stain out, too.

Ten days later it was Thanksgiving and the crisis was all but forgotten. I served a lovely meal, and the family relaxed and enjoyed

Cats and Comedy

themselves. And my mother-in-law even commented on how nice the oatmeal carpet looked.

— Laura McKenzie —

A Battle of Wills

Cats have a scam going — you buy the food, they eat the food, they go away; that's the deal.
~Eddie Izzard

Our cat, Rustle, is seventeen years young and is as willful as he is old. Recently, he has convinced himself that 4:00 a.m. is a perfect time to wake up and be fed. The battle begins strategically on his part, testing my strength and patience, but it quickly escalates to an all-out war.

At approximately 4:01 a.m., he innocently starts by tapping my face with his paw ever so gently like a baby's kiss, stirring me from my slumber. He often rubs his wet nose on mine and proceeds to lick my cheek or forehead with his raspy tongue. I meet his attempts with several sleepy groans, telling him that it is way too early to get up and pull the covers over my head. His incessant purring gets louder with each passing minute. I soon realize that his war machine is just warming up.

Rustle walks on and around me until he lands on my shoulder and begins pulling the blankets from me. I respond with a stern "No." Seeing how this is not working, he jumps off the bed with a thud and gallops down the stairs. I believe he has retreated and has given up due to my commanding presence and superior intellect. But I am sadly mistaken.

At 4:17 a.m., just as I lull myself back to sleep with my false sense of security, my cat stealthily creeps up to the bedroom like a silent

Cats and Comedy | 61

assassin. He pounces right on me and circles my head with his paws, which then pull on my thinning hair. Now, he has my attention. He proudly displays his derriere in my face, taunting me, as if saying, "This battle is far from over."

I cover my head with my arm, and he aggressively head-butts my elbow. I push him away. He returns, head-butting and pouncing. I push him away again and turn my back, only for him to jump off the bed for what I expect to be another frontal surprise attack.

But he switches strategies. He jumps on my wife instead, circling her head like an attack drone, pawing, pushing, and pouncing. I hear the words, "Go see Papa." I am betrayed by the woman I thought was my ally, but I guess at 4:28 in the morning it's everyone for themselves.

I'm now lying on my back, staring at the ceiling, wondering what on earth has gotten into this cat. Why now? Is he getting senile? Am I? What is the meaning of life? Why do we exist? What sins have I committed? Why am I being punished? Who really is the owner, and who really is the pet? I'm delirious with lack of sleep.

I have left myself in a vulnerable position and Rustle knows it.

He attacks like a Green Beret.

He jumps right onto my throat. As I gasp for air, he leans forward, putting his entire weight, all fifteen pounds and three ounces of him, on my jugular. With his nose nearly touching mine, he stares directly at me. He is no longer purring but meowing a guttural sound that would put the fear into any minister of the cloth. I hear his stern, commanding words, "Okay, buddy. Let's get serious. Enough of this pussy-footing around. You ARE going to get up. You ARE going to feed me. Or this WILL get ugly REAL fast, and I do mean UGLY."

I know exactly what he means. In previous battles, I picked him up, tossed him out into no man's land, and closed the bedroom door. There, he howled insanely, waking up the entire household, and then proceeded to throw up and release excrement. Other times, he simply retched on the bed, forcing me to clean up the mess.

He is right. It is ugly. War is ugly, and I decide that, at 4:45 in the morning, it is better to surrender than suffer more collateral damage.

And so, I maneuver my disheveled self out of bed. With my head hung low in defeat, I put on my old, worn-out slippers and tattered robe and slowly follow my conqueror down the stairs to his winning spoils. He leads me to the darkened kitchen where I step directly in the throw-up that he left earlier in the morning. It is his way of making certain I know my place in his world. As I clean the muck from my slipper and reach for his food, Rustle meows his victory chant, "I am cat. Hear me roar!"

—Manley Fisher—

Chance the Darkness

*A cat's plan for the day: 1% chasing its own tail,
99% controlling your life.*
~Author Unknown

No matter what the weather was like outside, darkness came to my home the day I accepted Chance as a foster. Not quite a year old, the small black cat slinked out of the carrier to hide under my bed.

"Hey, sweetie," I ventured, kneeling to offer him a treat. I got nothing in return.

Nothing but a glare from under the blanket.

No treat, food or toys could lure him from under the bed. All that bright day, I saw nothing of him but the occasional glimpse of moving shadow. Throughout the afternoon, I popped in to check on him.

"Sweetie?" I asked, but there was only silence.

After sunset, I went to brush my teeth. Coming into the room wearing my pajamas, I asked one last time, "You okay, Chance?"

Nothing. I shrugged and crawled between the sheets. It was strange to settle down to sleep knowing there was a monster under my bed, but I wasn't all that worried.

He was a small monster.

The following days were challenging, as the lurking shadow refused to eat out in the light of day. I had to risk pushing his food bowl — and my hand — into the murk he had claimed as his territory. For the first twenty-four hours, he refused all my offerings.

Cats and Comedy

Finally, almost two days in, I was rewarded by loud, lip-smacking noises from under the bed. Relieved, I left him to himself.

Chance decided, after days of hiding, to expand his territory. Able to roam the entire apartment, he normally kept himself confined to the bedroom unless tempted out by a fly or bee that had flown in through the open window in the den. Swatting at the creature, he would play for a moment, but then he seemed to remember himself and rush back to his sanctuary.

I was permitted to enter the bedroom, but only to leave food or to sleep. If I deviated from that, he would puff up, bounce, and dash for the gloom under the bed. So, it came as quite a shock when, a few weeks after first accepting him as a foster, Chance not only remained close while I put down his food bowl but actively reached out to touch my toes.

I gasped and then bent down to stroke his paw, but the movement broke the enchantment of the moment. Chance scuttled away from me to hide deep in his murky safe space.

I worried that I had frightened him, but the very next night, something light, something made entirely of shadow, skittered across the end of the bed, waking me, and was gone. Shooting up out of sleep, I called out, "What?"

Only silence answered me. Then, a terrifying wail split the night. The wailing went on for a few heart-pounding minutes and then faded into nothingness.

In the morning, there was a dead housefly in my shoe.

So, we went on for months. It was a strange, haunting time, filled with midnight yowling and gifts of dead spiders. From long experience with fostering, I knew we were on a promising trajectory, but Chance the Darkness was his own cat. He simply could not tolerate the touch of his human servant, allowing affection only from a distance.

And then, one day, it happened. Shockingly, as I spoke to him and held out a toy, Chance moved up to sit near my foot. Worried that he would run away again, I bent very slowly until I was crouching on the floor. Keeping up a constant stream of praise, I reached out to stroke his cheek. His soft fur rubbed against my fingers, and I felt a thrill of triumph. There was even, as I held my breath, the faintest purr. Then, a soft brush of tail against my face, a whirr, and he was gone.

I grinned stupidly for the rest of the day. The Darkness had chosen to love me as only a ghoulish thing could.

True to his nature, Chance decided after that to ask for affection in a weird way. Unlike many other cats, the types who roll over on their back or chirp lovingly, Chance the Darkness would stalk me through the apartment. Once I settled down at my desk or on the sofa, he would sneak in toward me until he was just inches away from my face, only to freeze in place. Ignoring him in irritation, I would continue to read or write, but it was no good. The Darkness had "caught" me and wouldn't go away until I reached tentatively to scratch his chin.

There was a heavy, expectant feel to his presence, almost like a thunderstorm waiting to break, and so I would give in. Each and every time. Then the Darkness would slink away to blink at me from behind the sofa.

Quite predictably, I failed as a foster with Chance. Under some dark compulsion, I found I had to adopt him. Just as predictably, the weird happenings continued. There were strange noises, gifts of dead bugs, and a lot of stalking, but then there was something new.

Chance began to turn into inanimate objects right around the time I started to need glasses. One day, I walked into the den to find the Darkness sitting in the armchair. He was a little blurry, but I knew he was there. When I tried to shoo him so I might sit down, he didn't move. Annoyed, I reached out to touch him, only to discover that he was cold and leathery to the feel.

Startled, I put on my glasses to find that, somehow, Chance had turned into my black purse. Picking it up, I turned around to find the Darkness looking up at me innocently from the floor.

"Seriously?" I muttered. I went to hang the purse in the hallway closet.

As my eyesight worsened, Chance played this game more frequently. When I bent to put on my shoes, they would sometimes jump up and run away. Black sweaters thrown over the back of the sofa would meow softly at me.

The whole experience left me unnerved.

It has now been fourteen years since the Darkness claimed my home. It can be said that I put up a good fight, but to be honest, it was halfhearted at best.

In that time, I have learned so much about shadow creatures.

When others speak of facing their own personal demons or struggling with dark thoughts that plague them, I always pause. There is a part of me — a large, unashamed part — that wants to recommend chin rubs and a nice bowl of chicken delight.

Or maybe a dead housefly.

That worked on my little monster.

— Alexes Lester —

Clever Cats

Feline to the Rescue

*I have studied many philosophers and many cats.
The wisdom of cats is infinitely superior.*
~Hippolyte Taine

"Mousey!" I called. "Mousey, where are you?" I knew my gray cat was nearby. She didn't stray far, but it was time for her to be home for the night. My pet door was left open during the day for her to come and go as she pleased, but I locked it at night.

My best guess was that I'd find her at Poppy's house. (Poppy was short for Penelope, which her grandchildren couldn't say. They called her Poppy, and the name stuck.) She often worked in her backyard flower beds or sat drinking a glass of iced tea on her patio. Mousey joined her when I was at work or away for a few hours.

Sure enough, there she was, chasing a moth that Poppy had disturbed while planting. "I see Miss Mousey is pestering you again," I said.

"Oh, heavens, no. She isn't bothering me at all. I love her company. Don't I, Mousey?" she cooed and reached out to scratch the cat's head. "Don't worry about her being over here. She's welcome anytime."

"Well, if you ever tire of her, just shoo her away and tell her to go home." I picked up Mousey and snuggled my face by hers. "You know Poppy's busy. You shouldn't be bothering her." Mousey rubbed against my face and stared into my eyes. I could have sworn she knew what I was saying.

I carried Mousey through the garage and into the house to the

Clever Cats | 27

utility room. I put her down by her bowl and opened a packet of her favorite cat food. "I don't mind you visiting Poppy, but remember where you belong and who feeds you."

As I petted and talked to the cat, the light above us went out. I looked up and decided I'd better replace it. I might need to see my way into the garage at night. My folding ladder hung on the wall of my garage on two hooks in front of my parked car. I lifted it from the hooks and turned to walk with it into the house. As I put one foot on the step going into the house and reached to turn the door knob, my other hand lost control of the ladder. My first thought was *It's going to hit the car!* I immediately twisted, causing the ladder to slam into the wall. It bounced back, hitting me, and caused me to fall. The leg and foot that had been on the step ended up twisted under me. The pain was excruciating.

After a few minutes, I tried to move but it was too painful. I pushed the ladder from the top of my body to the garage floor. As it clattered to the ground, I saw Mousey stick her head through the pet door.

"Hi, baby. It's okay. You can come out."

She walked gingerly down the step, being careful not to touch me. Her purring increased as she approached. When she was within reach, I laid my head back on the cement and petted her, letting the purring calm me. The pain subsided a bit as I let the calm surround me.

"What am I going to do?" I wasn't talking to the cat, but no one else was around, so I might as well have been.

As I calmed and felt a little better, I thought about plans of action. My cellphone was in the house. I didn't have relatives who would come check on me without a reason. People at work would wonder where I was but probably wouldn't check on me.

"Mousey, I'm in trouble. This could be bad."

About half an hour later I had an idea. "Mousey, go get Poppy." I gave the cat a little push. "Poppy. Go get Poppy."

Those bright green eyes looked at me as if to say, "You are crazy if you think I understand you." She turned her head and looked at me from head to foot. Then, she stared at my face.

I tried again. "Go get Poppy!" She knew the word "Poppy," and if

28 | Clever Cats

I said, "Let's go get food or go get a drink," she'd usually go straight to her bowl. It was worth a try.

Mousey's tail twitched, and she turned and walked regally to the pet door. She turned to look at me and then disappeared through the door.

I allowed myself to relax, trying to build up the strength I knew it would take for me to get to a position where I might be able to drag myself into the house—if I could even manage to open the door.

I started crying. Every plan I came up with seemed impossible. Then I heard knocking on the garage door. "Rita, are you in there?"

My eyes flew open. "Yes! Yes, I'm in here. Poppy, is that you?"

"Yes. How can I get to you?"

"Go to the back door. Come through the house."

I closed my eyes. *Thank you, Lord.*

The door from the house opened. Poppy stepped out, followed by Mousey.

"I'm so glad you found me!" I smiled through happy tears.

"Mousey wouldn't leave me alone. That cat meowed and meowed until I followed her. She led me straight to your garage door. I had no idea what was going on."

"Oh, Mousey, you are so smart and wonderful. I owe you lots of treats."

Poppy looked at me, and her tone became serious. "I don't think I can get you up. We are probably going to need an ambulance."

"Yes, we need to call one. My phone is on the kitchen cabinet. If you'd get it for me, I'll call."

The ambulance whisked me away, followed by Poppy. We were soon back at our respective homes, me with a badly sprained knee and Poppy volunteering to come over if I called.

As soon as I settled into my recliner, my incredibly talented feline snuggled into her usual position on my lap. She purred loudly while I caught up on much-needed rest. I will be forever grateful for her devotion and intelligence.

—Rita Durrett—

A Bitter Pill

The cat is, above all things, a dramatist.
~Margaret Benson

We watched the scene unfold, trying to hide the amused grins on our faces behind our hands as the veterinarian and her two assistants wrestled with our rescue brat. They had been at it for twenty minutes now, getting redder in the face and growing progressively more frustrated as time passed.

We had just arrived at our new home in Germany where I would be working on a NATO base as a professor for an American university. The first thing we did was seek out a good vet clinic for our brood of rescue animals. Because we were now in Germany, we collectively called our gang Bratwursts, or Brats for short.

Ingrid, the veterinarian we were assigned, was a kind soul who patiently issued new batches of medications for each of our senior rescue animals. We explained that our dogs all took their medicine without any problem because we could wrap the pills in something delicious that they would swallow in one gulp. The cats were craftier, though, eating the yummy food wrapped around the tablets, while leaving the pills intact.

So, we were open to suggestions, looking for tips and tricks to make giving a pill to an ornery cat less of an ordeal. Ingrid said that she'd show us a simple technique on how to do it. Easy, peasy, she said. She picked up Kika the cat and proceeded to give her a pill.

Clever Cats

Or so she thought.

Kika was the brattiest of our Brats and the most averse to taking pills. Ingrid learned that the hard way after wrestling with her for twenty minutes. Despite her best efforts, she and her two assistants were not able to get a pill down Kika's throat. Defeated, she ended up handing us back the Brat and the pill, telling us that we would have to work it out when the cat was calmer.

Because the animals knew and trusted me, I was able to soothe them enough to give them their medication at home. The dogs were easy because they figured they were getting a treat. Our oldest dog, Bubba, was particularly pleased with his extra tidbit, even trying to nab the bacon-wrapped medication from the other dogs. To Bubba, virtually everything was a snack. So, he would hover around the senior Brats until all of the medication was given out, hoping to snag an extra delicacy.

I individually pilled all the Brats and finally came to Kika, who, to my surprise, took her tablet easily on this particular day. I was thrilled that my brattiest Brat was finally coming around. I couldn't blame the Brats for spitting out medication, since I knew the pills could be bitter. So, I silently congratulated myself for becoming an expert at it.

The next time we dispensed medication, my husband watched in disbelief as I successfully gave Kika her pill. She had been such a tyrant before that now we couldn't believe our continued success. We gave each other high-fives as we watched her walk out onto the terrace, followed closely by her dog brother, Bubba.

This same pattern continued over weeks as we marveled at the new Kika, who now took her pills without a fuss. Congratulating ourselves one day after another successful administration of medication, we watched her cross the patio with Bubba in tow as usual. Suddenly, she stopped and coughed up something that Bubba gulped down in an instant.

We looked at each other. Mystery solved. Kika had learned to keep the pill lodged at the back of her throat, only to cough it up when we were out of sight. Bubba would then gobble up the evidence.

Sigh. Outsmarted by the Brats once again.

— Donna L. Roberts —

And the Rains Came

Intelligence in the cat is underrated.
~Louis Wain

The sun was setting behind the house, blinding us. Even so, when we got to the stop sign, we could tell something was wrong.

My mother, my three sisters, our brother baby, and I had just driven home to Montana after visiting Grandma in Indiana. As we parked, we realized that sometime after we'd last talked to Dad, our house had caught fire.

Curtains fluttered out the broken windows, and greasy black streaks ran from a hole in the roof to the eaves. Aside from what we had in our suitcases everything was gone.

"Where's Dad?" I said. He'd almost died the summer before, and my worst fear was that, this time, we hadn't gotten off so lucky.

With relief, we saw him trudging toward us in strange, borrowed clothes. It was a hot day, and a cloud of mosquitoes followed him. He was allergic to their bites, so he'd pulled a coat over his head.

We ran to him, crying, filled with a million questions. We'd lost everything, yes, but once again, we had all survived.

"I'm okay," Dad said, hugging us back.

"Is Monsoon okay?" my sister Adrianne asked, referring to one of our cats.

We'd gotten Monsoon the previous summer during the worst flood in Montana history. It had rained non-stop for days, and both

Sand Coulee Creek and the Missouri beyond had broken their banks. Dad had been in the hospital fighting cancer, so saving our home fell to Mom and me.

Although Mom was six months pregnant, we didn't lose anything. Dad recovered, and our house survived, but it had been horrible. To cheer us, Mom had brought home a Siamese kitten she named Monsoon because we got him when the rains came.

"And Snowy? Is Snowy okay, too?" Adrianne continued. Snowy was a stray we'd taken in. She'd had a litter the year before, and the death of one of her kittens had driven her crazy with grief.

"They're both fine," Dad said. "A little wild but fine. Monsoon's around here someplace. He's been sleeping in the house. Snowy, too.

"The Dawsons have offered us a place to stay," he went on, "until we decide what to do. For now, Dorothy has tea and sandwiches ready for you."

Mom finally spoke. "When did this happen, John?"

"Last night."

"Oh, my god, how?"

"I don't know," he said. "I woke up, and the room was filled with smoke. I couldn't even see the bedroom door."

We were silent. Even at our ages, we knew that in a fire most people died of smoke inhalation, sometimes in their sleep. What if Dad had just continued to sleep while the smoke killed him?

"I'm sorry, Joyce. All I was able to save was the saddle and some books by the front door."

"The rest is gone?" Mom asked.

Dad nodded. "I could've saved more, but I got the cats out first, and Snowy kept running back in. I think she was looking for her dead kitten. I had to go in after her twice."

Once again, we stood in stunned silence. Dad had actually gone back into a burning building to save a stray cat. We were both grateful to Dad for saving her and mad at Snowy for making him risk his life.

"I'm so thankful that you and the kids didn't make it home a day earlier." He shook his head. "I don't like thinking what might have happened if you'd all been here, too."

Clever Cats | 33

"I know," Mom said. "I'm just glad you woke up."

Dad shook his head. "It was the craziest thing. I was sound asleep. Monsoon woke me by standing on my chest, yowling down into my face. I'm not sure I'd have roused if he hadn't been making all that racket. I think he saved my life."

As we approached the destroyed house, a soot-covered Snowy appeared in the doorway. Monsoon was nowhere to be seen. The little cat who had arrived when the rains came, had arrived just in time. He had saved our dad and now guarded what was left of home, still making sure everything — and everyone — was safe.

— Leslie C. Schneider —

A Girl Named Joseph

The cat is domestic only as far as suits its own ends.
~Saki

It was a cold day in late spring when the slender, mostly black kitten we'd been feeding throughout the winter showed up again. But that morning, it was lethargic, with a runny nose and watery eyes. It barely glanced at the bowl of kibble before curling up into a tight ball on our kitchen table.

Our microchip reader found nothing, and even though the world was in quarantine due to Covid-19, I decided the cat needed to see a doctor. The problem was that no veterinarian would accept walk-ins. And it is impossible to schedule an appointment for a stray kitten that doesn't understand you made an appointment on their behalf for a specific day and time.

I rushed to place the kitten in a padded box and then drove like a madwoman to the closest animal hospital with emergency care, seventy-five miles away. Five minutes after the vet tech disappeared through the emergency-room doors with the box, my cellphone rang.

"Am I speaking with the person who brought the cat to the emergency room?"

"Yes," I answered.

"I am the veterinarian looking at the cat. This is not your cat."

"Yes, I know. I declared that on the form."

"I must contact the owner of the cat. Only the owner can authorize treatment."

Clever Cats | 35

"Oh, you mean the cat has a microchip?" I asked, dumbfounded. (Later, I learned that our home microchip reader was too new to read the older type of chip that was in the cat.)

"Yes, and you are not the owner."

"Yes, I already confirmed that."

"When I call the owner, can I give them your contact information?" she asked in a clipped tone.

"Of course."

Ten minutes later, the phone rang again with a different unknown caller. I answered it.

"Is this Leeann?" the caller huffed.

"Yes."

"My name is Karen, and Apple is my cat. Why did you steal my cat?"

I hesitated for a moment, searching for the right words. "I didn't intentionally steal your cat. I have been putting food out for her over the past six months, and this morning she showed up with symptoms of Covid-19 — watery eyes and a runny nose — so I took her to the vet."

"Oh, now I understand how she got to a hospital in Walnut Creek. My son visited me yesterday, and he lives in Walnut Creek. Apple must have jumped in his car when he was here. So, you must live near my son. I've been so worried about her. You know, she's fourteen years old."

"Oh, I thought she was a kitten. And, just so you know, my house is in Napa. I drove all the way to Walnut Creek to find a doctor who would take her."

"Napa!" Karen exclaimed. Then, we figured out that we lived three or four houses away from each other, but on different streets. Then, she continued, "I'm sorry I accused you of stealing Apple, but I have a reason. Do you know Linda and Tom?"

"I've met them. They live a few houses down from me."

"Well, they are awful people. Earlier this year, Apple didn't come home for at least two weeks. My daughter was in tears. We were really afraid that Apple was hurt or couldn't come home because she couldn't breathe from Covid-19 — all kinds of horrible thoughts. So, I made up flyers with Apple's picture and put them on every pole around town.

Clever Cats

Then, my daughter and I started going door-to-door, asking anyone who would answer if they'd seen my cat. Linda and Tom answered the door, and I handed them the flyer. They looked right at me and said they hadn't seen my cat. And then, you know what?" she continued without waiting for my response. "Apple came out from behind their legs and jumped into my daughter's arms!"

"That sounds terrible," I sympathized, "but I'm glad you got your Apple back."

"Yes, but that's why I thought you had stolen my cat — because those horrible people did!"

The vet said the cat had a cold, not Covid, and we drove back to Napa where I delivered Apple to her owner. A bit later that day, some neighbors on a walk with their dog stopped by, and I shared that morning's events with them.

Two weeks later, Ron, the neighbor across the street, happened to see me outside and motioned me over to his yard.

"I heard from Paul and Jill that you met Karen," he snickered.

"Yeah, and it took a while to explain to her that I already have a cat, so I have no need to steal hers."

His shoulders shook while chuckling. "What you don't know is that I've been taking care of Joseph for the past two years. He's been living with me. I even buy the special food he needs. My friend is a vet, and he told me that Joseph has a thyroid problem. That's why he's so small and eats a lot. Sure, he checks in with Karen every few weeks, but he sleeps every night in my house. A few weeks ago, I went on vacation, and I asked Linda and Tom to watch him for me."

He paused to wipe at the tears of laughter. "And that happened to be the one week in forever that Karen went looking for that cat! So now she hates them and still has no idea I'm the one taking care of her cat!" He winked at me while I was trying to stifle my own giggles.

"But are you sure we're talking about the same cat? The vet and Karen told me the cat's name is Apple. It is a small, mostly black cat with a little, white goatee on her chin?"

"Yep, that's Joseph," Ron assured me. "Pete down the street there," he pointed two doors down, "calls him Midnight." Then, he pointed

Clever Cats | 37

in the opposite direction. "Danni over on Elm calls him Shadow."

"But, Ron, the vet says it's female, and its name is Apple."

"Boy named Sue, girl named Joseph, all the same." I could still hear Ron's low-voiced cackle as I headed into my house to find my own cat and give her a big hug. It was wonderful knowing that everyone on the block was doing their best to look after our neighborhood friend.

—Leeann Lynton—

The Signal

It is impossible to keep a straight face in the presence of one or more kittens.
~Cynthia E. Varnado

I first met Ink when a telephone repairman was fixing some wires outside my house one spring afternoon. I went out to see how the work was progressing, and the repairman told me he was having fun while he worked, watching my cat rolling in the grass and chasing after bugs. But the cat he was pointing to wasn't mine. Not yet, anyway.

I had never seen that cat before. But the energetic female, with all-black fur on her upper body and legs and mostly white fur on her underside, was definitely having a good time. I put out some roasted chicken, which she scarfed down before running into the woods behind my house.

My mysterious new pal started visiting my backyard several times a day after that meal. She was petite, warm, and very outgoing. I named her Ink because I had worked at a newspaper, and her rich black fur reminded me of the printer's ink used on the presses.

As it turned out, Ink had a secret, and she wasn't going to share it with me until she felt I was ready to handle it.

Roughly a month after we met, Ink decided to break the big news. While she would usually eat and then run into the woods, on this one particular morning, she kept running in and out of the woods, making it quite clear that she wanted me to follow her. So, I did. Ink slowly

Clever Cats | 39

weaved her way through the woods, looking back several times to make sure I was still there.

We came to a massive boulder in the woods. There was a hole in the ground next to it, with two kittens peering out. Ink seemed relieved. She had found help for her little ones.

A visit to the vet revealed that Ink and her kittens were in amazingly good health for having been exposed to the elements for at least a few months with no real shelter. My wife Diana and I now had three new feline companions.

For their part, Ink and her kittens, all domestic shorthairs, made the leap from living in the great outdoors to the indoor life with ease. One of the kittens was a tiger-striped male. The other was a female tuxedo cat. The male kitten was a bit bigger than the female. After watching him traipse around the house for a few days, we noticed that he had a lumbering walk, just like Tigger of Winnie-the-Pooh fame. Naming him Tigger seemed very fitting.

His sister had a distinctive white band diagonally across the black fur on her left back leg, so naming her Stripe was an easy decision. Funny, Diana and I always referred to Tigger and Stripe as the "kittens," even after they grew up. Neither of them ever lost their youthful charm.

My house was a bustling place with these three new residents scampering around. Ink was not that old herself. The vet guessed that she was about two years old, if not a bit younger.

Once she was in the house, it didn't take Ink long to pick up on a habit of mine that I had never thought much about. When I get ready to go outside, do some chores, or work on a project, I rally myself for the task ahead by clapping my hands. I mumble to myself, "All right, let's get it done," and clap my hands a couple of times. I've done that since I was a teenager. It's a habit I picked up from playing sports, a personal pep talk. No big deal, right?

Well, it was to Ink. After she had been in my house for a couple of weeks, I noticed that every time I clapped my hands, Ink would run over to me. She'd look up at me with this quizzical expression on her face as if to say, "You rang?"

I didn't connect the hand clapping with Ink's timely appearances at first. But then the two kittens followed suit and would run up to me, right alongside their mom, every time I clapped my hands. All three stopped everything they were doing and responded to my hand clapping immediately.

If they were eating, sleeping, hiding, playing with a toy, or looking out the window, they zipped right over. They came from downstairs, upstairs, and one end of the house to the other. And they ran hard. It sounded like a stampede of paws as they raced along the wooden floors in my house to my side. They couldn't get to me fast enough.

Tigger would jump over both Ink and Stripe so he could reach me first. I'm not sure about Ink, but I think the two kittens thought we were playing some kind of game. Once, after this ritual started, I was watching a ballgame in the bedroom and started clapping my hands after an exciting on-field play. Within seconds, the gang was all there.

Diana pointed out that Ink and her kittens were interpreting my hand clapping as some type of signal. Without realizing it, I had taught a whole family of cats to come to me on command.

After a while, Diana wanted to try her hand at summoning the felines. We started off by both of us clapping our hands at the same time. Sure enough, all three cats came rushing over. Eventually, Diana would go it alone. In no time, either one of us was able to give the signal individually and the cats would quickly respond.

This unintentional signal I had developed with the Ink family came in handy. Stripe and Tigger loved to hide in clandestine places around the house, especially when they were young. When Diana and I couldn't find these frisky rascals, one of us would clap our hands, and Tigger and Stripe would suddenly appear.

If someone came to make a repair in the house, we always liked to herd the cats into one room and close the door. As the time for the repair appointment approached, one of us stood in the room, clapped our hands, and, within seconds, the Ink family was all rounded up, safe and sound. It was as if we had made some magical breakthrough in cat communication.

But, like all wizardry, you had to be extremely careful not to abuse it. So, at my house, when something exciting happened, we learned to

Clever Cats

let out a cheer, give a pat on the back, maybe several high-fives, perhaps a kiss on the cheek. But we never, ever clapped our hands — unless, of course, we wanted Ink and her brood to come running.

— Robert Grayson —

Dr. Callie

*Not all angels have wings.
Sometimes, they have whiskers.*
~Author Unknown

My sister Pat had the crankiest baby I've ever seen. Pat was tired from the birth and lack of sleep but there was no rest for her. That seven-pound baby, Terry, had the house in an uproar. She was diagnosed with colic, but no matter what my sister did, things didn't improve.

I offered to take my niece for the afternoon to give my sister a rest.

Callie, my calico cat, had never seen a baby and was fascinated. With tiny steps, she worked her way along the couch, creeping closer and closer to the baby until she was sniffing her. I put the cat on the floor but she wouldn't leave the baby alone.

I noticed that Callie was focusing all her sniffing on Terry's left ear so I let my sister know. We agreed that maybe all the crying and fussing was coming from an issue with that ear.

Pat called the doctor and was told to bring Terry to the office. After explaining what brought us there, the doctor examined Terry's ear. Sure enough, Terry was suffering from a severe ear infection — first diagnosed during Callie's "CAT scan"!

— Mary Grant Dempsey —

Herding Cats

Cats can teach us about contentment, thriving, and being content with what life gives us.
~Author Unknown

My grown son stood at my front door, holding a cardboard box and corrugated cat-scratching disk. "Mom, can you take care of Bucky? I have a problem."

"What's wrong?"

He told me that, the week after he and his bride moved into their apartment, a brand-new, black leather sofa was delivered, and it didn't take Bucky more than one night to discover that leather makes a great scratching post. The next morning, instead of breakfast, his wife gave him an ultimatum: "Get rid of that good-for-nothing cat!" So, the culprit was quickly offloaded to my house.

After he left, I opened the box and welcomed Bucky. I remembered how thrilled my then teenage son had been to discover a rare (at least for the Hudson River Valley) tuxedo cat, black with a white face and paws, at the animal rescue where he was fulfilling his community service requirement for his college applications.

He was proud to pay the adoption fees out of his own lawn-mowing cash, and he picked up food, cat toys and litter on his way home with his cat, just like an adult.

"He can live in my bedroom, Mom. I'll take care of him," he said.

Sure enough, he did take care of the cat, and we all enjoyed having Bucky around to keep us company when he went to school and work.

Clever Cats

Although I was sorry that my son couldn't keep him now, I was glad to have Bucky back. I missed my grown-up son, and Bucky made me a little less lonely.

Living with me, Bucky was on extra-good behavior. He slept in the soft, round bed I bought him and never scratched the furniture. Instead, he seemed happy to claw the empty cardboard boxes I got for him. He became my very well-behaved indoor cat.

However, I noticed that Bucky would stare longingly out the kitchen window for hours. I decided to take him outdoors as a reward. I even purchased a complicated cat harness and leash, and I imagined the pleasant walks we would take while meandering toward the Hudson River. We practiced buckling the harness and leash and walked through the rooms of my house.

Finally, I felt confident in Bucky's leash manners. One lovely, late spring morning, we buckled up and sashayed out. Bucky sniffed his new outdoor "room," and our walk was perfect, better than I had dreamed it could be.

Until the deer appeared on their morning walk to the Hudson. I had forgotten that deer still walked from the woods behind our housing development and continued past my house to the river.

I also forgot that cats are like wet spaghetti. They can miraculously wiggle through the most impossible obstructions. Before I could catch him, Bucky had wiggled out of the harness and raced after the deer. I raced after him. When I spotted the deer again, I could see Bucky herding. He ran back and forth, like a sheepdog, behind a fawn who had dawdled too long to keep up with the others. I had seen other cats following cattle in the pastures, but I know the phrase "herding cats" doesn't mean cats are doing the herding!

I kept my distance and was proud to see the baby rejoin the herd. Bucky had done his job.

He turned and ran back to me. I felt a little foolish carrying the harness dangling from the leash, but Bucky stood quietly. He finally pawed at it to let me know that it was time to put it back on him and continue our walk.

For years afterward, Bucky and I did our morning walks — he, in his harness and leash, believing this was the way it should be — and me chatting with walkers who thought it funny to see a cat acting like a dog.

— Sheila Hollihan-Elliot —

The Power of the Purr

> *Cats are cats... the world over! These intelligent,
> peace-loving, four-footed friends — who
> without prejudice, without hate, without greed
> — may someday teach us something.*
> ~James Mackintosh Qwilleran

My fifteen-pound tricolored rescue cat, Chamois, had recently taken up lying on my chest. She would settle in with her front paws and head on my right shoulder, and the rest splayed over me. I felt like I had to hold her up so she wouldn't slide back down into my lap.

Was it uncomfortable? Absolutely. Would I ever think to push away this snuggle muffin? Absolutely not. But then, during one of our snuggle fests, as she went to step away, I winced with pain. "Your little toe-beans hurt me today," I told her, rubbing the area. With this rub, my life was about to change. I had found a dreaded pea-sized lump in my right breast.

As a lot of women know, this was a life-altering moment. *This can't be happening,* I said to myself. I had always done self-exams, but lately, with everything going on, I had stopped. I was twenty-six years old, had an eighteen-month-old daughter, and was recently divorced. Now I would add this diagnosis to the stressors of my life. That "pea" led to a year filled with aspirations, biopsies, localized radiation and, finally, an all-clear from my doctor.

"You caught it early."

"You're so lucky it hadn't spread."

I heard this over and over from friends and family. It was 1993, and I was told that I needed to have a mammogram every three months for the next five years and then one every six months after that.

Did I credit Chamois for finding this lump and saving my life? Yes, I did! Did we snuggle as much as possible with her on my chest? Yes, we did!

Year after year, the mammograms came back with no problems. I remarried in 1997 and had another daughter in 1998. She breastfed for two years. After she stopped breastfeeding and my milk had dried up, I noticed that my left breast had a milk duct that was still producing. Over the years, I mentioned how it produced a stick, greenish-brown substance when I squeezed it. My gynecologist told me that all the tests were fine and to "stop touching it"; it would disappear. I stopped thinking about it. I kept going to the mammograms like they told me. All was good.

By September 2022, my beloved Chamois was long gone and I had a nine-year-old, orange rescue cat named Ellie.

Ellie had always loved sitting as close as possible to me, usually in my lap. But then she started splaying across my chest with her front paws on my left shoulder. At first, I didn't think anything of it. "Oh, she's so snuggly. I love being this close."

But there was a reason for this behavior. The mammogram that I had just completed came through as suspicious.

Here we go again, I thought.

I was sent to see a specialist in women's health. He ordered an ultrasound-guided biopsy in November, and when he wasn't happy with what he saw, I was sent for an MRI biopsy right after Christmas. Through all that time, Ellie kept lying on that area.

It turned out I had stage zero breast cancer. So we caught it early. I went for a bilateral mastectomy and reconstruction. Poor Ellie. I had to stay away from her until my drainage tubes were out. I spent eight days listening to her little meows on the other side of the bedroom door.

When the tubes were finally removed, she came and sat on the pillows that surrounded me — my "pillow fort," as my grandson called

Clever Cats

it. Ellie never attempted to lie across my healing chest. She knows things.

I've read many articles about the health benefits of cat purring, including reducing stress and anxiety, boosting immune-system function, and promoting healing and recovery. The physiological effects include increasing blood flow and reducing inflammation.

Did my two extraordinary cats reduce my stress and help me heal? Yes, they did. The power of belief and a snuggly cat can work wonders for the human body, and I believe it played a significant role in my recovery.

— Lynn Hendricks —

Cat-a-combs

One reason we admire cats is for their proficiency in one-upmanship. They always seem to come out on top, no matter what they are doing, or pretend they do.

~Barbara Webster

I was a Chief Petty Officer stationed with the U.S. Coast Guard in San Pedro, California. On duty one evening, I drove a golf cart-like vehicle to check the base perimeter. Along the way, I stopped at a beautiful vista overlooking the Pacific Ocean.

Fascinated, I watched as a flock of seagulls fought over a fish that one of them had caught. During the brouhaha, the fish was snatched several times by various birds and kept bouncing about in the air between them. This battle slowly moved inland toward my position until it was only a few feet above the sand and no longer over water. As the fish finally dropped onto the sandy beach, the birds also landed, commencing a ground assault.

Doubtless hearing or observing the scuffle, a glaring of at least twenty feral cats began to emerge from little tunnels, or cat-a-combs, all about the rocky area just ten feet below the ledge upon which I stood. Spotting the felines, the gulls ceased their aggression toward each other and appeared to look nervously about. Probably realizing they were no match for this new threat, they chose to leave the fish on the beach and fly away to safety.

Meanwhile, growling and hissing warnings to each other, the cats stealthily closed their circle around this mouthwatering feast. They began fighting each other for the delicious morsel. I had seen cats playfight, and even nip angrily at each other, but I had never witnessed an outright brawl like this.

Finally, a tiny kitten appeared. It walked nonchalantly through the melee and picked up the fish in its mouth. It didn't seem to matter that this catch was much larger and longer than the kitten's little body. Comically, once it had claimed a good grip, the little guy dragged the fish between its legs, walking its treasure nonchalantly back through the ruckus. Just as the kitten was about to disappear through a small hole in the rocks—a kitty-comb—the bigger cats ceased fighting and turned to stare in disbelief as their prize vanished before their bewildered eyes.

Moments later, the cats dispersed back from whence they came. They had just lost their potential dinner to a stealthy little furball.

—Timothy Nipko—

Neighborhood Visitor

*Remember, a well-timed meow can often
open more doors than a bark.*
~Author Unknown

"No. Absolutely not." I can still hear my mother's words and the panic in her voice when my father and I walked into our home with two adult cats in carriers.

"They were going to put them down." My dad locked eyes with my mom. "I just couldn't."

At the age of ten, I already knew my dad would win this battle, so I sat cross-legged on the floor and opened their cages. My dad had been bringing strays home my entire life, but we'd been without a pet for nearly six months. It was very unlike us. Today, while we were out, he had suggested we go by the shelter "just to look."

Well, the rest is history.

Over the next few days, my entire family, even my mom, fell in love with the tabby cats.

A few months of honeymoon bliss went by before the smell started. As the youngest child and the most naïve, I had no idea the rancid smell was caused by my precious cats.

Mom, on the other hand, knew, and she wasn't having it. I overheard my parents talking one night.

"If they're marking, they won't stop. We can't keep them," Mom whispered in harsh tones to Dad.

Clever Cats

"We don't know it's both of them," he pled.

"They were in the shelter for a reason. This has to be it."

Dad sighed. "They might have been feral before being picked up. Tom is always trying to get outside. He's probably rebelling. Why don't we try making them indoor/outdoor cats? Let's see if it helps."

After a long pause, Mom said, "It's not sanitary. If this doesn't work, we can't keep them."

"I know."

I was worried when the cats started going outside. Would they know how to come home? Would somebody take them?

My dad reassured me that they'd be fine. Cats are smart.

A few days passed, and the cats stayed safe and found their way home in the evenings. Best of all, the marking stopped.

We had one solid month before Tom didn't come home. We searched everywhere for him and posted signs, but we couldn't find him. Months later, we found him living with a new family a neighborhood over. My dad talked to them, and we found out that Tom — well, Rusty — had disappeared on them, and they didn't know what had happened to their cat until the day when he just showed up on their porch again.

Sometimes, I'd ride my bike by their house, and Tom would be sunbathing on their porch, tail twitching. I was glad that Tom had found his way back to his family.

Bo reveled in the extra attention he got after Tom left. At first, he spent more time at home, but then he remembered he liked the outdoors. Soon, we learned that Bo had started accompanying our mailman as he walked from house to house to deliver the mail. Quickly, he learned the mail schedule and started waiting for Mark, our mail carrier, where he parked his truck.

Mark would tell us, "I pull up, and there he is at the curb. He follows me for the route around your neighborhood and then veers off toward your street when I head back to my truck." Mark would shake his head and say, "In all my years, I've never seen anything like him."

As time passed, we would go days without seeing Bo, but he always came home. During a neighborhood garage sale, many of our neighbors were shocked to find out that Bo had a family and it was

Clever Cats | 53

us. Several of them confessed to feeding him and letting him inside on cold nights.

"Wow. We had no idea that Bo was making his rounds. We're sorry if he has been a nuisance for any of you," my dad apologized.

The murmur in the crowd was that he was great to have around.

One elderly lady in a wheelchair made a clicking noise with her tongue. Bo ran from his perch on the yard-sale table to jump onto an afghan covering her lap.

She stroked him from head to tail. "Your cat has brought great comfort. I found out I had cancer the very day I met this boy." She scratched between his ears and smiled. His purr grew loud enough to hear. "I don't know how he knows, but he comes on the days I need him most. I, of course, spoil him with a treat, and he then lies with me while I knit before drifting off to sleep. When I wake, he's gone until the next time. Thanks for sharing him with me."

My dad reached forward and took her hand between his. When she made eye contact with him, he said, "Bobbi, we will share Bo with you anytime."

Months later, Bo came home meowing and moping. He spent weeks howling and unsettled and not wanting to go outside. We found out later that Bobbi had passed away.

Bo spent many years being the neighborhood cat. He always seemed to find the person who needed him most. Until the day we had to say goodbye, he brought joy to all who encountered him.

After he passed away, we asked Mark the mailman to take Bo on one final mail route, to spread his ashes over the yards of all the neighbors who loved him.

— Heather Hartmann —

Chapter 3

Saving Kitty

The Power of the Purr

*If there were to be a universal sound depicting peace,
I would surely vote for the purr.*
~Barbara L. Diamond

I love dogs. My wife, Grace, loves cats. So, we have cats.

When we married, we agreed, "No pets." A few months later, we went to the nearby laundromat. While waiting for the clothes to wash, Grace looked through the storefront window, and I heard her say, "A kitty!" She rushed outside. She quickly returned holding a skinny, longhaired white cat that settled into her lap and began purring.

I knew what was coming.

She was named "Honky Cat" for Elton John's song. We wanted to have her fixed, but she went into heat, and Grace decided she should be allowed a litter. My brother had a huge, longhaired white male, and we "borrowed" him. Grace insisted we have a wedding for them, so we held a short marriage ceremony. Immediately afterward, the groom started the honeymoon in front of everybody.

Repeatedly.

Soon, Honky Cat gave birth to three white kittens and a mostly black one. They were named for the four apostles: Matthew, Mark, Luke, and Sam.

Okay, mostly.

Grace wanted to keep Sam. Sam showed his gratitude by purring all the time.

Seven years later, our son, Chad, was born. Sam loved Chad, and Chad loved Sam.

Sam tolerated Chad pulling his tail or whiskers. When Chad learned to walk, he often carried the hapless cat around the house in what had to be uncomfortable positions, including upside down. Sam never growled or scratched. Instead, he purred.

Four years later, in early December, Sam began to lose weight. A trip to the vet confirmed the worst. Sam was dying.

I was told to take him home until he began to be uncomfortable and then to bring him back so he wouldn't suffer. On the drive home, Sam purred throughout the trip, and I wondered how to explain death to a four-year-old.

Every day afterward was a blessing. We pampered Sam, and he purred his appreciation. And I still could not figure out how to explain to my son why we would be losing Sam. I lost hours of sleep over it.

Early Christmas Eve morning, Sam began to exhibit signs of pain. I wrapped him in a towel and left the house before my wife and son woke up.

I drove my son's best friend to the veterinarian. I held him as the needle was inserted and felt his last breath as he went limp. Tears ran down my cheeks.

The vet walked me out, his arm around my shoulder, trying to console me. His words failed to help. As we entered his lobby, there was a commotion. An older couple came in carrying a box of young kittens. They explained that the mother cat had been carrying a kitten across a busy highway and was struck by a truck. The truck didn't stop, but these people did.

The cat and kitten were dead, but they heard mewing. They looked inside the culvert that ran under the highway and spied kittens. They captured four, but one retreated into the darkness of the culvert, out of sight.

I was in a fog of my misery and left the building, got in my car and started it up. Then, what they had said hit me. I went back in and asked the couple where the culvert was. I asked the vet if he had a flashlight. He brought me one.

Saving Kitty

I drove to the spot they described and crawled inside the concrete tube. I didn't find the kitten. Instead, I found smelly mud, spiderwebs and roaches. LOTS of roaches! On hands and knees, and then on my belly, I pushed in farther, following the beam of the flashlight. No kitten, but I did alarm a large snake.

I slowly backed out, dripping mud and smelling really bad. Defeated. I started to drive back to return the flashlight and inform my child of his pet's death.

But a short distance away was a second culvert. I pulled off the road and headed to it. As I approached the opening, I heard the sounds of a frightened, hungry kitten. Again, I got on my hands and knees and peered under the highway overhead.

There it was! It had returned to the opening, but now it turned around and headed back into the concrete tube. I made a desperate lunge and banged my head on the top of the concrete tunnel, landing in a puddle of nasty water and onto a piece of sharp broken glass. But my fingers were wrapped around the frightened creature's hind leg!

It promptly showed its gratitude for me trying to save its life by sinking its teeth into my hand.

I let out a stream of words that my mother would have rewarded with a soap sandwich. I held on, though, and pulled out the hissing and scratching little guy.

As I held the soaked kitten to my body, it stopped fighting me and began the most pitiful mewing imaginable. I limped back to my car with mud streaming off me, blood dripping from several spots, and a huge bump on my forehead. I dug a towel out of the trunk of my car and wiped away as much filth from my body as possible. Then, I wrapped up the infant and held it in my lap as I drove back to the vet. About halfway there, the kitten began to purr.

When I walked into the vet's office, he whistled at my wounds and appearance. He examined and cared for the kitten as his assistant cleaned and bandaged my cuts, scratches and bite.

Then, I asked how we should care for our newest cat. He smiled and gave me careful instructions along with enough kitten food for a week.

Then, I headed home to talk to my son about life and death, endings and beginnings.

He named his newest friend Furrball. It should have been Purrball because he did that virtually nonstop.

He enriched our lives for twelve years. Often, I'd stretch out on the couch to watch TV and fall asleep. I'd awaken with him wrapped around my neck, purring with joy.

— Chip Kirkpatrick —

21

Meow Loudly

*Cats need to meow because we humans
are generally so unobservant.*
~John Bradshaw

It was a cool April night in Maine, on the eve of Easter. My extended family had journeyed north to Mom's house near Moosehead Lake to celebrate together. After greeting everyone in the house, I had snuck outside for some deep breaths.

The cold, fresh air helped for a moment. But then, despite the din inside and the traffic nearby, I heard a quiet meow. I looked around and called, but no felines came running. Eventually, I went back inside. Tiger, the orange Hemingway tabby, and fluffy gray Charlie were there, but I couldn't find the dark calico named Chocolate. This wasn't unusual, though, since she was the most skittish and independent of the bunch.

Perhaps it was a neighbor's cat that I'd heard.

For the rest of the evening, I got caught up in preparing Easter dinner and talking with siblings I hadn't seen in several months. I forgot about the soft meowing until I was tucked into my childhood bed. That's when I heard the cat again.

I got up and started searching. First, I checked the adjoining bathroom, which was small and clearly empty. I heard the meow again and looked out the window. Soon I was back outside.

I kept hearing the meowing, but I couldn't see anything. I returned inside for a flashlight, and my brother, who clearly thought I had lost my mind, offered to help nonetheless. We searched and listened, eventually pinpointing the sound to the basement bulkhead door, which was still buried in deep snow.

Back inside, we clambered down the dusty basement steps, ducking our heads as we moved toward the older section. Our flashlights shone on the stone walls. We began searching through piles of forgotten tools and an old weight bench. We could hear the meowing loudest right at the bulkhead door. We called out, and the meows grew closer together. The sound was right there! But we didn't see any cats.

Giving up, we returned outside and started chipping away the hardened snow from the doors. When we finally pried them open, we found… nothing.

Maybe we were hearing wrong. We checked the rest of the yard, beneath the front steps, the roof, the trees, and even the shed at the far back of the property.

My brother reasoned that we should get some sleep. It was late. Soon, everyone would be awake and eagerly looking for the Easter Bunny's trail. We couldn't spend the entire night searching for a meow.

Still, when I tried to sleep, it was nearly impossible. Every time I managed to doze off, I would hear another meow. I must have managed to sleep at some point because I was jarred awake around 5:00 in the morning by my brother. Something had occurred to him.

We went back outside and opened the bulkhead doors again. There was still a faint meow. Then my brother shone his flashlight on the external wall. It was made of cinderblocks that were staggered so that you could see the half the cinderblock beneath each one… and the opening inside the blocks.

Maybe the cat was in there… and maybe it was Chocolate. When we went inside and asked my mom, she realized she hadn't spotted the cat for at least a day.

There was only one thing to do. With a hammer and chisel, we tried to break away the top layer of cinderblocks, but the tools were inefficient. It took forever just to remove one block.

That's when my mom called the fire department. You hear stories of people calling them to rescue cats, and it seems like overkill, but what else was there to do?

Saving Kitty | 9

The first two firefighters to arrive were smirking—until we showed them the bulkhead wall, and they heard the meows themselves. Their faces grew concerned and puzzled.

Before long, a half-dozen volunteer firefighters had found their way to our yard, sacrificing their Easter morning to strategize how to safely extract a cat from a cinderblock wall. The solution ultimately came down to a masonry saw and prayer—and later, once they spotted the first bits of fur four layers down, rescue claws. The meows became louder as the pile of broken cinderblocks grew.

There were cheers when she was finally lifted out, wrapped in a blanket, and taken inside to warm up and have food and water. Chocolate was tired and spent most of Easter napping, but she was back to normal within a day.

Eventually, the cinderblock wall was repaired, this time with cap blocks added to prevent a repeat. And life went on as though it had never happened, except for the memory of those persistent meows for help and the desperate searching.

Imagine if Chocolate hadn't kept meowing, if she'd given up…

—Charlotte Louise Nystrom—

Fostering Joy

*Volunteers do not necessarily have the time;
they have the heart.*
~Elizabeth Andrews

We talk about how "hard things are hard" in our family, and when our cat passed abruptly from a blood clot on her spine, that was definitely hard on us. We were devastated.

Even after many weeks, my husband and I realized we weren't ready for a new cat. But we read about an opportunity at our local animal shelter that made us consider something new: becoming a foster family.

Fostering a pet can happen for multiple reasons. Sometimes a cat needs home care because of a tough transition into shelter life from an owner's passing, a family move, or another major life disruption. Other times, the cat may benefit from socialization around people, or it needs to be quarantined from the other animals in the facility. That was how Tiki landed in our lives.

He was a six-month-old, shorthaired, orange-and-white stray. He had been brought in by a good Samaritan who found him in an abandoned car, tick-ridden and with heartbreaking burn marks on his skin. When the shelter technician held Tiki for the first time and started removing the parasites from his ears, Tiki simply purred. He was so grateful to be in someone's loving arms.

Despite his friendly demeanor, Tiki wasn't adopted from the shelter. He was there for months, and then an upper respiratory infection rampaged through the cats in the shelter. When they started sneezing and coughing, they needed to be quarantined.

Tiki was very ill, one of the least likely to survive. But we couldn't turn him away when we were asked to take him. Luckily, under our care, he improved by leaps and bounds. He was also a delightful guest — grateful, affectionate, and playful. He was so good that he even took his medicine like a champ.

After a few weeks, Tiki was ready to rejoin the population of available pets at the shelter. It was a bittersweet return, for he had wiggled his way into our lives and been such a happy addition to our home. We could only hope that adoption would now be on the horizon for him.

As we stepped into the foyer of the animal shelter with Tiki in his carrier, there was a man looking to add a third cat to his family. Two cats already resided on his farm, and I immediately thought about how social Tiki was. He was bound to get along with the man, his wife, and his four-year-old son, as well as the existing cats.

We watched through the large glass window of the cat room as the man met Tiki. We held our breaths, hoping that little Tiki would finally find a permanent home. And he did!

To see a foster cat adopted warmed our hearts and justified the hard work we did in getting Tiki well again. It also helped ease the emotional challenge of returning him to the shelter. Since he was only there for a short time, it was a smoother transition than we could have imagined. He wouldn't have to adapt to shelter life again.

As we left the shelter that day, one of the staff members reminded us: "See? Fostering saves lives!" Indeed, Tiki had a long journey with plenty of uncertainty along the way. But he earned his happy ending, and we played a role in helping him get there. Our own hearts were mended, too, in the process of fostering, knowing that our actions made a difference.

So, even though hard things are hard, we also know this: There can be real joy on the other side of hard things — for cats and humans alike.

— Audrey Wick —

Patched Up

*In this life we cannot always do great things.
But we can do small things with great love.*
~Mother Teresa

I'd agreed to pick up my friend's mail and change light bulbs as needed after he moved out. On one of my visits to the empty house, I saw a skinny gray cat lying in a rain puddle by the front door. Since I usually carry pet food in my car, I opened a can for the sickly-looking feline.

I placed the open can in the dry spot below the door's eave. He slowly dragged himself up; it was obvious that he was very weak. He was so hungry that he inhaled the food. I thought I should get him to a vet and tried to pick him up, but life on the streets had made him wary, and his fear gave him the strength to run from me.

For the next three days, I returned to feed him. He was always waiting — no longer in a puddle — but just on the side of the house. As I shut my car door and popped open a can, he'd emerge from the house's shadow. He had a voracious appetite, but he still looked pretty sick. His eyes were runny, and his coat was dull. He allowed me to stand near him while he ate, but every time I tried to touch him, he took off.

Finally, I rented a humane trap from the feed store. I set his canned food inside, but he refused to go in. The first two nights, I ended up giving him the food anyway, because I didn't think he'd go inside the cage to get it.

On the third night, I loaded the trap with all-white chicken and left the cat alone with it while I went to the store.

Less than an hour later, as I pulled into the driveway, I saw the cage door down. Bingo! The cat was waiting inside.

As I lifted the cage into my back seat, I noticed the cat's fur seemed to be moving. He was moving restlessly too, as if something was biting him. I had a new Buick with a capacious trunk and decided to place the cage in there. That turned out to be a very good idea.

I rushed the cat to the twenty-four-hour veterinary clinic and the first things they noticed were armies of fleas and lice marching all over his body, and mites in his ears. They bathed him twice in a special solution to kill the bugs before admitting him to their isolation ward for his upper respiratory infection.

A week later, after he'd been tested and neutered, I took him home. He was FIV-positive (i.e., kitty AIDS), but that didn't scare me. I'd had an FIV-positive cat before, and he had died of old age.

Before his release from the clinic, a fungus had been discovered between his toes, and I was instructed to bathe his feet in a warm, sudsy solution daily. He'd freaked out when I got him home, so I didn't expect him to cooperate. He must have sensed that I was on his side, though, because he reluctantly submitted.

What started out as a challenge became some of our best times together. I'd place the tub of warm water on a table and then gently lift Patches, so named for his patchwork coat, into it. He'd stand with only his feet getting wet while I cooed encouraging words and petted him beneath the chin. When his soak was done, I'd place him on a fluffy towel while I rubbed each foot dry. If his loud purrs were any indication of his feelings about the procedure, I'd say it was the equivalent of a hot-stone massage at a five-star hotel.

Soon, his purr greeted me every time I entered the room. He would lean his head against my arm as I placed his food before him. Between bites, he treated me to his friendly gaze and allowed me to pet him while he ate.

Things were looking up. Patches began gaining weight, and his mangy coat, now free of lice and fleas, was replaced by silky gray fur. Even a splendid fur coat can't hide a lifetime of hard living, though.

Patches appears to have survived a number of fights, and he's got the scars, broken teeth and torn ears to prove it.

His imperfections make him all the more endearing to me. I'm just glad I was there when he hit rock bottom and seemed to lack the strength to pull himself up from that rain puddle. My discovery of what could have become a watery grave for a sickly cat led to a bond that I wouldn't trade for the best-in-show winner at a cat competition.

—Marsha Porter—

How I Made Three Cats Happy

*People who love cats have some
of the biggest hearts around.*
~Susan Easterly

I have always been an impulsive person, and it's gotten me into a lot of trouble in the past. But, somehow, I've never changed. So, I bought my Persian kitten, Shireen, completely on impulse. I hadn't planned to acquire another cat, as my Snoopy seemed entirely happy on her own. But Shireen was a gorgeous, longhaired kitten, just three months old, with the cutest little flat face. She was the last of the litter, and the breeder had reduced the price substantially. I'm a sucker for a bargain, and I decided to take her home. After all, I reasoned, I had often had a multi-cat family in the past. Surely, Snoopy would like Shireen as much as I did.

I was delighted to find that Shireen and Snoopy got on well almost immediately. The breeder had said that Shireen had always lived with other cats and really liked being with them. But then, just three weeks later, Snoopy was killed on the road outside my house. I never learned how it happened.

I grieved deeply for Snoopy, and perhaps somewhat surprisingly, Shireen grieved, too. She wandered around looking for her new friend, and then just sat there looking sad. It wasn't natural for a kitten to do that, and I was worried about her. She obviously hated being on her own, particularly as I was out at work most of the day. I decided to get another cat, perhaps not so much for me but for little Shireen to have a companion.

A few days later, I was telling a friend at work this sad story. Wendy had a solution. A neighbour of hers had recently rescued two young male cats who had been badly treated. She was keeping them in her garage and urgently needed to find a home for them. Would I take one? It might be the perfect solution for everyone.

To be honest, I wasn't that keen on the idea. Did I really want a potentially disturbed older cat as a companion for a lonely kitten? Would that work out? It went against all the advice for rehoming cats that I'd ever heard. But I said perhaps I would have one, and I took a cat carrier to work the next day, planning to go and see the two cats when Wendy and I finished for the day.

When I saw Velvet and Domino, I almost burst into tears. They were very young, barely out of kittenhood. They were sitting in a corner of the garage, shaking and almost clinging to each other, obviously completely traumatised after their bad experiences. I didn't know exactly what had happened to them before they had been rescued, but it clearly hadn't been good. It was obvious that I couldn't separate them, as they needed each other.

So, again on impulse, I said to Wendy, "I'll take them both."

"Are you sure?" she asked, quite startled since she knew I had been slightly ambivalent about having one of them in the first place.

"I have to," I said. "Look at them. They need each other, and they're scared stiff. You can't put them through more trauma by separating them."

So, we put Velvet and Domino together in my cat basket, and I took them home. It might have been a crazy idea, but I felt I had to help them. I carried them into my front room, where little Shireen was sitting forlornly by herself. But when she saw my cat basket and its contents… well, everything changed dramatically. She stood up and just stared at it, absolutely transfixed. I don't think I'd ever seen a cat smile before, but Shireen really did smile in obvious delight. If she could have spoken, I'm sure she would have said, "Those are cats!

Saving Kitty

That's just wonderful."

I let Velvet and Domino out of the carrier, hoping to make some tentative introductions. But the two boys had other ideas. Still quite terrified, they took off in different directions. Within seconds, there was no sign of them, although they had to be in my living room as the doors were closed. Little Shireen just stood there, looking all around, clearly mystified. Had she just seen two cats, or had she imagined it?

I searched the room, then the rest of the house for good measure, but there was no sign of the two new cats. From past experience, I figured they had probably gone up the chimney and would emerge when everything was quiet, probably at night. So, I closed the doors and left food out for them overnight. Sure enough, the following morning, I found sooty pawprints, and the food I had left out was all gone. They clearly weren't so frightened that they couldn't eat, which was encouraging. Hopefully, they would come around in time.

Telling little Shireen that we'd both have to be patient, I continued to leave food out, and assumed Velvet and Domino would emerge in their own time. And I really hoped that when they did so, they would get on with Shireen, who so obviously wanted to meet them.

My efforts were rewarded within a few days when the boys started to come out for brief periods during the day, particularly if there was food around. They were still nervous around me, but they didn't seem at all bothered by Shireen, who was much smaller than they were and obviously not a threat. Maybe this would all work out after all. So, I bided my time and hoped things would continue improving.

This situation carried on for about two weeks, with Velvet and Domino becoming gradually more and more confident. I wasn't sure how they felt about Shireen, and I didn't know if the three cats would ever become friends, but then something amazing happened. I came home from work one day and found all three cats lying together on the bed. Velvet and Domino were sitting on either side of Shireen. Velvet had a paw around her, and Domino was looking at her adoringly. They all seemed relaxed and happy, and Shireen was purring loudly, obviously delighted with her new family. We had made it!

After that, the three cats became great friends. It was lovely to see, and I was very happy with my new multi-cat family. Despite a difficult start, I had managed to go from having one sad little kitten and two traumatised rescue cats to having three well-adjusted and contented cats. It seemed that, for once, my impulsiveness had paid off.

— Helen Krasner —

Unexpected Blessings

Your heart knows the way. Run in that direction.
~Rumi

George and Jack came into my life unexpectedly. I had gone to our local pet store to buy fish food. I had lost my previous cat the year before and didn't feel ready for another one, but I always looked into the big black cage to see the cats available for adoption.

On this particular day, there were three: two large orange ones and one black one. The black one was to be adopted with another cat that was at the vet that day. As I looked in the cage, George, a champagne color, came over right away, making sure I knew he was there. The other orange cat was lying in a hammock looking very relaxed, like one cool cat. He never took his eyes off me, though. So he wasn't quite as cool and detached as he might have been pretending to be.

He was George's brother, Jack. They had come from a hoarding situation where the owners had twenty-two cats. With both owners passing away, twenty-two cats now needed homes. I was told that Jack and George would have to be adopted together. Well, seeing as I had only come in for fish food, this would require some serious thought on my part. Could I afford two cats? Was I ready to take on that responsibility?

I went home but returned the next day to have another look. Three other women were standing outside the cage, admiring the cats. But the funny thing was, Jack was lying in that hammock and staring right

Saving Kitty

at me again. He never took his eyes off me. I felt like he was telling me, "I want to come home with you." George was busy pouring on his charm. I decided it wouldn't hurt to fill out an application, so I picked up two on my way out.

The next day I was returning to the store with the two forms filled out, but I was still unsure. So, I did what I always do when I have a decision to make: I prayed. I said, "Lord, if I'm meant to get these cats, show me something orange." I decided that was too general of a request, so I modified it to something more specific: an orange car. You don't see many of those.

As I drove down the country road toward town, I came to a railroad crossing that I cross every day. There are thirteen houses on the other side of the tracks, all on the east side of the road. On this particular day, as I drove by, I noticed that every single driveway was empty except one. And, yes, it had an orange car parked right down by the road. It was like God was saying, "I can't make it any more obvious than that." I smiled a little, gave thanks, handed in my applications and waited for word. The next day, I found out that these two six-year-old cats would be coming home with me.

For the first couple of months, everything was wonderful. I had the two sweetest cats ever. But then I noticed something was wrong with Jack. I couldn't put my finger on it; it was subtle but there. After a few trips to several different vets, the diagnosis was heartbreaking. This big, beautiful, everything-you-would-ever-want-in-a-cat character had Feline Infectious Peritonitis. I was told it was almost always fatal, and by the time he was diagnosed, the best option was to put him out of his misery. I was devastated.

With Jack no longer around, George came into his own. Big time. He had that "extra something" — beautiful long hair and a face that would make you smile just because. He immediately took over the house. Not that he hadn't done some kitty things prior to Jack's passing, but this seemed like an open invitation to celebrate all things George. He was insanely magical. He was love on four legs. If I was on the couch, he was on my lap. In bed, he slept beside me, right up by my head. I have a light on my headboard that works by touch. Many

Saving Kitty | 73

times, I would be awakened in the middle of the night by the light, which had been activated by George.

If I was on the computer, he needed to be sitting right there, watching the screen with me. He would play the piano. I had to strap down my TV so that he wouldn't knock it over. Every flat surface was bare and for good reason. Anyone who has ever had a cat knows what I mean by that. And talk. My goodness, George could hold a conversation better than most people, always wanting to tell me of the goings-on of his day when I arrived home from work.

The new gregarious George never met a person he didn't love. His charm was always the biggest thing in the room. Any person he met loved him back as well. Children frequently came to my door wanting to see George, who would willingly oblige by being the sweetest cat they had ever seen.

Two years after Jack passed, George needed all his teeth pulled out. I had never experienced that with a cat before, but after a few rough days, he rebounded. Sadly, a few months later, George began losing weight, and his appetite waned. After another visit to the vet, the diagnosis was again devastating: lung cancer. How does a cat get lung cancer? The next couple of months were spent giving him the best life possible. Letting go is the hardest thing to do when all you want to do is hang on.

Two beautiful creatures came into my life and were taken too soon. What I wouldn't give to have my headboard light wake me up in the middle of the night now.

I went from no cats to two. Twice the blessing, but unfortunately it was double the loss. Still, I would do it all again. Bringing them home was the best thing I ever did.

—Laurie Heard—

Urgent Care

*Cats know how to obtain food without labor, shelter
without confinement, and love without penalties.*
~W.L. George

When Bugs arrived at my beach house, he couldn't have been much more than four weeks old. I found him curled up outside my door, malnourished, covered with fleas, and barely moving. In truth, when I brought him inside and placed him in a shoebox, I was certain it was the box I'd bury him in.

He was too weak to hold up his head, so I cradled him in the palm of my hand and fed him warm condensed milk with an eyedropper. I figured that if he made it until morning, he might just survive. And survive he did. By the next afternoon, he was sitting up on his own, but he was still the most pitiful-looking creature I'd ever seen.

If he was to have any chance to grow stronger, I'd have to free him of the hundreds of fleas plaguing him. I knew he was much too weak to endure poisonous flea powder or spray so I began the tedious process of removing them by hand. And with every flea I removed, the more alive he seemed. And the more optimistic I became that he would live.

Bugs grew bigger and healthier every day. More confident and independent. And as he did, it became clear that he didn't like the confines of my house. He'd sit on the window ledge by the back door as if waiting, staring outside for hours. Unlike many cats who enjoy the coddled, pampered life of an indoor cat, Bugs missed the outside world.

As the weeks passed, I hoped he'd outgrow his curiosity—if that's all it was. I hated the thought of returning him to the elements that had sent him to me in the first place. But he didn't change. I had to face the reality that, although I'd come to think of him as a domestic cat I'd rescued, he was actually a feral cat longing to return to the wild. So, I did what I thought was fair.

I got him his shots and had him neutered, figuring that was my responsibility. Then, after a few more weeks when he didn't outgrow his yearning to be free, I opened the door and offered him freedom. As he scampered down the driveway and out to the alley, I knew that's where he belonged. (I set his food dish just outside the door in case he changed his mind.)

As days turned to weeks, I came to accept that Bugs was a free agent, so to speak, with his own life to live. When weeks turned to months, I wondered if I'd ever see him again. I imagined him strutting down the alley; maybe I'd see him, and he'd remember me. But that didn't happen. I resigned myself to knowing that I'd helped another living creature survive.

Then, very late one night a few months later, I heard a mournful cry outside the back door. Even though his voice had deepened, I knew it was Bugs. I opened the door, and there he sat. The whole side of his face was covered in blood.

When I looked closer, I realized that he had a three-inch, multi-barbed fishing hook stuck halfway through his cheek. Two things were apparent: He knew he was in serious trouble, and he remembered that I'd helped him before, even though that was months ago.

I didn't relish what I knew I had to do.

I petted his head for a moment and then left him sitting by the open door while I raced inside. I hurriedly collected wire cutters, pliers, a clean towel, alcohol, hydrogen peroxide, and cotton balls. I dropped the tools in a bowl and dumped in the alcohol.

When I returned, I persuaded him to lie down on the towel. I then explained to him what I was going to do. I could only hope that on some level he understood what had to be done. The hook had to come out. And the least damaging way was to push it through.

He sat there trembling and whimpering as I removed the wire cutters from the alcohol. I hated the idea of putting them into his mouth. But, fortunately, the eye of the hook was protruding just outside his lips. If I could persuade him to open his mouth the tiniest bit, I could easily snip off the end. But would he let me?

I placed one finger into his mouth and forced it open just enough to expose the hook eye. Then, before he could change his mind, I snipped it off!

But now the hard part. I had to pull the razor-sharp hook out through his cheek.

Stroking his back, I wrapped my arm around him and told him I was sorry for what I was about to do. Removing the pliers from the alcohol, I held him firmly against me and steadied us both. Then, as carefully as I could, I latched onto the barb of the hook and, in one fluid motion, yanked it through his cheek!

He recoiled and jumped out of my arms, but he didn't tear off as expected or claw me as many cats would. Instead, he ducked under a lawn chair and hid in the shadow, crying. I sat there near him most of the night, hoping he could make some sense of it all.

Just as the sun came up, Bugs came out into the light and reclaimed his spot on the towel next to me. I needed to swab peroxide onto the wound but wasn't going to hurry him. A while later, he let me pet him, and I knew I'd never have a better opportunity.

Dumping peroxide on a cotton ball, I gently dabbed it onto the open wound. He again took refuge under the chair—but just for a few minutes.

After a second treatment, I went inside and got him a bowl of warm condensed milk. When I checked on him a while later, the bowl was empty, and he was gone. I'd planned to treat him a few more times when he returned, but he never did.

I think I saw him once in the distance, but I can't be certain. And that's okay.

If he's ever in trouble again, he knows where to find me.

—James R. Coffey—

Saving Kitty

Can't Judge a Cat by His Cover

There is no such thing as an ordinary cat.
~Colette

When I first laid eyes on Jeffrey, a giant streak of a black cat with a bloodied ear, I thought, *My God, that's the most feral cat I've ever seen.* In all my years of taking care of a colony of homeless kitties, I'd never encountered such a fierce-looking junkyard dog of a cat.

At the first sight of me, he dashed in a fury toward the storm drain at the end of the parking lot and disappeared. After I'd watched him slip under the cement grate for several days, the name Draino popped into my head. Not very original, I admit, but apt.

So, Draino he became for the next several months.

Each day when I fed the parking lot Gang of Eight, including Cutie2, Bojangles, Tuxedo, The Professor, and others, I noticed Draino watching from a distance. By the time I reached the entrance to his underground home to leave him some food, he had already disappeared. This ritual continued for several months. Whenever he heard me calling for the kitties, he would pop his head out from beneath the grate but slip back under as soon as I approached. His ear needed medical attention, but there was no way I could get close enough to examine him.

Over the next several months, I noticed that instead of disappearing

Saving Kitty

down the drain, as usual, Draino now sat on top of the grate, staring, while I fed the other cats. He was no longer so quick to run away when I approached him with a handful of food.

Where had he come from? What was he thinking?

I surprised myself at how easily I had dismissed Draino in the beginning just a "feral" cat, unlike my other sweet, friendly, homeless but civilized kitties. How easily I had made a judgment, and a harsh one at that, about someone who seemed so wild, so desperate. I had unwittingly fallen into the trap of thinking that there were "good" kitties and "not-so-good" ones. Our other kitties were "good" because they let me pet them, came when called, and were beautiful. Draino didn't measure up. I had disregarded him and hoped he would just go away.

He apparently had other ideas.

Gradually, I began to feel guilty for calling him Draino. It wasn't his fault that he looked like hell. Who knew what he'd been through?

I thought perhaps the name Jeffrey would be more to his liking. More Ritz-Carlton, less trailer park.

Over the next many months, Jeffrey insinuated himself into the group of eight. Those kitties didn't exactly hand out engraved invitations, but little by little, hiss by hiss, growl by growl, they worked through their issues.

Eventually, after more than a year, he started to come closer and closer to the feeding station. And then, one day, when I bent down next to him, he let me lay my hand on his scruff. He froze but then allowed me to gently massage his neck for a few minutes.

Now that he had become Jeffrey and was no longer Draino, and he let me pet him, I could see his battered and bloodied ear in more detail. One day, it looked like it was healing on its own, but the next it was bloody again, probably from his scratching it.

His new status as Jeffrey ushered in a moral dilemma I'd not had to face when he was Draino. Should I spend time, energy, and money to trap him and take him to the vet?

The problem with having chronic pain and fatigue, the result of an auto accident, is that people so afflicted often look normal. I didn't look decrepit enough to need help, nor did I like to ask for it. Even though my body was racked, I still harbored an image of my pre-accident self as one of health and physical competence. I would go to almost any length to keep from admitting that there was something I could not do.

But I couldn't not help Jeffrey.

My friend Katherine agreed to help me trap him. We went to the parking lot where we set up the metal trap that I had borrowed from Fix Our Ferals in Berkeley. We were a ridiculous sight on our fool's errand, trying to keep the other cats from entering the trap to snatch up the tuna I'd placed at the back, praying to the cat gods to usher Jeffrey into it. Several of the drivers entering the parking lot stopped and rolled down their windows to watch, some smiling, others staring at us as if to say, "Who are those crazy cat ladies?"

Finally, the gods heard our pleas. Jeffrey sneaked in and sprang the trap — but we had forgotten to ask the gods to keep him there. In less than a nanosecond, he backed out before it shut on him.

Now what?

I called another cat rescue friend and asked for guidance. She thought her drop trap would be more effective. I could borrow it if I would drive the twenty-five miles to San Rafael and meet her.

For a normal person, no big deal; for me, a very big deal, what with the sitting, the bending, the lifting. But, in for a penny, in for a pound; I gulped down some Advil and took off.

I met Ann at the Petco where she held her adoption events. She dragged over a huge drop trap made of white PVC tubing covered with netting. We emptied my trunk of all its junk and piled the contents in my back seat. After we hoisted the trap into the trunk, we tied down the lid with bungee cords and fastened a red rag around the trap's bottom to alert other drivers.

Back home, Katherine met me at the parking lot and set up the trap. She waited in my car while holding onto the cord attached to the stick that propped up one end of the trap.

I called for Jeffrey, petted him a little, and then backed away as he ducked under the trap to gobble up the tuna. Katherine yanked hard on the stick. Ka-boom! The trap flopped down. We gingerly transferred Jeffrey from the drop trap to the smaller metal one for transport. Our vet examined him, cleaned his ear, gave him shots, and kept him for a week until he healed.

By the time we returned him to his outdoor home, his transformation from junkyard dog cat to sleek, handsome prince was complete. Which just goes to show that you can't judge a cat by his cover.

—Rosie Sorenson—

Fearsome Feral to Pampered Pet

If we treated everyone we meet with the same affection we bestow upon our favorite cat, they, too, would purr.
~Martin Buxbaum

I first saw Mia when she was outside with her mama. A feral-cat colony near my home had been relocated when apartments were built. A couple of the cats eluded capture, and Mia's mama was one of them.

My neighbor Ryan was leaving food under the fir trees behind our houses for any cats left behind. I walked by one evening and saw two gray shadows — a full-grown cat and a half-grown kitten — race across the road back to the woods. Life is hard for feral cats on their own, and that was the only time I saw the mama cat.

Two years later, I was out on my deck when one of the fir trees started shaking. I went over to it and looked up in the branches. Peering out at me was a little cat.

"What are you doing up there?"

She kept staring at me as if she was asking for help.

Wondering what could be keeping her there, I looked at the base of the tree. A huge, gray tomcat was looking up at her. I clapped my hands and he ran off. I backed up to give the trapped cat some space but she took off.

I checked with Ryan. He'd been feeding the gray tom for a while and thought there was a second cat sometimes. We decided he would feed the tom, and I would feed the other one. It took her a while to figure it out, but soon the little tortie would show up near my deck every evening at dusk for dinner, looking like a gray ghost in the dim light. She was quite wild and would flee when she saw me. I had to retreat up on my deck, out of her sight, so she would come back and eat.

Within a month, she tolerated my presence if the food was under the deck and the steps were between us. I moved the bowl a little each day until it was out on the grass. I sat on the steps and spoke softly to her while she ate. She was beginning to trust me.

The first time I touched her, I barely grazed the tips of her fur. She leaped back like she'd gotten an electric shock. I kept trying. I had to be careful; to her, movement meant danger. Amazingly, she began to let me stroke her, but only if my hand wasn't in her direct view.

Over several months, I slowly moved the bowl up the steps, across the deck, and near a chair where I could sit. I named her Mia and called her when I took out food. She'd answer with a meow and pop up from under the deck. By then, she wanted me to stroke her back while she ate, and she started twining around my ankles to greet me and lounging on the deck chairs when she was done.

It was December and getting colder outside. Ryan's wife Julie and I put a shelter under my deck for her, but she wasn't interested. She'd disappear into the woods every evening, and I started worrying about her out in the cold.

I thought my cat days were done when my previous two cats passed, but I was wrong. "You know you've got yourself another cat," Julie said.

"No, she's too wild."

"She wants to be inside with you."

"She's a grown feral. She can't live in a house."

"Kirk was a year old, and he adjusted." She'd gotten him while caring for a feral colony, and he was a great cat.

Mia started coming up to the patio door and looking in the kitchen. My dog furiously wagged his tail on the other side of the glass. I told Julie what she was doing. "Try to get her into a carrier," Julie said.

Saving Kitty | 83

"Kirk went right in one for me."

I borrowed a two-door carrier from her. Two weeks later, just before Christmas, Mia went all the way in to get her food. I closed both doors and took her to the vet. It had taken six months.

They wrapped her in a towel, and, to everyone's surprise, she allowed them to examine her without incident. She was two to three years old and had a tipped ear, which meant she'd been spayed. I learned later she'd been trapped by another neighbor after she'd had kittens. She was considered too aggressive to be re-homed, so she was spayed and released.

I brought her home and put her in one of the basement rooms with a litter box, food, and water. She slept in a little cubbyhole and came out when I brought down food. But the third day she got spooked and disappeared. I set up a camera and saw she had gotten access into the finished ceiling and was coming down while we slept, eating and using the litter box and retreating back into the ceiling.

I was frantic, but I found an online group that coached me through it, telling me this was normal for a feral. After three weeks, she hid in a closet instead, still only coming out at night. I finally realized it was the first time in her life when she was warm, fed, and safe, and so she slept. I went down every day and talked to her so she would hear my voice and remember I was her friend.

Six weeks later, she trotted out of the closet when I came down, meowed hello, and twined around my ankles. I stroked her back while she ate just like I used to. When she was done, she went back to the closet to sleep again.

A couple of weeks later, I left the basement door open at night and put food on paper plates all around the house so she could hunt for it. Every morning, the food was gone.

The first time she came up during the day was in March. A week later, she was staying upstairs until movement or noise sent her whizzing back down to her closet. Another month passed, and she had favorite places to laze in the sun, often near the dog. By summer, she was sleeping on my bed.

Mia is now a spoiled house cat who has no desire to go back

outside. She bats at toy mice, lunges at ribbon toys, and naps on soft beds. She lets the dog know who's boss and sleeps with me at night, sometimes waking me when she burrows against my side or snuggles under my arm. She's content to watch the birds, squirrels, and chipmunks from the windows.

Some people think an adult feral can't adjust to being a house cat. Mia is proof that a feral doesn't have to stay wild. With her, it just took patience, time, and a lot of love.

—Joan Friday McKechnie—

Rehoming Tom and Jerry

The greatness of a community is most accurately measured by the compassionate actions of its members.
~Coretta Scott King

My elderly neighbour, Pauline, had been ill. One day, she stopped me as I was passing her house.

"Helen, I may have to go into hospital," she said, looking worried. "If I do, would you look after my cats?"

"Of course, I will," I said. I thought no more about it until I got a quick phone message several weeks later.

"Helen, they're taking me into hospital now. Can you feed the cats, please? There's dry food in the tin, and milk is delivered three times a week."

For the next three weeks, I fed Tom and Jerry. They were semi-outdoor cats, living in an uncovered porch; they'd always lived there. But it was December and extremely cold. The cats had a bed and a bit of shelter, but snow blew into the porch, and the temperature plummeted in our Derbyshire Peak District village. Their milk and water froze over, and I worried about them, wishing I could make their situation a little better.

My wish was granted, but not in a way I either expected or hoped for. Pauline passed away just after Christmas, and her grieving daughter didn't want the cats. Concerned about what might happen to them,

I offered to take over, telling her I was involved in animal rescue and could find them a home. She agreed, and I breathed a sigh of relief. They would be safe. Then, I began to panic. I had five cats of my own; I couldn't take on any more. And the local animal-rescue centres were full to bursting, with long waiting lists. What was I to do?

I decided to use the Internet to spread the word and hopefully find the cats a home. I posted a picture of Tom and Jerry on Facebook. I also told the whole story on the forums of a freelance writing site that I was involved with. And I emailed everyone I could think of.

Meanwhile, I mentioned it to the rescue-centre staff, who were helpful and reassuring. They would put Tom and Jerry on the waiting list, but could I keep looking after them for now? I could, but Pauline's house was to be let as soon as possible. Okay, they would mark it as a possible emergency. But I renewed my home-hunting efforts for Tom and Jerry, hoping to take the pressure off the rescue centre, which I knew was struggling to find homes for all the unwanted cats in the area.

It's amazing what modern technology can do, and soon emails began flooding in. People told their friends, who passed on the message. An Irishman in Norfolk said he was trying hard to find a home in his village. A woman in the U.S. had relatives in my area of the U.K. and would try to get something done. Someone even offered to put up a temporary website for Tom and Jerry and get their plight publicised worldwide!

However, it was an old friend of mine who finally found a home for them. Ramona's friend Julie had recently lost her own two cats, and she would be happy to take on Tom and Jerry. Julie and I talked on the phone, and she sounded perfect. She and her husband Brian lived on a country lane in rural North Wales, which would be ideal for two Peak District countryside cats who had little road sense. They had rehomed adult cats before and were prepared to give them space and time if they were nervous. They asked about the cats' previous lifestyle, what they ate, where they slept—all the right questions. Then, they arranged to drive over the following weekend to pick them up.

I had left the cats in Pauline's porch, as that was their home. It was now a little warmer, and I wasn't so worried about them. However, I would have to confine them if Julie and Brian were to be able to collect them. This turned out to be far harder than I expected. I managed to catch friendly Tom, but the more nervous Jerry took one look at the cat carrier and bolted. I put Tom in my conservatory, where he seemed quite happy, but Jerry would no longer let me near him.

I borrowed a humane trap from the rescue centre, put strong-smelling food in it, and placed it in the porch, next to Jerry's now empty food bowl. If I fed him, he'd never go in the trap. Over the next twenty-four hours, I caught and released three of the neighbours' cats! But not Jerry; he was far too wary for that. In fact, he'd completely disappeared. I phoned a friend in cat rescue, who just told me to persevere.

The next day, it snowed again. In the morning, I went to check, and poor Jerry was sitting by his food bowl, looking cold and miserable. The trap was there, but he wouldn't go in it, and he ran off as soon as he saw me. What was I to do? My friend said to be patient as it could take weeks. But how was Jerry to survive with no food in this weather? It was now Friday, and I called Julie, telling her we might have to put things off until the following weekend, but I'd let her know.

That afternoon, my doorbell rang. It was another neighbour's little lad.

"The cat's in the trap."

"Pauline's cat?"

"Yes."

"Wow!"

I dashed over, and sure enough, there was a very miserable Jerry, trapped at last. Incredibly relieved, I put him in my conservatory with Tom and called Julie to say that the Saturday pick-up was on. I then started to worry about how I was going to get two very wary cats into carriers for the long journey from Derbyshire to North Wales.

In the end, it was much easier than I expected. Trapped indoors, Tom was easy to catch, and even Jerry gave up and uttered little more than a token hiss. We soon had them in the car and off to a new home. And I could settle down for a cup of coffee and an unbroken night of sleep without worrying about "my" two outdoor cats — for I'd become very attached to them.

I phoned Julie the following day, and Tom and Jerry had settled in well. Understandably, they were still nervous, but Tom had slept on a chair by the woodstove and was just about allowing himself to be stroked. Even the cautious Jerry was eating normally and didn't seem too upset. I assured Julie that it was merely a matter of time and to be patient. The two cats had had a traumatic time; it was bound to take them a while to settle down. But hopefully they would soon realise that they had a perfect new home.

And they did! I kept in touch with Brian and Julie, and Tom and Jerry turned into happy North Wales cats. Their rehoming had been a success.

— Helen Krasner —

Chapter 4

What a Character

Hidden Treasures

There is no such thing as "just a cat."
~Robert A. Heinlein

It was love at first sight when my wife Diana and I walked over to a pet-adoption event at a local pet store and saw the cutest long-haired tuxedo kitten ever. She couldn't have weighed more than six pounds soaking wet. That face was sooooo adorable, and her long fur stuck out all over the place. Her short, fluffy tail just added to her allure. How could we not take her home?

To our surprise, this small bundle of fur was not a kitten at all. She was a full-grown cat, about a year and a half old. But, no matter, she'd found her home. What this tuxie lacked in stature, she made up for in stamina. She was energy personified.

When we first brought her home, she started racing around the house. She hasn't stopped since. This frisky feline runs like Tom the cat from the *Tom and Jerry* cartoons. She revs up her legs about five seconds before the rest of her body. She seemingly gets everywhere in the house in the blink of an eye.

My wife and I are both writers, so we decided to name her Byline. It was a fitting name, as it turned out, because as soon as she came into our lives, she began writing her own story. That includes clawing and scratching everything paper and wood in the house, but when she looks at you with that sweet, innocent face after scratching the doorpost, how can you be angry?

Most of all, Byline loves cat toys—all kinds of cat toys. She welcomes each new toy with the same zest as the one before. And she never seems to lose interest in any of them. With boundless energy, she carries her toys from room to room to play with them in different areas of the house.

Several years in, Byline had amassed quite a collection of toys and made time in her busy schedule to play with all of them daily. Then, one night, we saw her doing something odd. After she was done playing with her toys, she went around the house and put each one away in a particular place: a fish on a rocking chair in the living room, a red bird on the hall table, a mouse on the sofa, a frog on the bookcase, a catnip-filled strawberry on my desk downstairs.

There seemed to be a pattern to it all. She began doing this every night and put every toy in the same spot where it had been the night before. Every toy had its place, and in the morning, she would get each one and play with it. It would take her quite a while to put away everything each night, but she'd do it very systematically. There was always one toy that she would take to bed with her. That would vary every night, but other than that, her routine stayed the same.

After several weeks of watching Byline's ritual of putting away her toys each night, Diana and I couldn't resist putting this clever feline's system to the test. So, we switched around some of the toys, putting them in different places than Byline had assigned for them.

One of the first toys we moved was the catnip bird on the hall table. We put the fish there instead and put the bird where the fish had been. I was sitting in the living room when Byline came by. When she glanced at the hall table, she stopped short. She jumped on the table, picked up the fish, and brought it to the spot where it was supposed to be. She removed the bird from that place and brought it back to the hall table. This cat was serious about having everything in its place.

The next night, we moved several more cat toys around to different places than Byline's designated spots, just to see what would happen. I got up in the middle of the night and found that Byline had moved all the toys back to their rightful places.

It didn't take Byline long to tire of us switching her toys around. One night, we noticed that the toys were missing when this feisty feline went in to sleep. But they were all out in the open again in the morning. Byline must have figured that if we couldn't follow her fairly simple method for keeping the toys organized, she'd be better off hiding the toys until she wanted them, rather than having us misplace them.

Now, we have no idea where Byline hides her toys. I'm sure one day I will move a big piece of furniture or a heavy bookcase and find a treasure trove of cat toys. But, until then, this wily feline is keeping this secret all to herself.

— Robert Grayson —

The Cat with Six Names

Time spent with a cat is never wasted.
~Sigmund Freud

My husband Chris, a handyman, couldn't believe what he was hearing. "I had to choose," Mary said, self-righteously. "The apartment owners where I'm going only allow one pet."

Our neighbor Mary was moving out that fall and leaving her cat behind. She was keeping her yappy little dog.

After our two beloved cats died, we swore we were not going to get another. We didn't want to go through the pain of losing a pet again. Nevertheless, Chris called and told me the sad story of Mary's abandoned cat.

"Poor little thing," I said. "Yes, bring her home."

But when he tried to catch her, she ran away into the bushes.

We saw her infrequently running around our mobile-home park. I left cat food and water on the porch, which she would only eat when I was safely inside.

Gradually, by crouching down and speaking softly, I earned her trust and she let me approach her. I noticed that she sounded like she was crying while she was eating, as if the food, even though it was soft, was hurting her.

That winter, she roamed outside in the cold and rain. She became thin, and her coat matted. She now allowed me to pet her, but when Chris tried to pick her up and examine her teeth, he was rewarded with scratches.

In the spring, we left the door open and put her food in our house. Cautiously, she came in and ate and then ran back outside. By then, we had stopped calling her Mary's cat and named her Missy. That fall, when the weather turned colder, she began staying in and finally settled on Chris's lap.

It had taken a year, but we were finally able to take Missy to the veterinarian. She laughed at us. "I think you'd better change your cat's name. It's not a girl; it's a boy." We renamed him Mister. But the other news she gave us wasn't funny.

"Your cat needs all his teeth pulled, his gums scraped, a flea treatment, antibiotics…" She just kept ticking things off on her fingers.

"How much is this going to cost?" Chris asked.

"Probably between six hundred and one thousand dollars."

I wanted to cry. On Social Security, we didn't have the money for this, especially for a senior cat who might not last much longer. We paid for the visit and a shot of penicillin and went home feeling hopeless and sad.

Every four months, I hosted my writers' group at our home. One month, Mister came in while we were reading our chapters and began eating. Betsy, one of the authors, stopped mid-sentence and said, "Whatever is wrong with your cat?"

I explained Mister's problem and our lack of money to fix it. After everyone but Betsy had left, she said, "I'm going to call Grady."

Betsy and Grady are hardcore cat people like us. When she shared Mister's plight, he said, "Get everything done up to one thousand dollars."

We were so grateful and relieved. We called the next day and were able to get Mister in for all his procedures.

When I told the staff what had been done for our cat, they shaved off some charges, and the total came to six hundred dollars.

Mister healed quickly and filled out. We bathed and brushed him. His gray, black, and white coat was now soft. He ate without pain. He was still an indoor/outdoor cat, so he would meander around our

What a Character | 95

mobile-home park.

One day, another neighbor called Chris and said, "Will you please come and get this kitten? It's wandering around in the middle of the street and will get run over."

Then, Chris called me and told me the sad story of the kitten whose eyes were completely crusted shut, with no mother in sight.

I sighed. "Okay, bring her home."

I fed the tiny mite with an eyedropper filled with goat's milk and put a hot-water bottle under the blanket in her bed.

Mister didn't like the kitten, Muffin, because we were paying him so much attention. He began staying away, not even coming back at night.

Weeks later, Chris was doing some maintenance work in our park. Mister sauntered up the driveway.

"Well, hello, Mister," Chris said. "Where have you been?"

Jean, the lady he was working for, said, "Mister? No, that's my new cat, Buster. He just showed up here. He keeps me company at night, sleeps on my bed."

Another day, while Chris was repairing Heather's porch, Mister came to be petted. Heather said, "Oh, my cat Pickles likes you, Chris. He's more of an outdoor cat."

So, we were obliged to share Mary's cat/Missy/Mister/Buster/Pickles with our neighbors, but we didn't mind since he came home for cameo appearances.

We had an opportunity to move from Oregon to California two years ago to be near our daughter. When we sold our mobile home, we told the lady that it was likely our jointly shared cat would show up on her doorstep asking for a handout.

"Oh," she said, "I've always wanted a cat."

So, we said fond goodbyes to our furry friend without a guilty conscience. After getting settled at our new residence with Muffin we called the new tenant to find out if Mister had shown up.

"Yes, but he's afraid of my dog. Steve who lives across the way says that the cat you described is his cat. He says he's the nicest cat he's ever had. He calls him Peanuts."

Sure enough, we visited the mobile-home park a year later, and there he was on Steve's porch. We went again this year. Stiffly, he walked toward us, winding around our legs as we petted him, a senior cat in a senior mobile-home court, a cat with six names.

— Ramona Scarborough —

As Cunning as a Fox

*My relationship with cats has saved me
from a deadly, pervasive ignorance.*
~William S. Burroughs

During my London days, I lived in a ground-floor apartment overlooking a beautiful garden. The building-management terms stated that the garden was for "viewing, not using."

Well, those of us on the ground floor ignored that, climbing through our windows to picnic out on the lawn during warm spring days, much to the consternation of a particular resident on the top floor. Donna didn't have this convenient garden access, yet we constantly invited her to come through our windows to join us.

However, it seemed Donna preferred to make a hobby out of writing complaint letters to the leasehold management company instead. A fellow apartment owner's party that got too merry on a Saturday night? The management company would send a polite letter expressing "a resident's" dissatisfaction. The other residents and I had invited Donna to all our parties. Yet, like the garden picnics, she declined before complaining "anonymously" about what she saw as rule-breaking.

During the furtive picnics on the lawn with my fellow ground-floor neighbours, my longhaired, grey cat, Roscoe, would jump through the window and join us, hoping for titbits from our sandwiches.

"It's such a lovely garden," Shelia said. "Roscoe should at least be allowed free access to it, not just when we're out here."

What a brilliant idea, I thought. I got my then boyfriend to install a cat flap beneath the wood panel under my window.

Days later, I received a letter from the management company telling me a resident had complained about the newly installed flap and that my cat had been seen sitting in the garden.

How mischievous of him!

I read through the lease and then wrote back, stating, "There is nothing here that advises one's pets can't access the garden, nor anything that forbids a cat flap. Roscoe is doing no harm apart from sunbathing and chasing the odd butterfly. I can't imagine why a resident would complain, unless, of course, it's the neighbour at number 27, whom I'm sure you hear from regularly."

The management company's response was brief, if not a little tongue-in-cheek. They agreed that as my pet was causing no harm, they would be prepared to "let sleeping cats lie."

Shortly after, Donna came up with a new plan to keep my cat out of the garden. She began a ritual of throwing cooked chicken out of her top-floor window onto the lawn, hoping to attract foxes. We lived not far from an open woodland and were aware that some foxes were about.

The foxes began visiting our garden each evening. I quite enjoyed watching these furry, red critters as they sat peacefully in a circle waiting for chicken pieces to drop from heaven. As they only came at night, the ritual hardly curtailed Roscoe's afternoon garden explorations.

Then, one evening, there was a knock on my door. On opening it, Donna stood, her jaw clenched in annoyance.

"Please, can you get your cat out of the garden?" she said.

An icy wave of fear washed over me. *Oh, no. The foxes.* "Is my cat okay?"

"He is, but it's not fair," she said. "Look out your window."

I rushed to the sitting room and peered through the glass. I then stifled a laugh at the scene before me. The foxes sat in a circle as usual, their pointed faces turned up towards Donna's dark window. Amongst them sat a smaller, grey, longhaired animal. I watched as Roscoe rose taller within the circle, standing now as he stared up towards Donna's

What a Character |

window. Then, he let out a long, impatient meow.

"'He did this last night, too,' Donna said, her tone sharp."

"And do they let him eat with them?"

"Let him?" She grimaced. "I'll show you what this cat of yours does."

She left the apartment. I walked back to my sitting-room window and waited. The light came on through Donna's window. She appeared there a moment later with a bowl in her hand. On seeing Donna, Roscoe let out another meow, this one longer and louder.

Donna threw down the chicken pieces. As the stringy meat landed on the ground, Roscoe confidently sauntered towards the middle of the circle, where most of the pieces had landed, and sat himself down to eat. The foxes then followed his lead, gently eating the chicken pieces nearest them, behind Roscoe.

Bravo! I thought. *What a courageous cat.*

I've since looked it up, and I now know that the word for a group of foxes is a "skulk." Yet, as I watched Roscoe and his fox followers convivially enjoying their chicken dinner that night, the word that came to me was "pack." For, if every pack had its leader, these foxes had ordained my fluffy Persian cat as theirs.

Eventually, the companionable outdoor dinners ceased. Donna sold her apartment and moved away. The chicken pieces from heaven stopped, and the foxes slowly returned to the woodland. However, Roscoe, my lovable, mighty Persian cat, remained in charge of his little territory, strolling his garden, day or night, whenever the mood took him.

Then, occasionally, just to remind him how he became leader of a pack of foxes, I would treat him to an evening chicken dinner in my kitchen.

— Karen Storey —

Tail or No Tail

Things are not always what they seem; the first appearance deceives many; the intelligence of a few perceives what has been carefully hidden.
~Phaedrus

I was thirteen when we moved from the city to a large house in the country complete with a horse barn and fifteen acres of land. The house sat on a hill behind five acres of manicured front lawn.

My family members were all animal lovers. We had a house cat and a small dog when we moved there, and we soon added four horses, a large farm dog, and several barn cats. One day, when we'd lived there a couple of years, I walked down to the mailbox at the end of our driveway and found a very tiny calico kitten with only a tiny stub of a tail. I'd never seen a cat without a tail before. I picked her up and carried her back to the house with me.

"Mom, look what I found in the front yard."

"Oh, my, she's not very old. Was she alone?"

"Yep. Where do you think she came from?" I asked. Our closest neighbor lived a half-mile down the road.

"I don't know. I've heard of people dropping off kittens or puppies in front of nice-looking houses in the country. I guess someone could have thrown her away." Mom took her from me. "She doesn't have a tail! She must be a Manx. They're rare."

"Can we keep her?"

"We'll see. First, we'll need to see if someone has lost her. Maybe she wandered away from home."

When my dad got home from work, Mom showed him our new arrival with the stub of a tail. "I think she's a rare Manx," she repeated, beaming.

"Don't be silly," Dad said. "No one would throw away a valuable cat. It's obvious that her tail got cut off."

"Cut off?" I exclaimed in horror. "How could that happen?"

"I don't know, but if someone threw her away, they weren't good cat parents. Maybe she got it caught in something, or maybe someone cut it off to be cruel. I don't think she's a Manx."

"Well, I do," Mom said defiantly.

After asking all our neighbors, we didn't find where she'd come from, so Stubby, as we aptly named her, became a member of our family.

For that first couple of years, Mom and Dad had an ongoing, good-natured disagreement about whether Stubby was born without a tail or had somehow lost it. When friends and relatives visited, Mom would proudly show off her rare Manx cat while Dad would just laugh.

Then one day, she got outside and got pregnant by the neighbor's tomcat, who, of course, had a long, bushy tail. My parents' debate kicked into full gear. Mom was convinced that we were about to have a litter of tail-less cats, while Dad was convinced that he would finally win the argument when they were all born with long tails. They even put some money on the bet, and my brother and I got involved, me betting on tails and my brother on no tails.

As the weeks of Stubby's pregnancy passed, we all waited in eager anticipation. Then came the big day. She had four beautiful, healthy kittens — one with no tail, one with a stub like hers, one with a short tail about an inch long, and one with a full, long tail. Mom won the bet. It was obviously a genetic trait. Dad graciously admitted he'd been wrong all along.

It was easy to find homes for the short-tailed cats as Mom proudly advertised them as Manx. Stubby had another litter before we got her fixed, also with varying lengths of tails. Throughout my childhood, I enjoyed having litters of kittens from several different cats we owned, but I never enjoyed one as much as Stubby's and the variety of tails. The little, discarded cat had definitely brightened all our lives.

—Jill Haymaker—

Taming the Tank

If you would know a man, observe how he treats a cat.
~Robert Heinlein

A small gray cat streaked from our wooden shed. "There she goes again," my mom said.

Felines seemed to collect at our house, but this one hung around more than most. A couple of weeks later, we heard mewing coming from the back of the building. *Uh-oh.* While their mama was away, we found five tiny kittens huddled together behind a pile of planks.

My family provided for them the best we could, but we dared not venture too close, unwilling to risk a nasty scratch from their fierce protectress of a mother. Bringing the kittens into the house was out of the question. Their mom would never allow it. Still, many dangers awaited her babies.

When the kittens grew old enough to venture from the garage, neighborhood kids chased them up and down the alley behind our garage with shopping carts. We couldn't stay outside twenty-four hours a day and help Mama Cat protect them, so adoption seemed the best option. We eventually found them all loving homes and sneaked them away one by one while their mother went off hunting mice.

Unfortunately, Mama Cat didn't learn from her first experience and had another litter. And another. We could only adopt out so many babies and never succeeded in catching her to have her spayed.

With each pregnancy, her little body became broader and flatter

What a Character

until one day my mother said, "She looks like a tank."

Watching her waddle at top speed toward anything that threatened her children, I had to agree. As myriad infantrymen have learned, nothing withstands a tank. We all backed down when Mama Cat came after us.

All except my boyfriend, Stan. For some reason, Mama Cat took a shine to him. Maybe because he sat for ages murmuring to her, Stan eventually reached the point that he could scratch her behind the ears — for a few moments anyway. Then, she would skitter away.

My mother marveled that Stan could achieve such a feat with our little tank. The wheels began turning. Though Mom desperately wanted to stem the flow of kittens, she had a more immediate concern. A legion of fleas had taken up residence on Mama Cat and threatened her health because they could infect her with tapeworms next.

Mom handed my boyfriend a flea collar. "Do you think you could put this on her?"

Stan looked doubtful but took it. "I'll try."

Scratching Mama Cat was one thing, but buckling a collar around her neck? Quite another.

It took more than an hour of coaxing, sweet talking, and bribery with cat treats, but when Mama Cat finally bolted away, she was wearing the collar. Stan's feat took on mythical proportions. Now, anything was possible, right?

Making an appointment for spaying at the vet's office was more an act of faith than anything else. Our faith in Stan. Mama Cat's faith in Stan. And Stan's faith that he would survive an encounter with the tank.

Anyone who has tried to force an unwilling cat into a box has an inkling of the challenge he faced. Multiply that by a feral tigress who had defied capture for years, and a clearer picture emerges. Stan took a deep breath, positioned the pet crate on its side in our downstairs entry hall, and coaxed Mama Cat into the vestibule. The rest of us stayed out of sight while Stan sat on the steps and waited. Like an old-fashioned Pong video game, our little tank bounced from one wall to another, trying to find a means of escape, but gradually she quieted and even made forays into enemy territory for brief petting. Stan's deep, gentle

What a Character

voice soothed her further, and thanks to time, tenacity, and strategically placed treats, she stepped into the box. With deft movements, Stan flipped up the carrier and closed it.

I ran down the stairs to cheer him, but Stan gloomily shook his head. "She'll never trust me again."

However, a funny thing happened. Once Mama Cat recovered from surgery, she accepted Stan's attention more willingly than ever. He said she thought the sadistic box had trapped her, not him, and that he had been her sole ally. I'm not so sure. Maybe it was because Mama Cat had finally found a man who had her best interests at heart, and she knew a good thing when she saw it — as did I.

No longer needing to pose as a tank who took on all comers, Mama Cat eased into our family. Although she'd had a hard life, surviving the only way that she knew how, Mama Cat allowed herself to trust again and find love with us. Along the way, she taught me the traits to look for in a man: gentleness, constancy, loving kindness. We both decided Stan was a keeper.

— Tracy Crump —

Never Name a Cat After a Natural Disaster

Most of us rather like our cats to have a streak of wickedness. I should not feel quite easy in the company of any cat that walked about the house with a saintly expression.
~Beverly Nichols

On September 10, 2017, Hurricane Irma made landfall on Cudjoe Key in the lower Florida Keys as a Category 4 hurricane. One hundred forty-nine miles to the north, I was in lockdown with my mom and my partner in Memorial Hospital Miramar, where my partner had been admitted after throwing her back out while helping me put up our storm shutters. My then ninety-year-old mom and I were allowed to spend the night in the hospital with her instead of going home to ride out the storm.

In the hospital's lobby, seventy-five pregnant women and their families camped on inflatable beds. The pressure of a hurricane can induce labor. The hospital officials were taking no chances that the women would go into labor at home with no emergency vehicles able to get to them.

Six miles to the south, another female was going into labor in the crawl space above my mom's garage. She was part of a colony of cats that had "adopted" my mom after my dad passed. No one knows where the cats came from. But we considered them guardian angels sent by my dad to care for and comfort my mom.

We had tried to round up the cats before the storm and get them to a safe place, to no avail. I was particularly concerned for the pregnant cat whose kittens were imminent.

As I locked the door to my mom's house before leaving that day, I said a silent prayer that they would all be safe.

After two nights of lockdown in the hospital, we were finally allowed to go home. I dropped off my mom at her house and promised to return the next day to help clean up the debris in her yard.

There was no sign of the cats, and even though animals know how to find shelter during storms, Hurricane Irma's winds had been pretty rough, and I was worried.

My worst fears were put to rest the next day when I looked inside a large pot in my mom's front yard and found a momma cat and six tiny kittens.

Days passed, the kittens grew, and the neighbors took turns feeding them. Everything was back to normal, except for the occasional sounds from my mom's attic and faint, intermittent meowing that we thought was coming from the cats outside.

One morning, there was a loud thump inside one of the walls. My mom was having some work done around the house, and she asked the handyman to see if he could determine what it was.

He located the source, opened a hole in the wall where the sound was coming from, and out popped a surprised but very feisty kitten.

She had been left behind in the attic after birth, and the momma cat had climbed up each day to feed her. During an exploratory trip around the attic, the kitten fell through one of the beams and landed on the floor behind my mom's living room wall.

We named her Irma.

That was our first mistake.

Hurricane Irma caused widespread destruction, but it was no match for the psychological terror her namesake kitten would inflict on her family of humans.

My mom would insist that the cat "never comes in the house." But I would open the door, and a foot away from me, I would find the tiny terror staring at me, daring me to go inside.

To this day, the minute my car pulls into the driveway, she prances over to me and demands food, and I am not allowed to even say hello to Mom before feeding Irma. Doing so risks a look of disapproval so strong that I melt on the spot.

That look is her secret weapon. It's a combination of cuteness and caution that instantly hypnotizes me. The words coming from my mouth sound like a mother talking to her newborn.

"Oh, you little baby waby cutie pie! I wuv you, little Irma. Sorry, sweetie weetie."

I mean, what is that? I used to be a grownup human. What happened to me?

It's then that Her Royal Highness of the Hurricane allows me to pick her up, but only so she can give me an earful of everything that has happened since my last visit.

She also loves to tease me by rubbing up against my leg and allowing me to pet her. But if I do so for too long, she'll slap my hand as if to say, "That's enough. I'll let you know when it's okay to approach me again."

She's tiny, but she reigns through intimidation. We had her spayed, thinking it would help her mood, but it did the opposite. Instead of calming her down, she used this as an excuse to punish us for messing with her private parts.

If I put out a bowl of food for her, no cat dares to get too close.

If I fill bowls for her and the other cats who also call the neighborhood home, she will eat from all of them while the other cats (usually twice her size) sit in a corner waiting for the queen to finish before timidly eating whatever Irma leaves behind.

Like the hurricane she was named after, Irma can be unpredictable and quickly change her mood. My mom, her accomplice, excuses Irma's behavior with a smile and a reprimand.

"Oh, look how cute she is. Give her some more food before she

What a Character

wastes away!"

It's like the two of them have formed a pact to remind me that, even though I am my mom's only human daughter, Irma is just one cute feat away from overtaking me on the favorite-daughter scale.

Despite — or perhaps because of — her quirkiness, I adore Irma. She not only knows this, but she uses it as a weapon against me, knowing I will do whatever she asks.

When I complain to my fellow cat people that Irma is a spoiled brat, they smile and offer this as solace: "You named her after a hurricane. What did you expect?"

— Barbara A. Besteni —

The Cat Who Wouldn't Squeak

A meow massages the heart.
~Stuart McMillan

"Look what I've found in the bushes!" my husband announced as he came in the back door, carrying something gray and scrawny.

"Not another cat!" I sighed.

"Not another cat!" echoed my mom, who lived with us.

I glanced at our Maine Coon mix, Milot. Maybe I was delusional, but I thought I could see her shaking her fuzzy head.

So, I promised the new kitty to a friend. But first I took it to the vet, who diagnosed it with an injured kidney caused by a fight with another animal. I decided to nurse it back to health before I gave it away because I couldn't give my friend a damaged kitty, could I? It's not that he was so beautiful, but he was hurt and alone, after all.

Do you know what a Cornish Rex looks like? Certainly not like our gorgeous Milot. This one had a very long face and large ears. But he had the softest fur.

I learned that nature only gave Cornish Rexes one layer of fur, while most other cats got two, so Mother Nature made it softer.

Larry named him Squeaky, although I wondered why since he never uttered a sound. We were accustomed to Milot, who was a "talker." She'd sit on our bed and yak loudly, as if relating the events of her day.

While recovering, Squeaky would sit on the floor and watch us chat. Wherever Milot was, so was he. He was smitten with her, following her around like a puppy, if you'll excuse the expression.

From across the house, Mother could sometimes be heard yelling at us to pipe down because she couldn't sleep. That's how much noise our Milot made.

Once you nurse a cat to health, you can't help but fall in love with it. This new cat turned out to be the sweetest! When Mom realized what a prize he was, she decided she wanted him for her own.

"I need my own cat. You have Milot. I have no one. I want Squeaky to talk to, to sleep in my room, to cuddle."

What could I say? I may have been old enough, but I was still not strong enough to go against my mother's wishes. I gave in completely, conveniently forgetting about giving away the cat.

But instead of hanging around Mom, Squeaky became Milot's shadow, always hovering in the background. He adored her. He'd listen to every meow she made, fascinated, but he never uttered a sound.

"What made you name him Squeaky?" I asked Larry one day. "He hasn't made a noise since he's been here."

Mother decided to take the situation into her own hands like she did everything else in the household.

"Leave it to me!" she said. "I'll teach him to meow like a normal cat."

"Go for it!" conceded Larry, with a smirk. "Good luck."

Each day when I'd get home from work, I'd catch Mom locked in her room with "the cat-in-training." The seven-pound prisoner-kitten would be placed on her dresser. They'd be eye-to-eye, and Mom would coach him.

"Speak! Meow! Say something."

Squeaky was a boy of few words — actually, none.

Occasionally, a tiny murmur might escape his lips, but it would hardly be called meowing — more like he was pleading to be released from Mom's clutches.

After a few days, Larry approached Mom, teasing, "How are the speech classes going?"

"Nothing yet. Not *my* fault. He'd be fluent by now if you hadn't

What a Character

named him Squeaky."

Mother was a toughie.

If she left her door open for a second, Squeaky would charge out as if escaping from the clinker. Stalking Milot was much more fun than speech lessons from that tyrant.

Eventually, Mom assumed Squeaky didn't like her. She became discouraged. Not one to accept responsibility, she blamed Larry.

"It's your fault he can't meow. What kind of ridiculous name is 'Squeaky' anyway?"

One day, I took Mom into the hospital for some minor surgery. The surgery turned out fine, but unfortunately, as sometimes happens afterward, she suffered a minor heart attack. I was with her in the hospital when it occurred. It was frightening, as one can imagine. The doctors took over her care, and as soon as she was stable, I called home to give Larry the news.

"Pray for Mother. She had a slight heart attack. But she's going to be fine," I quickly added.

He asked what time it had happened. When I asked why he needed to know, he said, "A couple of hours ago, Squeaky started howling like I've never heard a cat howl before."

It had been two hours since Mom had suffered her heart attack. A bizarre coincidence?

Thankfully, Mom recovered and was released a few days later. While driving her home, I called Larry to tell him we were on our way.

"I know," he replied.

"How do you know?" I asked.

"Because Squeaky started howling again."

The cat who wouldn't squeak had found his voice. Arriving at our front door, Mother and I could hear this thunderous and joyful wailing from inside. As we walked in, Squeaky wrapped himself around Mom's legs with such passion and delight that it brought tears to my eyes. Mom was elated.

While Mother recuperated, Squeaky, the cat who finally learned to squeak, never left her bedroom. He stayed glued to her, showering her with love, affection and babbling. He stayed on her bed or followed

What a Character

her wherever she went.

Mom healed completely. When Squeaky realized his services were no longer a matter of life and death, he went off to fulfill his own dreams. Every morning, he'd search for Milot and spend the day following her around. But, in the evening, he returned to Mom's room to chat, cuddle and sleep. He was her cat at last!

Often, the noise coming from Mother's room would keep us awake. Squeaky's meow was the loudest. It was Mom talking to Squeaky or Squeaky talking to her. I never knew what they said. I only know we had to keep telling them to keep down the noise so we could sleep.

The cat who never squeaked still didn't talk to anyone else but Mom. And when he did, it came from the heart.

Mother always got her way.

—Eva Carter—

A Spa Day

Who among us hasn't envied a cat's ability to ignore the cares of daily life and to relax completely?
~Karen Brademeyer

When the weather is rainy and dreary, I need a project to make me feel cheery. If I don't have much on my daily calendar, I quickly turn this bad day into a special spa day. It is not my personal spa day, as you would expect, but a fun "Cat Spa Day."

I have four female cats, which immediately puts me in the category of "A Crazy Cat Lady." I see nothing wrong with the fact that I love cats because they add happiness and meaning to my life. Since the foursome are all rescue felines, I have given them a healthy, happy home and companionship.

My life is full and well-balanced. I enjoy writing and leading my weekly prompt-writing group, gardening, cooking, entertaining family and friends, designing fancy broaches, and painting. And, of course, being a nurturing mom to my cats and box turtles.

Spa Day is very important to me and my cats. After lunch, I carry them into the bathroom, one at a time, to brush them, clean their ears with a cotton swab, brush their teeth, cut their nails, and wash and comb out any fur balls they may have. Depending on the day, they may or may not be enthusiastic about being groomed. They all accept their beauty treatment, though, because they have no choice. This is a spa day in which they all must participate.

What a Character

Cookie, my largest and fattest black-and-white cat, needs a forklift to get her onto the bathroom counter where I work my magic. She is both heavy and floppy. Baby, a multi-colored cat, is shy and plays with the water in the sink. Little One, my orange cat, needs a lasso to catch her and two strong hands to contain her. She is my Olympic jumper and never stays in one place for more than a few minutes. Brenda, my youngest and sweetest black cat is calm and collected and lets me have my way with her with no resistance.

Usually, after finishing up the first cat, the others can sense that they are next and try to hide somewhere in the house. I can find them easily, as their hiding places tend to be under the bed, a throw blanket or pillow on the couch. A tail sticking out is a dead give-away and so predictable. "Gotcha!" is the last thing they hear before entering the bathroom, and "Nice, clean kitty" is the last thing they hear after they've been glamorized.

Personally, I have never attended a girl's spa day nor do I have any future plans to do so. I watch the housewives on television as they enjoy their spas, a luxury that has become their lifestyle, not mine. I will continue to pamper myself and don't need any help in the process. A hot bubble bath with candles glowing in the bathroom and soft music playing is my version of a spa day. I can give myself a facial and manicure, and with the phone turned off, I am totally relaxed. A regular spa day would be both time-consuming and expensive.

It is fortunate for my cats that they can enjoy a free spa day with someone who loves them, cares for them, and attends to their individual needs… me! Although they don't thank me or leave a tip, and instead wiggle and squirm in my arms, I enjoy the satisfaction of seeing the end results. It takes a lot of time, energy and preparation for a cat spa day, and I am sure they are grateful when it's over, like I am. They even get a hug and a spritz of perfume when leaving the bathroom.

I guess I do qualify as "A Crazy Cat Lady" after all.

— Irene Maran —

Barry on Board

*A cat's rage is beautiful, burning with pure cat flame,
all its hair standing up and crackling blue sparks,
eyes blazing and sputtering.*
~William S. Burroughs

My family was not happy about our upcoming move from the large city in the south of the province to a small town up north where I'd accepted a new job. It was an excellent employment opportunity for me: more money, better prospects for advancement, and a chance to put my engineering skills to practical use. So, my wife Lillian put on a brave face and assumed an upbeat attitude for my benefit and to encourage our two children.

But Ryan, age five, and Chloe, ten, were not taken in by their mother's positivity or Dad's tales of how wonderful the northern town was, what with the natural beauty of the growing community, and all the new houses, buildings and recreational facilities. The kids did not want to leave their friends and the unlimited shopping and entertainment options available in the city.

"Big house — all our own — huge front and back yards, forest, lake, beach, fresh air!" I enthused, extolling the swimming, boating, fishing, camping, hiking, golfing, curling, skating and other activities available. "Way more exciting than the polluted, crowded, concrete jungle we live in now."

Ryan and Chloe glanced glumly up at me, seated on cushions in the tiny, nearly empty living room of our rented side-by-side.

"It'll be an adventure!"

Our cat, Barry, was sitting on a packing box, staring at me with his shining blue eyes, the perpetual smile on his black-furred face widening with delight at my rah-rah antics, his gleaming, white fang teeth showing.

I pulled out my car keys and dangled them in front of the attentive cat, rattling them. "It's a big change, but it'll be worth it in the long run."

Barry playfully shot out a paw and smacked my key-gripping fingers with his pad.

"See! Barry has the right attitude! He's giving me a high-five to the move!"

Chloe rolled her eyes. Ryan sighed and looked away.

Barry dramatically turned on me early the following morning. We had finished loading up the car with the rest of the stuff remaining in our side of the duplex we'd called home for ten years. The moving van had departed with our furniture two days earlier.

It would be an all-day drive to our destination.

Barry the cat sat on Ryan's lap in the back seat of the car, next to Chloe. Barry was bobbing his head around in an agitated, alarming manner, his mouth open, his furry body quivering.

When I started the car, Barry yowled, long and loud, almost shattering the car windows and everybody's eardrums. He hadn't been in a car ride since Ryan and I had picked him up as a kitten at a friend's house and driven him home two years prior. That raucous howl, and his blue eyes, belied his part Siamese heritage.

I grinned in the rearview mirror. "Here we go!"

Barry bellowed another yowl that overwhelmed the enclosed space of the car, like a ship's horn unexpectedly going off, but nowhere near as melodious.

I pulled away from the curb. Our adventure had…

Barry leapt off Ryan's legs, clawed up the back of the seat and clambered onto the ledge under the rear windshield. He crowded up against the glass, staring out at our retreating old home, hunched down, ears flat, his body shaking like he was about to lunge at some

What a Character

prey, panting heavily with his long tongue hanging out. He let out another yowl that shook the car.

    For eight hundred plus miles!
    Fourteen and a half hours!
    Yowling! Howling! Growling!
    Panting! Pacing! Prowling! Clawing!
    Hissing! More yowling!

    Ryan gave up trying to coax some calm into the cat after thirty minutes. Chloe huddled against the opposite passenger door, trying to avoid contact with the cat. My wife and I stared straight ahead at the road. Each one-hundred-decibel yowl sent chills racing up and down our spines.

    When we (frequently) stopped for a bathroom or mental-health break, or a bite to eat, somebody had to stay with Barry in the car to prevent him from tearing up the interior. And, despite it being a warm day, we had to keep the windows almost fully up to keep Barry from squeezing through and racing back down the highway.

    Nobody spoke for the final four hundred miles of our tortuous journey.

    Except Barry, whose crazed energy was relentless.

    Whatever goodwill about moving I'd built up before, Barry had now shredded with his road rage.

    When I finally drove up the driveway and rocked the car to a stop, I had to snatch Barry from the back seat and rush the squirming, spitting, yowling cat through the house and out into the expansive backyard. A small, sour cheer arose as I slammed the back door on our pet.

    Everybody avoided Barry for the next two days, too busy unpacking and getting adjusted to our new surroundings to care much about the cat, other than to feed and water him. There was still a lot of ill feeling towards our furry family member.

    Barry was occupied anyway, sniffing and poking around, exploring every nook and cranny of the large house, bushes, trees and rock garden in the yard. He got to watch the abundance of birds, squirrels and rabbits that inhabited the woods in back of our home.

On the third morning at our new place I jingled the car keys at the kids slumped on the couch in the living room. Morale was still lower than the local mineshaft. "How 'bout we try that hotel coffee shop for breakfast today?" I said brightly and bravely. "Then go on a tour of our beautiful new hometown?"

The kids listlessly fidgeted and groaned.

The excitement and eagerness for which I'd been wistfully striving came from a most unexpected source.

Barry suddenly shot out of the kitchen, from where he'd been eating out of his food bowl, and charged into the living room, apparently triggered by the sound of the jangling car keys. He leapt up into Ryan's lap and playfully batted a paw at the keys I was dangling, meowing. His eyes shone, the smile on his furry face showing off his fangs and the tip of his tongue.

We all gaped at the cat, amazed at his display of joyful anticipation.

We piled into the car, Ryan clutching our purring, rubbing pet. They sat in the front with me, with Lillian and Chloe in back. Laughter and chatter filled the vehicle as the kids and my wife and I marveled at Barry's enthusiastic antics.

He stretched out with his back paws on Ryan's knees and his front paws up on the dashboard, gazing out at the passing homes, big lawns, wide streets, tall trees, and distant, sparkling-blue waters of the lake. His fur, fangs and eyes shone in the bright, clear sunlight. With a feline's temperamental and wise nature, he'd sized up his new home and was now showing his approval.

Barry was "on board" with our move, and the happy cat lifted all our spirits.

I let out a yowl of delight. Everyone (two-legged) gleefully echoed it!

—Laird Long—

Wait for Me!

Cats are a kindly master, just as long as you remember your place.
~Paul Gray

Rusty was born on our farm. As a kitten, he lived in the stall next to my horse. I worried about him more than the other farm cats because he would head off on his own and go exploring, even when he was too young to safely do so. He also seemed compelled to add a different twist to whatever activities his siblings were engaging in. If they were sunning themselves in front of the barn, he was sprawled on the window ledge of the chicken coop. I could never figure out how he could get up there when he was such a young kitten.

When Momma Cat started to take the kittens a little farther from the barn, and they were learning to climb trees, Rusty decided that climbing my horse's tail was a lot more fun! Fortunately, my horse did not object to it, and she would stand quietly as he practised his climbing skills. When he reached his destination and sat on my horse's back and surveyed his kingdom, her tolerance and his determination made them quite the team.

One day, Rusty was climbing her tail as usual, but the horseflies were especially bad. My horse swished her tail, and Rusty went flying. It took him a couple of days to plan another strategy, and then he had it!! He would wait until she was happily grazing and then climb up her face and walk along her neck until he reached the middle of her

What a Character | 121

back. Then, he curled up for his nap.

It became the norm to see my horse grazing in the pasture with Rusty sleeping on her back. When he awoke from his nap, he would wait until she put down her head and then make the trek back down her neck and leap to the ground from between her ears.

As Rusty became heavier, my horse wasn't quite as convinced that she needed a big cat hanging on her head. Whether it was coincidence or a well-thought-out plan between the two, they came up with a new strategy. She would walk over to the gate in her pasture, and Rusty would climb up the gate post and then leap to her back.

One day, I was planning on going for a ride in the country. My horse was saddled, and we were ready to go. Then, I remembered that spraying myself with a bit of mosquito repellent might be a good idea. I tied my horse to the gate, and when I returned Rusty was sitting in the saddle. I put him on the ground, got on my horse, and headed down the lane. I turned around to make sure that all was well and could see him running along behind.

I turned back and put Rusty in the barn. But he got out and followed us. Once again, I turned around and this time I locked him in the vacant chicken coop. It was screened, and I felt he would be safe there until I returned. I gave him food and water to distract him and assumed he would be happily sleeping when I returned.

I made it down the lane and turned around to check. No Rusty. I was happily riding down the road, enjoying the wonderful smells and sounds of summer in the country. I saw a tractor pulling large equipment coming down the road towards us. The farmer pulled over and shouted to me. He laughed and said, "Did you know that you have a cat following you?" And, sure enough, there was the escapee determined to find out where we dared to go without him!

The farmer said he would wait until Rusty caught up to us as he didn't want to risk running over him or scaring him with his equipment. I admitted to defeat and let Rusty ride home in my lap.

That was the beginning of what became our weekly routine. Our routes included busy grid roads between farms and the ditches alongside a busy highway. Locals would recognize us and slow down when they saw the horse and rider coming down the road with the orange cat peering at them from the saddle. The most frequent comment was "I can't believe that darn cat likes to ride a horse!" Strangers on the highway would often slam on the brakes and wait for us to catch up, so they could have a better look at the cat sprawled across my lap at the front of the saddle.

The three of us covered many miles together over the years, and I wouldn't have changed a thing. That little cat taught me to step outside the norm and to just go for whatever feels right. His determination and persistence to do things "his way" were valuable lessons in how to live life to the fullest.

— Brenda Leppington —

Chapter 5

Changed by the Cat

Respect

Respect is one of the greatest expressions of love.
~Miguel Ruiz

The winter winds howled and blew icy rain against the back door of the house. My sister Gail stood in the doorway frantically calling into the night for the cat who had disappeared earlier in the evening. Inside her spare bedroom, four newborn kittens cried out for their mother.

Gail was a cat lover. Through the years, many feral cats had found their way into her garden, and she fed and cared for them. Most had been unapproachable, but that never seemed to bother her. I was irritated that she was helping yet another, probably ungrateful, feral cat. This one had appeared when she was about to give birth, and Gail had welcomed the cold, starving cat into her spare bedroom and left her there until the birth of the kittens.

When the kittens arrived, the mother cat fed them during the day, and Gail would let the mother cat out to wander in the evening. The cat would disappear for an hour or two and then rush back to the house to feed her kittens.

On this night, the weather suddenly turned horrible, with snow and freezing rain. I received a frantic phone call from my sister asking if I would drive around with her and try to spot the missing cat. I agreed, but soon the lack of visibility made the task impossible. We gave up, and I went home to bed.

Morning brought no relief in the weather. Gail had been up most of the night checking the back door, but no cat had appeared. She went into the spare bedroom to check on the kittens. They were warm but noisily hungry. By this time, Gail was beginning to wonder how she would care for the orphaned kittens.

Suddenly, Gail heard a cry at the window. When she looked up, she saw the mother cat balanced on the freezing cold air conditioner that jutted out from the house. Her fur was plastered to her body, and ice had formed on parts of her back. Flecks of ice blew against her coat, but she remained un-moveable — steadfastly watching over her baby kittens inside the house. Her paws were buried in the icy snow. Apparently, she had been there all night during the storm.

Gail ran out the back door and managed to extricate the cat's paws from the snow. The momma cat wasted no time in dragging herself into the house and back to her kittens. The hungry babies swarmed their mother, oblivious to her cold, wet fur.

When Gail told me what had happened to the mother, I cried. I had viewed her as just another feral cat, but her faithful duty toward her kittens touched me. How could one not respect an animal who had put her own life at risk for the protection of her babies? All night long, in the freezing rain, a mother cat sat bravely watching her newborns through the window, desperate to get in. It was one of the most beautiful examples of selfless love I have ever seen.

— Judy Kellersberger —

The Twinkie Effect

One must love a cat on its own terms.
~Paul Gray

When my husband and I were first married, we owned two cats: Buster and Bubbles. They were our kids back then, and our lives revolved around them. Buster was the rascal, and Bubbles was the prude. They got along mostly, except when Buster kicked into play/attack mode! They were a good pair, nonetheless, and our animal world felt complete.

Then, when I was pregnant with our first son, a church member brought us Twinkie, a stray they'd rescued. Could we possibly give this little black kitty a home?

We took her, but within a week, we discovered the dirty little secret that the church member hadn't noticed. Young Twinkie was pregnant. And she was very young and not equipped to be a mama.

When her little tribe arrived, she spent more time playing and wrestling with them like a sibling than mothering them. She always retained a bit of her wildcat mannerisms.

We homed out all the kittens, and Twinkie stayed, but she was always like a dark shadow on the sidelines, not like a real family member.

It could have been her wildness, or perhaps she just had a boring personality — we didn't know. She just didn't click with us like the other cats did. We fed her and cared for her, but we never really bonded with her.

Changed by the Cat | 127

Years passed with Twinkie in the background, and our family grew to include three sons. One day, my husband said, "I think I will do an experiment on Twinkie. Every time I pass her by, I will pet her and say something nice to her. I want to see what will happen."

I didn't give that much thought. Twinkie just existed in our home, and I figured that was how she'd always be: quiet, aloof, and boring.

I chuckled while watching Greg tell Twinkie how beautiful she was, patting her head as he passed her, and chatting with her sometimes. She just sat on the porch railing, awkwardly enduring it.

It was probably several months later, maybe more, when we realized that something was changing. When Greg sat down, he'd suddenly have a black cat slinking over to sit beside him.

Also, Twinkie started subtly perking up and talking a little. We'd never even heard her voice before!

The most interesting thing we noticed happened when Greg knelt down for his morning prayer time every day. Twinkie began rushing over to hop up onto his back, remaining there the whole time.

Twinkie was becoming friendly!

Fast forward to me as a harried home-school mom with three middle-schoolers. We often butted heads, and I felt discouraged.

I started to wonder if the Twinkie Effect would work with people… particularly in the family. Could a lackluster kid or parent be transformed by consistent attention and friendliness? Of course, I knew it was possible in theory, but what would it take for me to break out of my grumpiness so that I could try it?

Old habits are hard to break, especially for moms who have uncooperative children. We think they need to change pronto, and they have the same opinion about us!

But something started to click for me when I thought of how friendly Twinkie became after the consistent little attentions. These attentions weren't even big, just pats and nice words, but they had a beautiful effect.

Our family has lived through challenges and stressful times recently. We became five people and three cats living in less than 300 square feet of space when we opted to live in our camper while building our house.

Changed by the Cat

I decided that I could at least give as much as my husband gave to Twinkie. I wanted to train myself to give a smile every time I passed by my children and husband.

At first, it was hard. Making myself smile felt fake, especially when my kids were acting like rascals.

My boys eyed me suspiciously, like, "What? What are you smiling at me for?"

I'm not saying it changed instantly, but with time, it has gotten easier. Soon, I hope it will be more automatic, but I remind myself that it will always be a choice.

I am actually getting some smiles back, even if they are goofy ones. They laughed at me for smiling at them! Sometimes, I make sure to give a cheesy smile, and then they almost can't help smiling back. It feels better than scowling.

A win is a win.

The Twinkie effect works.

—Laurie Spilovoy Cover—

Life Lessons from My Cat

Cats are not antisocial; they're selectively social.
~Author Unknown

When my husband passed away suddenly in 2013, I was devastated. Friends who were worried about me being alone told me I needed to get a pet. Of course, the dog lovers all suggested I get a dog, and the cat lovers all suggested a cat. For me, it was an obvious choice. I have always been a cat person.

I put my name on a list to be notified when new kittens came in at the local shelter. One day, I got the call and went up to see a litter of adorable tabbies.

They had them all in a room together, and prospective pet parents could go in and play with the kittens. There was one tiny thing that didn't want to come out and associate with any humans. Being an introvert and a loner myself, I knew she was the one for me. I named her Miesha because it means gift from God.

My husband's old office became Miesha's room. It has two glass-paned French doors that allow Miesha to see what is going on in the house. And there is also a large window through which she can see the front gardens. When I am home during the day, Miesha has full run of the house, but at night she stays in her room to sleep. I need my sleep too badly to have a kitty climbing all over me or meowing at night. So, she has her own room filled with kitty toys.

Miesha has never been a lap cat. She doesn't like to be picked up. Everything about her seemed to be introverted. We would sit together on the couch, but if I tried to pick her up and hold her, she would run away. We got along very well that way. And, like me, she has always been pretty selective about who she warms up to.

As the years went by, I started to develop health problems. I had chronic fatigue symptoms. I was very tired and weak a lot of the time. But Miesha, being a cat, would often get the zoomies and run back-and-forth across the house. One day, I was especially weak, and she was being frisky. She ran between my legs, and I fell over her and tripped. Although I had never broken a bone before, I knew right away that my wrist was broken. I got a cast on my right arm, but even my left hand wasn't very usable. And, for some reason, my legs got very weak after that, so I had to use a walker.

I became very cautious about letting Miesha out of her room. Even though I had the walker for support, she would still get under my legs and walk between the wheels of the walker. It got to the point where I kept her in her room a good percentage of the time.

Less than a month after I broke my wrist, I had a TIA and heart attack. I ended up in the hospital for almost a week. At first, I had a few friends stop by the house to feed Miesha. Eventually, I hired a pet sitter who was recommended by a friend. It was a little weird having a complete stranger come to my house when I wasn't there, but I needed to make sure that Miesha was taken care of. When the sitter came over, I could see and hear her from my hospital bed on the video-doorbell display on my phone, and she would start talking to Miesha even before she walked in the house. It made me smile to know that Miesha was in such good hands.

Once I was discharged from the hospital, I was still exhausted and weak on my feet. So, I kept Mary the pet sitter coming twice a day and I got to see her in action.

Mary not only fed Miesha but played with her, brushed her, kept her room clean, and brought her new toys. The cat was in heaven. Mary even trained Miesha to lie down on a special mat when she wanted Mary to brush her. Of course, Miesha missed having full run of the house. But I couldn't really let her out unless I was just sitting in one place.

At times, I would look in Miesha's room and almost be jealous of how well she and Mary were getting along. But how can you really be jealous of someone who is giving your fur baby so much love? I had thought that Miesha was so much like me and didn't really need or want a lot of attention. But now I saw a whole new side to her.

Seeing this major change in my "introverted" cat had an effect on me, too. Since I had started to look forward to our twice-daily visits from Mary, I realized maybe I wasn't as much of a loner or introvert as I had always thought. Mary started bringing her granddaughter Abby with her some days. Since I don't have children or grandchildren of my own, Abby added a whole new level of joy to my days.

Our pets teach us lessons in different ways. I'd always called myself a loner. I never needed a lot of people around me. I was kind of like little Miesha before I adopted her, hiding away from the rest of the humans, not really thinking I needed that kind of interaction. But watching how Miesha changed when she was around Mary made me realize that maybe I really did need more connections in my life. Not just anybody, of course. But maybe it was worth making the effort to meet some people whom I did want to let into my little world.

I still don't like crowds or a lot of people, but I'm happy to say that I have made some changes and developed new friendships that have become a huge part of my life. I've learned that just because I'm a loner, it doesn't mean I have to be alone. And Miesha seems to like these new relationships as much as I do!

—Betsy S. Franz—

A Senior Cat and the Value of Memories

It is impossible for a lover of cats to banish these alert, gentle, and discriminating little friends, who give us just enough of their regard and complaisance to make us hunger for more.
~Agnes Repplier

I was nervous as I walked into the local shelter with my husband. I'd spent the past few months grieving for my soul cat, Jimmie, a tiger-striped cat with tons of personality, sass, and a love for cuddling. We had a sweet kitten at home, but she was my husband's cat. I was missing my companion and my lap was empty in the evenings. It was time, I'd decided, to give another rescue cat a home. With trepidation, thinking that maybe each of us is only ever granted one special connection with a cat, I walked into the room of kittens with the shelter volunteers, hoping against all odds I'd form another special bond.

My husband and I played with kitten after kitten, and he tried to talk me into one of the playful white cats or the gray one stalking a toy. They were adorable, but something wasn't clicking. The shelter volunteer asked if I'd like to see the senior-cat room before making a decision. I nodded, despite my husband's warnings that an adult cat wouldn't live as long.

We walked into the communal cat room, and dozens of cats greeted us. I walked around, spending time petting cat after cat, wondering which one I should pick. And then I saw him.

A colossal black cat popped out of a tiny cat-condo bed. He was the biggest black cat I'd ever seen, and he walked right up to me, his green eyes locking with mine.

"Him. It's him," I said, an inner knowing taking over.

The coordinator began to tell me the story of Blackie, as he was called. He'd lived with an elderly lady who had gone into a nursing home months earlier. His four cat siblings had all been adopted already, but he was left because he was almost thirteen. No one wanted a cat that old, she explained.

My heart was stuck on him. My husband warned that it was a bad idea. "He won't live long, and then you'll be heartbroken again," he warned. But it was a risk I was willing to take.

We loaded Bob, as we'd decided to rename him, into a pet carrier. The shelter staff clapped as my husband carried him — it took two hands on the bottom to support his eighteen-pound size. They told us they'd worried that Bob would die in the shelter because no one would give him a chance.

I'd like to say that as soon as we got Bob home, we were best friends. That wasn't the case. Bob hid under our bed for almost three months, only popping out when we were at work or sleeping. I was devastated, my still grief-stricken heart wanting nothing more than to connect with him. I was patient, though, earning his trust slowly, week after week.

And then, finally, Bob came around, and I got to see what a sweet personality he had. He was nothing but kind to the kitten we already had, and although he didn't want to play with her, he would let her cuddle with him in the evenings. He loved sitting on our kitchen mat by the fridge, meowing for snacks throughout the day. We learned his favorite food was roast beef, and he only loved one toy, which was shaped like a doughnut. At night, he would cuddle on my lap and even wrap his paws around me. For two years, he helped fill the void left by my soul cat, making new memories with me as we celebrated holidays and even just the regular, in-between days. I even had the opportunity to put him in my second published novel, a sweet romance featuring an elderly lady with a beloved black cat.

On Black Friday two years after we adopted Bob, he suffered a stroke and passed away. It was gut-wrenching to experience another loss so soon. I cried my eyes out and wished we had more time.

Still, after the sudden shock of his loss settled in, I realized that I didn't regret picking Bob. In the two years he lived with us, I learned so much. He taught me patience. He was there to cuddle with me on the hard days, his sweet, green eyes steady and dependable. He taught me that sometimes the best things in life come in unexpected ways. He taught me that it's never too late to adjust to new environments or challenges. After all, at twelve, he'd had to undergo drastic change but still maintained his sweet personality. Most of all, he taught me that senior cats have just as much love to give as the younger, more popular kittens.

I still think about Bob all the time and the impact he made on our lives. I feel grateful we were able to be there for his final two years.

If you're thinking of adopting a kitten, I hope that when you go to the shelter, you'll think of Bob. I hope that when you're considering a young, playful cat, you'll wander over to the seniors there, too, and give them a chance. It isn't always about the quantity of time you have together — it's about the quality of the memories you make. Most of all, it's about the fact that you really can make a big difference for that one cat who needs you most.

— Lindsay Detwiler —

A Cat's Love Throughout the Years

What greater gift than the love of a cat?
~Charles Dickens

My younger son, Jim, wanted a cat for his tenth birthday and began a campaign to wear me down. Jim thought of every possible positive a new kitten could bring into our lives. "It will be cute! It will help wake us up in the morning! It will keep us warm in our laps!" I finally gave in and accompanied Jim, his brother Van, and my husband Gary on a trip to the local shelter.

We perused the cages to see which kitty struck our fancy. Of course, there were many adorable kittens, but none of them quite stood out as "the one" until my husband called out from the end of a row of cages, "Hey, how about this little white one?" We all ran over to see this potential contender. The "little white one" that Gary spotted was a kitten who was solid, unblemished white, the blinding white of newly fallen snow. Not a mark or freckle on him. The only other colors we saw were the pink of his ears, nose, and paw pads plus the green of his eyes.

We asked to hold him. The soft purr and contented snuggle of this little, white kitten sealed the deal. I was instantly smitten, and we named him Loki after the Nordic god of mischief. I thought his name was tongue-in-cheek. Such a sweet, angelic kitten could never live up

Changed by the Cat

to the reputation of the god Loki.

I was wrong.

Loki had the sweetest face I've ever seen on a kitten, but his heart was that of a little imp. That kitten's capacity for mischief was unmatched. Toilet paper, yarn, cups on the counter—all fell victim to Loki. The most familiar refrain in our house was an exasperated cry of "Loki!" as his latest messes were discovered.

Goodness, we loved him. And it seemed the more we loved him, the more that love was returned by our Little White Menace. No one could watch TV without Loki on their lap. A bathroom visit or shower had feline supervision. Bedtime was time for snuggles and purrs before our kitty settled in against one's chest or back. He came running and mewing at the sound of the can opener because it meant the possibility of a tuna treat. If the house was empty and Loki was alone for any length of time, the family's return would be greeted with loud and repeated meows asking, "Where were you? I missed you!"

This small bundle of fur had wormed his way into our home and our hearts.

As my sons grew and went off to college, Loki's "ownership" of family members changed. He had showered all of us with great affection, but with my sons out of the house, I became our kitty's favorite person. As I experienced the pain of an empty nest, I comforted myself with my last baby at home and became "Loki's Mama." I watched my once-rambunctious kitten grow older and more sedate, but his love never wavered, even as we both aged. He grew thinner, and the sweet roundness of his kitten face disappeared, much as the fullness of my face began to settle into hollows and creases. Loki's plush fur thinned and lost much of its sheen, just as my hair color dulled and faded.

I used to run an easy three miles with no strain but now found myself more and more winded toward the end of my workouts. Loki no longer attempted his youthful leaps to high countertops but contented himself with easier jumps to the living room couch. So, we aged together, but nothing dimmed the sparkle in those beautiful, green eyes of his, and age didn't diminish his want and need to be in every part and place of my daily life.

Why do pets live such relatively short lives compared to ours? I asked myself this question many times as Loki passed his seventeenth birthday, and his body grew weaker and frailer. Finally, my sweet kitty could barely struggle to his own feet. I tempted him with his favorite tuna to no avail. His appetite had vanished, and I knew it was time. The only thing that stayed young were his bright green eyes, and they gazed into mine as the vet administered the final injection. My sweet boy's eyes closed, never to reopen.

It's been over two years since Loki died, and I've adjusted fairly well, but every now and then I find myself looking for him out of the corner of my eye or listening for his mews as I return from running errands. We all love and lose pets and grieve, but this hit me so hard, far harder than I expected.

Loki was my final baby. My other babies had grown to be young men and were living their own lives, but a small white cat became my companion as we aged together and so many things changed for both of us.

— Liz Palmer —

Cute Kitties and Barbie Dolls

Kittens can happen to anyone.
~Paul Gallico

I am the eldest of three, and with two younger brothers, my parents did not bat an eye when I was still playing with Barbies in sixth grade. I was playing happily with my siblings, and my brother's G.I. Joes needed girlfriends, so what was the harm?

My classmates were not so understanding. We might have only been eleven, but we were in middle school now. Girls weren't supposed to play with Barbies and baby dolls anymore. We were supposed to be interested in makeup and boys. I had a large storage bin under my twin bed full of dolls. It was so full that I couldn't even attach a lid to it. Due to all the teasing, I started playing with the dolls less and less, but I still would take them out on a rainy day, neither wanting to give in to the bullies nor wanting to grow up yet.

My cat Strawberry was a black tabby with the most beautiful green eyes. She would sleep with me each night and greet me every day when I got home from school. When we found out that Strawberry was pregnant, I couldn't have been more excited. I got a big basket and as many old sheets as I could find, so Strawberry and her kittens would be comfortable. As Strawberry got bigger, she began to sleep in my bed less and less and in her basket more and more.

Two days before the vet's estimated due date, I was playing at a friend's house. My mom came to get me early because she hadn't seen Strawberry all afternoon and was worried about her. I immediately jumped in the car, knowing that she was probably hiding somewhere having the kittens. As we drove home, my mom explained that my brothers had their friends over and were being awfully loud, so Strawberry probably didn't feel safe in the basket I made her.

When I ran into my room, I heard the cries of tiny kittens. I looked all over my room, but I couldn't find where the cries were coming from. Finally, I peeked under my bed, and the cries got louder. I tried to pull out my Barbie bin, but it wouldn't budge. I peeked under again and saw that Strawberry was blocking the bin from being pulled out. I told her that it was me, and it was okay. She came out right away and jumped on top of my bed. I gave her a kiss on the head and a scratch behind the ears, and I told her what a good kitty she was.

"Now, let's see what you did," I said to Strawberry.

I finally was able to pull out the Barbie bin and found sweet, tiny kittens… surrounded by a sea of blood-covered Barbies.

"Oh, Strawberry, what did you do?" I said, laughing. My mom came in around this point, and what began with soft "oohs" and "aahs" for the kittens turned harsher as she took in the massacre.

We laughed together as I carefully moved each kitten safely into the basket that I had made for them as Strawberry purred at my side. She had five kittens: Cleo and Leo, the twin white Siameses; Jason, the black fluff ball; Spike, an orange tabby; and Stormy, with beautiful tortoiseshell coloring.

As I admired the kittens, my mom looked through the Barbie bin. She tried to be positive and suggested that maybe a few would be salvageable. I looked over at her holding my *Princess and the Pauper* Barbie that looked like she had just stepped off the set of *Carrie*.

I told my mom that I appreciated the positivity, but that I thought it was false hope. I wasn't as upset as I thought I would be. It was time to let go of my Barbie dolls. Sometimes, childhood slips away

Changed by the Cat

without you realizing it, and other times it ends with something really momentous, like a bin filled with bloody Barbies.

—Jessica Lorin Wood—

Belle

Cats are endless opportunities for revelation.
~Leslie Kapp

Like a lot of young couples, after we were first married, my wife and I spent a few years enjoying being childless. We traveled occasionally, slept in on the weekends, went to movies whenever we wanted, and watched friends start families and feel overwhelmed by the demands. We would talk about when we would start a family, but it always seemed to be something we would do when the time felt right. We both worked full-time, and I think we wondered what kind of parents we would be. When our discussions about starting a family became more serious, we did what a lot of couples do: We got a pet first.

My wife is a dog person, and I'm more a cat person. I was able to convince my wife that leaving a rambunctious puppy home alone all day probably wasn't a good idea, nor was it fair to the dog. Cats, I explained, were perfectly happy to be left alone. In fact, they preferred it as it gave them more time to do their favorite activity: sleep.

So, we headed off in search of a kitten. As luck would have it, there were a few kittens to choose from, and my wife picked out a little gray-and-white shorthair tabby she named Belle after a character in her favorite Disney movie. Belle was so small that her voice wasn't even fully developed. Sometimes, she would try to meow, and nothing would come out.

Belle quickly adapted to life with us at our small home. She loved to zoom up and down the hallway, in and out of bedrooms, before finally curling up in the corner behind the recliner and falling asleep. Soon, her favorite spot became the back of the couch where she could look out the front window as the world went by.

Sleeping in on weekends became impossible as Belle would sit at the entrance to our bedroom howling to be fed or, even more annoyingly, jump up to sit in the window above our bed, watching the birds outside at the feeder with her tail swishing inches above our heads.

Belle loved her cat toys, chasing them and batting them about, but her favorite toys were a small, wadded-up piece of paper and an empty box, thereby proving that the best toy for a kid or a cat is an empty box.

She also developed a taste for yogurt. Whenever one of us would open a yogurt container, she would come trotting into the kitchen. We wouldn't scrape the excess yogurt off the lid. Instead, we'd place it on the floor so she could lick it clean. She would slide the lid all over the linoleum floor, eventually pinning it under the cupboards, or more frustratingly, it would disappear under the stove. She would lie on her side with her little paw desperately trying to retrieve the lid, convinced it had a morsel of yogurt still on it.

And, like dealing with a child, there were moments of worry. She got mites in her ears, which my wife carefully and lovingly cleaned every night for a couple of weeks. And there was one incident when she tangled with another critter, needing an emergency weekend trip to the vet for stitches and antibiotics. She recovered just fine and was soon purring in our laps like before.

After a few years, we became relatively confident in our parenting abilities. After all, we had kept a cat alive. So, we decided to have a child. Our son soon came to love Belle as much as we did, and we always called her his older sister, reminding him that she was older than him by about five years.

Eventually, Belle began to slow down. She was less active, slept more, and put on a few pounds. Don't we all? She would still chase small balls of paper and lick yogurt lids, but less frequently, and her favorite place at night was curled up in front of the fireplace.

She grew old, and when she started not being able to digest her food, we knew it was time. With heavy hearts, we said goodbye, and my wife took her to the vet, who said she went quickly and peacefully.

I dug a hole in the backyard under a tree by the bird feeder and placed her in it. I covered her up, and with each shovelful, I felt tears welling in my eyes. When the hole was full, I got down on my hands and knees, smoothing over the dirt.

My wife and I stood there silently for a few moments remembering the joy and fun she brought into our lives. Most of all, we were grateful that the small gray-and-white tabby cat helped two young adults decide if they could be parents.

—John Danko—

Two Lives — One Kitten

> *If purring could be encapsulated, it'd be the most powerful anti-depressant on the pharmaceutical market.*
> ~Alexis F. Hope

The second I heard the soft mewing, my heart sank. As I walked down the stairs, looking under the piles of clothes and overturned furniture that littered my daughter's disaster of a bedroom, I knew what I'd find. And there it was. Hidden in a box, stuffed behind the nightstand, I found a five- or six-week-old calico kitten.

As I lifted her into my palm, she barely registered any weight. So tiny. So young. So incredibly beautiful with a big, black patch over her eye and vibrant colors splashed across her minuscule body. It was all so tragic.

It was my daughter's nineteenth year, and one of the worst of her life. Struck down with severe bipolar disorder at thirteen, she'd struggled with the disease for six years but had always been relatively compliant with her doctor's orders and her regular therapy.

Until she became an adult.

Then, she decided that she didn't want to be mentally ill anymore, and if she stopped taking her meds and refused to acknowledge the disease, it would just go away. Right?

Changed by the Cat

The result of this had been months of rapid cycling as she vacillated from the giddy highs of mania into the suicidal depths of depression and back again. It was a roller-coaster ride of near-death experiences punctuated by terrifying episodes of poor judgment. Yet, no matter how much her doctors or I begged, Katie would not consent to being hospitalized or taking her medication.

Many people caught up in this cycle of ups and downs engage in gambling, shoplifting, or other risky behavior. During this period, Katie did none of that, but she stole kittens (or took them from the feral cats behind the grocery). This little ball of fur was not the first pet stowed in a box in the corner. We'd already given away five stray kittens before this, and I was beside myself. Finding a home for one stray during kitten season was hard enough. We were now on number six, and I had long ago run out of friends and acquaintances willing to add a pet to their families.

But keeping her was out of the question. First of all, we already had a cat and dog. But, more importantly, I couldn't let Katie keep the fruits of her bad behavior. I couldn't let her profit from stealing these strays from their mamas — whether she was mentally ill or not.

So, while I brought food and a litter box for the night, I made Katie place an ad to adopt out the kitten — immediately.

The request was met with much wailing and gnashing of teeth. The cat was a stray. She needed it. It needed her. She'd be compliant if she could have it. If I was a good mother, I'd understand how much she loved and needed that kitten. I'd understand that this kitten could change her life.

Ten minutes after the ad was placed, we got the call.

As I pulled the phone to my ear, I heard the crying first.

"Oh, my gosh! Is the kitten still available? Please say 'yes.' We need her. My daughter needs her. Oh, please God, tell me that you haven't given away the kitten yet!"

After I assured the caller that I hadn't placed the kitten, this woman begged me to give it to her. When she asked why we were rehoming her, I explained that my daughter had her but was disabled and couldn't take care of her. Then, she told me her story.

She wanted the kitten for her daughter, Abby, who was also nineteen and disabled. Abby had been a normal, happy girl until her sixteenth birthday. Then, soon after, she called her mom to get her from school as she had a headache. By the time her mom got to school, Abby was in agonizing pain, and Mom had rushed her to the hospital. By the end of the day, her daughter was permanently paralyzed from the neck down.

Abby had handled her fate with real heroism throughout the rest of high school and had even graduated with honors. But, as her friends went off to college and began their adult lives, Abby had fallen into a deep depression at the prospect of spending the rest of her life alone in her bed.

As time passed, Abby had become less and less interested in interacting with life — until she saw Katie's kitten. "That's her! That's her!" she'd called to her mom. "I dreamed about her last night. I saw her in my dream. I knew she would be mine, and she looked just like this!"

And I knew in my soul that Abby was right. As Katie wept, I packed up the kitten and put her in the car. Katie had agreed that Abby needed the kitten but didn't have the heart to hand it over herself. I drove an hour in the night while that other mom did the same thing. There, at midnight, I handed her that tiny kitten as we both hugged and cried about our newfound camaraderie and shared pain. Yet, while I knew I'd be going back to my own heartbroken child, I had real faith that I was doing right by that kitten and right by Abby.

For the next few days, our house was silent with mourning.

Katie wouldn't talk. She'd barely look at me. She wouldn't eat. The mania that had sent her out finding "stray" kittens had turned into a deep despair at the loss of that tiny friend. Katie believed she needed no help — but she also had no hope.

Until the pictures came.

Three days later, my phone lit up — not just from the screen's illumination but from the joy filling the room from the message.

The first picture showed Abby with a cat toy in her mouth. The long straw stood out from her lips as colored feathers dangled from a string at the other end, and our sweet calico stood on Abby's chest, batting at the toy. The next was quieter. In it, Abby lay sleeping peacefully in

Changed by the Cat | 147

her bed, but there, tucked up in her hair, was her new companion, sound asleep.

Abby and the kitten had instantly bonded. And, as if she knew, the kitten hung out on Abby's head or played around Abby's mouth so that the two could interact.

"It's given Abby something to live for," wrote her mom.

Soft tears trailed down Katie's cheeks as she silently stared at the phone.

"That kitten has healed Abby," Katie said.

"Yes," I replied.

"But she was also meant to heal me," Katie said, as she watched the screen and stayed perfectly quiet.

"Do you think?" I asked.

"I know. And that's why I think you should call the hospital. It's time for me to go. I need to heal me."

And, in that moment, two lives were changed by one little kitten.

— Susan Traugh —

A Scrap of Forgiveness

*Anger makes you smaller, while forgiveness forces you
to grow beyond what you are.
~Cherie Carter-Scott*

When I heard Speckles hissing in the next room, I immediately went to find her and our kitten. I witnessed Scrappy step closer to touch noses with our senior cat and greet her with a trill. That prompted another hiss from Speckles plus a swat toward the kitten's face. Scrappy was quick enough to avoid any damage. When Speckles scampered away, the kitten thought it was a cat-and-mouse game. She followed close behind the tempting tail. Speckles pivoted and confronted the kitten again, and then she escaped through the pet door.

For nine months, this same routine had been occurring. Speckles rejected every one of Scrappy's attempts at friendship. I thought surely our youngster would give up any day, but Scrappy was persistent. That gray tabby eagerly greeted Speckles the same way over and over again. There was never a sense that Scrappy kept track of the number of second chances she offered Speckles. Her forgiveness was unlimited.

Nine months earlier (which seemed a lifetime now), my husband Tim and I were enjoying retired life. We had no children and lots of freedom to come and go. Tim had golf outings, I had volunteer work, and we both participated in church activities. Our senior tortoiseshell had been an only cat and protected the entire house and yard, as well as my husband and me. We supplied her food, water, and shelter, and, in turn, she practically took care of herself.

All that changed when Scrappy showed up, probably dropped off in our neighborhood, and then hid in our garage. In all fairness, we hadn't consulted Speckles about the new living arrangements. I had been so smitten with the adorable tabby that I just assumed everyone would love her, too. So, we read up on how to introduce a senior feline to a young kitten.

None of the tips worked.

After less than a month, Tim constructed separate areas for eating and cat napping. Speckles kept her domain of the outdoors and the porch. Scrappy was being raised as an indoor cat. All seemed fine until the cold Indiana winter temperatures made the outdoors not such a desirable option. We closed off our bedroom for our senior cat's comfort so that she could come indoors when needed.

Occasionally, Scrappy snuck into the room. That's when Speckles' hissy fits would commence. Tim and I got used to their behaviors and accepted this as our new life during the winter months.

One Sunday, before church services, I volunteered as a greeter by the front door as the congregation entered. I handed out bulletins, said some warm, welcoming words, and offered handshakes. Then, a husband and wife approached. The four of us had been best friends. Our friendship ended after a nasty disagreement. They left the church for another one in town. We hadn't been on speaking terms for more than twenty years.

However, three months ago they had returned to our church, and I had not been pleased to see them. So, I didn't pretend to welcome them as I handed them bulletins. My greeting ended there, and I really thought my indignation was justified.

When we returned home, Speckles rushed from the chilly outdoors into the warm house ahead of us. Scrappy eagerly scampered in from the other room — not to greet us, but Speckles. I heard the kitten's special welcoming sound and watched her rubbing noses. It got the same catty reaction from Speckles. Scrappy took it all in stride, as she always did.

This time, I took notice of Scrappy's example of friendliness and

150 | Changed by the Cat

forgiveness. Time after time, I witnessed her vulnerability, to the extent that she could be hurt again. Yet she held nothing back in her exuberance to greet Speckles.

I was ashamed of my earlier immature behavior at church. I had practically hissed at the couple as they walked in. Holding onto a grudge was not how I wanted others to see me. Couldn't I offer a scrap of forgiveness? It would not be easy for me. But twenty years of resentment had to end.

I immediately sat down, said a prayer, and wrote a simple "Welcome Back" message to the couple. The next day, I would mail it. I may never hear how the communication was received, but at least I had made an attempt.

Thankfully, I rescued a little kitten with mature wisdom and a big lesson in teaching me how to offer friendship and forgiveness.

— Glenda Ferguson —

My Furry Assistant

*Play is the only way the highest intelligence
of humankind can unfold.
~Joseph Chilton Pearce*

The quiet hum of the refrigerator and the steady whir of the ceiling fan filled the kitchen, a subtle soundtrack for my afternoon of grading. I sat back in my chair, eyeing the stack of student research papers with a mix of focus and fatigue. I usually found that a brief escape into fresh air helped break the monotony of grading, but today the idea of facing that searing Arizona heat kept me glued to my spot — grateful, at least, for the cool embrace of the AC.

Just as I was about to dive into another round of grading, I heard a faint rustling — the unmistakable sound of a welcome distraction. I looked up, and there she was — Angel, my furry, four-legged muse, making her grand entrance with the grace of a queen fully aware that all eyes are on her.

Angel wasn't just any cat; she was my shelter rescue, a fluffy bundle of black-and-white fur with the biggest, most inquisitive eyes I'd ever seen. I still remember the day I found her, curled up in the back of her cage, looking unsure of her surroundings. But when I approached, she'd given me a slow, deliberate blink, as if to say, "I'm ready to go home now." Since then, she'd made herself the queen of the household, and her timing had always been impeccable — especially when it came to lightening the mood.

She paused in the doorway, surveying the scene with narrowed eyes as if assessing my progress. "Hey, Angel," I greeted her with a warm smile. "Come to lend a paw? Maybe you can explain to this freshman why Wikipedia isn't the ultimate source of wisdom."

Angel responded with another slow blink, the feline equivalent of a wise nod — or perhaps a subtle reminder that she had more pressing matters to attend to. And then, she pounced — on a shadow, on the wall, on the floor. It didn't really matter as long as it provided a challenge. Her paws skidded across the tile.

I chuckled. "Nice move, kitty. You sure you don't want to switch places? I could use a little break from this research madness — and from pretending the AC is winning the war against the September sun."

Angel, now sitting upright with the grace of royalty, licked her paw with an air of supreme indifference. But I wasn't fooled. I knew she was just warming up. Sure enough, before I could finish writing "Reddit is not a peer-reviewed journal" she sprang at the curtains, claws out. Part superhero, part acrobat.

"Angel, no!" I said with no conviction as I watched her swing. "Those curtains aren't a jungle gym, you know."

She dangled there for a moment, wide-eyed and clearly exhilarated by her own bravado, before gravity — not for the first time — intervened. With a surprised meow, she plopped to the floor in a heap of fluff. I couldn't help it — I burst out laughing. "You're giving me more excitement than these research papers, that's for sure!"

Angel looked up at me, her expression one of pure determination undaunted by her brief encounter with gravity. A few seconds later, she was back on her feet, ready for her next daring act — a fierce battle with an invisible opponent, complete with pouncing, swatting, and dramatic rolls that would make a stunt double proud.

I watched her antics, the weight of the papers before me growing lighter with each of her moves. How could I resist joining in? Before I knew it, I was on the floor beside her, wiggling my fingers like a makeshift cat toy. Angel, always up for a challenge, pounced with the precision of a ninja.

"You win. You win!" I laughed as she pinned my hand down

Changed by the Cat

with both paws, looking as pleased as a cat who had just outwitted the world. "I surrender to your ridiculousness — and to the fact that at least I don't have to wear a fur coat in this heat."

Angel blinked at me with those big, contented eyes, as if to say, "About time, human." She released my hand and rubbed her head against my fingers, her purrs humming through the quiet room like a soothing melody.

And just like that, the stack of papers seemed more manageable. With Angel by my side, how could I possibly stay stressed? She was a one-cat comedy show, a master of distraction, and a professional mood-lifter, all rolled into one fluffy package.

"Thanks, Angel," I whispered, scooping her up into my lap as I leaned back against the wall. "Who needs a vacation when I've got you?"

Angel curled up, her purrs growing softer as she drifted off to sleep, her mission accomplished. The papers were still waiting, but they no longer loomed so large. Even the warmth in the room felt a bit more tolerable. After all, with a cat like Angel around, there's always a reason to smile — even when the work is piling up.

As I sat there with Angel asleep in my lap I marveled at her timing. Somehow, she always knew when to step in, reminding me with her playful chaos that life — and grading — shouldn't be taken too seriously. Sometimes, all it takes to turn around a daunting day is a bit of furry fun, a blast of cool air, and a cat who knows exactly how to bring it.

—Julia Gousseva—

Chapter 6

Quirky Cats

Chloe and the Beanie Babies

My dear, I'm a cat. Everything I see is mine.
~Rick Riordan

I had three cats. That's not exactly true. One of the cats, Chloe, made it known that she did not belong to me. She adored my husband. When we sat on the sofa or double recliner, she sat on his lap or between us. If I tried to snuggle with him, she swatted at me with her paws. Once when he was holding her, I attempted to kiss him on the cheek, and she swiped me with her paw and then put her head on his shoulder.

Chloe did love something else besides my husband, however. It was my collection of Beanie Babies and small stuffed rabbits, which I kept on a dresser in the guest bedroom. Chloe liked to carry them one by one, as if they were newborn kittens, to the sofa in the den where she would snuggle with them. My husband and I often watched as she carefully carried a Beanie Baby or rabbit in her mouth, placed it on the sofa, and then headed back to get another one. After she had arranged them just the way she wanted, she would snuggle with them. Laying a paw across one or two of them, she would take a nap. Each night I would put them back in the guest room.

Chloe and her sister were spayed, but she must have had a maternal instinct that was fulfilled by those Beanie Babies. On one occasion, Chloe, holding a Beanie Baby by the scruff of its neck, jumped up on the recliner and laid it on my husband's lap. She was entrusting him with one of her babies. I waited for her to bring me a Beanie Baby, but it never happened. She snuggled with the remaining Babies as always.

When I dared to take the Beanie Baby from my husband's lap, Chloe leaped off the sofa and swiped the Beanie Baby onto the floor. Then, to our surprise, she nipped at my foot, picked up the Beanie, and put it back in my husband's lap.

I soon discovered that my little collection of Beanie Babies was getting worn from constantly being carried in Chloe's mouth. I arranged them on a shelf where I was sure that Chloe could not reach them. We came home one evening from a dinner date to find Chloe lying on the sofa — you guessed it, with the Beanie Babies. Neither my husband nor I could figure out how the cat got to the shelf. I suppose nothing was going to stop her from rescuing her "babies."

Subsequently, I put the Beanie Babies and rabbits on the guest bed. My thinking was that she would just snuggle with them on the bed, and I wouldn't have to risk her falling while jumping onto the shelf. Chloe had other ideas. She continued to bring them to the sofa in the den and occasionally gave one to my husband to babysit. Each evening, I collected the Beanie Babies and put them back in the guest room while Chloe meowed at me in protest. I tried leaving her with one "baby," but she wanted them all.

Finally, I put the Beanie Babies in a drawer. I hated to take them from Chloe, but it was that or more wear and tear on them. Big mistake! Chloe stopped eating and lay on the sofa, lost without her babies. As she grew more and more sad, I found myself feeling guilty. Those Beanie Babies were her kittens. She was their mother and, like a loving mother, had doted on them, entrusting them to no one but my husband. So, I gave in. Chloe got her babies back, and she went right back to snuggling with them.

But now she hid them — under the bed in the guest room. From then on, that's where they were stashed when Chloe wasn't mothering them on the sofa.

— Carol Gentry Allen —

Trading Stuff

A cat will do what it wants when it wants, and there's not a thing you can do about it.
~Frank Perkins

Sometimes, you can provide a pet with everything, and it's still not enough. At least, it wasn't for my cat, Star.

Like a lot of folks, I have small collections of things I've gathered throughout my travels or from gifts. Whereas other parts of my life may not be organized, my collection is. That's why, when I came home one afternoon and found a small figure of a fairy lying on my living room carpet, I was not only surprised but alarmed. That little statue had been displayed on a shelf in my office.

I live alone, and no one is ever in my home without me. So, when I found that two-inch fairy lying there, I fled outside. Then I walked around the house, but I didn't see any signs of intruders. No screens were out of place. No doors had been tampered with that I could tell.

I needed to go back inside to see what had moved that fairy. I thought about calling the police to escort me. But then I decided I would just leave the front door open so I could get out fast, and I ventured back inside.

I crept through the kitchen, then the bedroom, but nothing seemed amiss. My jewelry, which only had sentimental value, was all there. But there was something missing: my cat.

Had someone stolen Star? I called out, but there was no response. I hurried into the laundry room where I kept her food bin and shook

158 | Quirky Cats

it hard, knowing that if she was okay, she'd come running.

Seconds later, I heard her familiar mewing, and she came trotting up to me, tail high in the air and purring.

I slowly crept to my office, where the door was closed. I kept it shut off from the rest of the house because many of my collectibles are breakable, and I didn't want Star tampering with them.

I sighed in relief when I saw that my computer was there. Star had followed me into the office, and I ignored her cries. I simply assumed she was hungry as it was dinnertime for both of us.

I walked over to the shelf where my fairies dwell and immediately solved the mystery of why my collectible had been found on the living room floor.

On the shelf where my fairy was supposed to be sitting, I spied a catnip mouse. It was one of Star's favorite toys. She'd managed to open the door of the office, remove a small item from the shelf, and replace it with something of value to her. And then somehow, she'd exited the office, closing the door behind her.

I put the fairy back where it belonged, tossed the catnip mouse down the hallway and left the office, closing the door behind me.

Noting that the house was, indeed, safe, I went about making myself supper, fed the cat, and proceeded to watch the evening news.

Sometime after the news was over, I heard loud bumping coming from the hallway. I got up, peeked around the corner, and saw Star jumping up and hitting the spring-latch office doorknob with her paws.

Her efforts proved worthwhile as the door eventually opened. Star darted into the office and came out with the same fairy in her mouth. I simply stood where I was and watched as she dropped the fairy in the foyer and then darted to her toy box. She came back with a rather tattered toy gecko. Then she scooted into the office and left the gecko on the shelf where the fairy had been.

There was something about the fairies that attracted her. I don't know what it was, but this happened several more times before I installed a simple hook-and-eye latch on my office door. I did give in on the fairy, though. It was made of resin. She couldn't swallow it, and I didn't see any harm in letting her have it if I saw no signs of her chewing on it and ingesting parts of it.

In the days to come, when I left the door open for her, she retrieved the other fairies, as well as a stuffed owl, a dragon figurine, and a gnome. All were about the same size. She always left a replacement object, something of value to her that she traded for something that was of value to me.

I asked a vet about this. He told me that some cats are notorious for taking things and giving other things back as replacements. While he didn't know why my cat was doing this, we believed she was trying to teach me how to hunt. Or she was bringing me stuff simply to trade.

Now, I'm content letting her take what she wants. But how do I organize my new collection of used catnip toys?

—Candace Sams—

Kitty Didn't Attack People

Cats are connoisseurs of comfort but experts in chaos.
~Author Unknown

The text message sounded like an emergency. "He's attacking me."

Another one came in. "I'm hiding in the bathroom."

My girlfriend, who later became my wife, had recently moved in with me. She had met Kitty before, but she's not really a cat person and hadn't spent much time around him. Still, I knew that Kitty didn't attack people. He was a big, white ball of fluff who minded his own business. Also, he had a strong connection with me and left everybody else alone. He lay around for the most part, unless he deemed something worthy of investigation.

I didn't know what my girlfriend was texting about. There was absolutely no reason to hide in the bathroom. She was being a bit dramatic. Kitty was a gentle friend.

I couldn't help but laugh as I walked into our apartment after work. My girlfriend was looking at me with such intensity. I asked her what had happened.

"I thought I'd clean the sheets and make the bed..."

Oh. Oh, boy. I forgot to mention something to her. Yeah, it all makes sense now. Kitty always ferociously attacked the sheets when you tried to make the bed. I realized I should have shared that bit of

Quirky Cats | 191

important information.

My girlfriend said that Kitty was in the other room when she walked by with the freshly washed sheets. She placed the fitted sheet on the bed and pulled the corners down over the mattress. She found the side of the flat sheet and flicked it over the bed. Kitty came out of nowhere with wide eyes, hair up, claws out, and hypersensitive reactions to any movement of the sheet.

My girlfriend tried pulling the sheet away from him. *Oh, no! No, no, no, no, no! Never pull the sheet! That's what he wants you to do.* That's Kitty's trigger. Pulling the sheet sends him into action.

He pounced on the spot where the sheet started to rise off the bed and began to scurry up the material leading to her hands. His claws were shredding through the sheet. She dropped it and ran into the bathroom, slamming the door behind her.

She could hear him outside the door. Thuds, scurries, and growls filled the air as Kitty took revenge on the bedsheet that was most certainly trying to destroy him. He would emerge the victor.

My girlfriend waited until the chaos subsided and silence resumed. She opened the door, just a crack. She looked for him. Braving the danger, she ventured into the bedroom and tried to assess whether or not this territory was still dominated by that fluffy white cat. He had retreated to the living room where he took a well-deserved rest.

Somehow, the bed was made when I got home. The fortitude and courage she mustered in that moment to accomplish the impossible in the face of danger will forever shine as a signal of strength.

Kitty didn't attack people. Those sheets, though… Kitty didn't like those sheets.

—Elton A. Dean—

A Hairy Problem

No amount of time can erase the memory of a good cat, and no amount of masking tape can ever totally remove his fur from your couch.
~Leo Dworken

The other day, I walked into my closet and heard a strange noise. My pants were purring. It took me a moment to realize that my garments should not be making sounds. Then, I parted my pants. Sure enough, one of the cats had taken up residence on the shelf behind my pants, where he could liberally shed all over my clothes.

The shelves behind my clothes are a popular hangout for my three cats. I wouldn't mind so much, except that I routinely find myself unintentionally wearing a fur jacket. Generally, it's not a big deal. That's what lint rollers are for. (Seriously, you thought they were for lint?)

But on my way to church one day, I glanced down at the right sleeve of my jacket to find it covered in cat hair. That side must have hung toward the shelf. The other sleeve was clean. This was rather embarrassing as I didn't have my lint roller with me, and I didn't particularly want to show up to church with mismatched sleeves. Furiously, I attempted to brush off cat hair while at a stoplight.

This was not only ineffective but also annoyed my teenager. I'm not sure why it annoyed him, other than the fact that everything I do annoys him. He felt obligated to point out the second the light turned green, berating me for my distraction in trying to de-fur myself and

Quirky Cats

failing to gun the engine. Geesh! I love backseat drivers in the front seat.

The other irritating habit that the cats have besides shedding all over my clothes is pushing anything off the closet shelves they don't want in their way. I frequently walk into the closet to find shoes, boxes, bags, purses, or other items that previously lived on the shelves rudely shoved onto the floor.

This would be a minor aggravation except for one other objectionable habit that my cats have: They pee on things that are left on the floor. It's particularly exasperating when they are the ones who are responsible for said items being on the floor in the first place. But they don't discriminate. They pee on things my son leaves on the floor, as well. Despite being repeatedly told to pick up his stuff from the floor, and despite going ballistic when he finds his things smelling like cat urine, his brain still fails to get the connection. You'd think he had to do the laundry!

You might wonder why I put up with a creature who complicates my life in so many ways. It's simple. The law says I'm legally required to care for my son until he's eighteen. Oh, wait. You meant the cats. Well, that's simple, too. They bring me such joy!

— Ellen Fannon —

Matching Agendas

*Every meal you have is automatically a cat's meal too.
They just let you think it's yours.*
~Author Unknown

"Leo, again?" I asked, followed by a sigh as I removed my tortoiseshell cat from our kitchen counter for the fourth time that day. This time, he had opened the toaster-oven door, pulled out the shelf, and licked the grease remaining on the pan from the bacon we'd cooked that morning. The time before, he had managed to open a Tupperware container of cooked hot dogs I had left on the counter. We were minus two hot dogs by the time I caught him.

Leo never used to be so mischievous with food—not until the veterinarian told me that Leo needed to lose two pounds, and Leo's sister, Precious, needed to lose four. The subsequent, gradual reduction in their three meals per day did not go over well with them, especially Leo. He became a scavenger and hunter.

He could find any small piece of food dropped on the floor or stove top. He hunted down dishes my kids left out and licked them clean, and then threw up because of the rich food. He even started crying at my feet when I cooked meat. I was getting very frustrated at how careful we had to be with everything related to food.

One day, as I was sitting on the sofa stewing over the new Leo who had emerged in recent months, my husband sat next to me to discuss travel plans.

Quirky Cats

"I was thinking that doing house swaps would really help us save money on lodging when we travel. And the people who stay at our house would agree to take care of the cats," he said with a smile. "This could really open up new opportunities for us."

I squeezed his hand where it rested on my leg. "That sounds amazing. I really wish we could do that. But I just don't see how it would be possible without lodging Leo somewhere, and I don't feel comfortable doing that. He would be miserable."

"I think it would be fine for him to stay here," my husband responded. "He is a sweet cat. People would love him."

"No, people would be really put out by how diligent they'd have to be at putting away and cleaning up everything once they are done cooking and eating. They wouldn't even be able to leave dirty dishes in the sink because Leo would lick them and then throw up. It would be a nightmare."

"Well, let's think about it," he said. "We could travel more and go to some fabulous places by swapping homes."

When he walked out of the room, I turned my gaze to Leo where he rested on the skirt under our Christmas tree. Leo had shades of red and green on his fur from the lights hanging above him. I walked over to the tree, knelt down, and scratched his head. Leo opened his eyes and gazed at me with such a relaxed, contented look.

"Okay, buddy, you need to learn to be this relaxed and content with the food we're giving you. Otherwise, you're going to drive me crazy and limit our ability to travel. Got it?"

Leo emitted a low purr and then lowered his head back onto the tree skirt.

The next morning, I found Leo using one of his front paws to open the door of the closet where we stored the cat food. The door had a latch that was getting old and not holding securely. Leave it to Leo to figure that out.

"Ahh, no!" I shooed him away and leaned a heavy item against the door until I could replace the latch.

I opened our front door and let him out for his second time that day. "Go, hunt!" I encouraged him as he meandered onto our front deck. He spent hours outside every day. Why didn't he kill rats, mice, or some other enticing delicacy to supplement his diet?

While I cleaned the kitchen dishes, I thought about how much easier his sister was. *Perhaps,* I thought, *we will not get other male cats in the future. And maybe it would be best to have him adopted by another family.* I was at the end of my rope with Leo. I couldn't stand much more of his antics.

Later that day, I sat down to read. Leo immediately jumped onto my lap and nestled in for a long nap. He purred consistently even when I didn't pet him.

The next morning, I found him nestled between my kids on the sofa. My kids took turns petting Leo and saying sweet things to him.

"You're such a cutey, Leo," my daughter said as she leaned over and gave him a kiss.

"Good boy, Leo," my son said as Leo rubbed his head against my son's hand and purred loudly.

I realized in that moment that adopting out Leo was not an option. Our kids would be crushed. Admittedly, I would be, too.

The next day, I sat at my computer, ready to find a solution to the problem. I figured there had to be a way to get Leo over his food obsession.

We tried all sorts of possible solutions that I discovered during my research, from giving Leo time-outs in a bathroom, to positively reinforcing good food behaviors, to lifting him off the kitchen counter and petting him to distract him from his food pursuit. Nothing worked.

Then, we decided to move from San Diego to a suburb of Portland, Oregon. I no longer had time to research possible solutions to Leo's poor food behavior because we were busy with showing the house and making plans for our new life in Oregon.

Suddenly, we were on the road, our belongings ahead of us in a moving truck. It was hard to believe that Oregon was becoming a reality. Things had moved quickly when we finally found a buyer for our house.

Oregon was a complete change for all of us, the cats included. It was greener, quieter, more spacious, and relaxing. It seemed as if time

Quirky Cats

had slowed. We were able to take deep breaths and not feel pulled in five different directions at once. It was as if a reset button had been pushed.

Our new home had larger windows that looked out onto a backyard with loads of squirrels, something never seen before by our cats. I purchased Leo and Precious their first cat tower and placed it by a window where they could lazily look outside all day.

And then, after living in Oregon for a few weeks, I realized it had happened. Leo rarely made his way onto the counters. He was too busy sleeping on our deck, watching squirrels, squeezing himself into the enclosed part of the cat tower, catching moles, or investigating the woods behind our home.

We moved to Oregon because my husband and I wanted a more mellow, outdoorsy and green life for us and our kids. Little did we know that Leo needed the same kind of change.

— Heather Harshman —

Kat in Wonderland

There are few things in life more heartwarming than to be welcomed by a cat.
~Tay Hohoff

My name may have lent itself to the nickname Kat. And I'd always been a bit standoffish — a shy, introverted homebody who relished her time alone. But that's where the similarities between felines and myself ended.

Or so I thought.

I was never a cat person. I had always shared my life with dogs. I knew them and loved them. And, most times, they loved me, too. So much so that, by my tenth birthday, I'd even started to earn a few bucks dog-sitting for locals.

Tending to cats was never in my pet-sitting oeuvre until I turned twelve. That's when a childless couple who lived up the block from our family called in the midst of winter and asked if I'd consider taking care of their cat, Dixie. The couple had to tend to a "sudden family matter," and they were desperate for a cat sitter for about a week.

I was leery but thought, *How hard could it be?*

"Oh, there's nothing to it. Dixie practically takes care of herself," the couple told me at our meet-and-greet. "Dixie's very independent. She's more like a boarder in the house than a companion. All you need to do is stop by once a day on your way home from school, put down some water and cat food, and clean out the litter box."

Quirky Cats | 69

Thus began my very first cat-sitting job.

Every afternoon, I'd slip the neighbors' house key into their brass doorknob and step into their quiet living room brightened by the sunshine glowing through shut-tight windows. The stillness inside felt eerie compared to the uproar I was accustomed to when visiting the houses where I did my dog-sitting.

There was never any sign of a four-legged feline, but I went about my duties.

Water down? Check.

Food in bowl? Check.

Litter box clean? Check.

When the couple called to check in after a few days, I told them, "I guess Dixie's fine. I have yet to see her."

The couple, on two phone extensions, were audibly charmed. "Oh, that's just Dixie. Not to worry," they assured as they asked me to stay on into the following week.

Day after day brought more of the same. The only telltale signs of Dixie's existence were finding her water and food bowls empty and little presents left in the litter box.

I wasn't complaining. This was surely the easiest pet-sitting gig in the history of my short life. But there was something unsettling and unnerving about never having seen this cat. She was like a puzzle I felt challenged to solve.

Burning curiosity irked me enough that, on the ninth day, I stopped at the local pet shop and purchased a shocking-pink cat ball with a jingly bell inside in the hope it might win over Dixie.

But when I showed up at the house and gave the ball an enthusiastic rattle, with the bell joyfully tinkling inside, I was only met with silence again.

Dejected, I left the ball in the middle of the hardwood floor on my way out.

The next day, my spirits lifted when I spied a glimmer of pink among the once orderly sofa pillows that were now strewn upon the floor.

From the foyer, I stared at the ball, listening for sounds of life.

But all I heard were whistling eddies of hot, forced air passing through the central heating vents.

I picked up the pillows and put them back on the sofa.

When I pushed open the front door the following day, a playful jingle sounded. A ball of pink rolled into the room with me and stopped at a lamp overturned on the floor.

I set the lamp back on the end table, relieved there was no damage.

Dixie was really toying with me!

On the twelfth day, when I walked in, the pink ball was sitting next to a hardcover book with its feathery pages open on the floor.

It must've fallen off the coffee table...

I reached for it and discovered an illustrated, hardcover copy of *Alice's Adventures in Wonderland*. I'd never read the timeless classic by Lewis Carroll.

Perhaps I was meant to?

With book in hand, I flipped on the table lamp, plopped onto the sofa, and cushioned by those pillows, I tilted the book toward the light and started to read the story aloud.

It didn't take long to become completely engrossed in the surreal adventures of Alice, her menacing journey down the rabbit hole, and her trying to find a way to access that beautiful garden.

And just as the Cheshire Cat entered the story, I gasped. As if coming to life right off the page, a real live cat — three dimensions colored in shimmering, slate gray — took a resolute leap onto the lamp table next to where I sat reading.

Why, it was Dixie!

"Oh, hel-lo," I said, mesmerized by her wide, green eyes.

Despite the pounding of my heart, I did my best not to scare her off. I decided to play her game: hard to get. I simply picked up reading the story aloud right from where I'd left off.

With every page turn, Dixie snuggled closer. She pressed her body against mine — her thumping tail curled and looked just like the grin of that Cheshire Cat. As I stroked her velvety fur, she purred with pleasure.

From that day until the couple returned, Dixie and I found common

Quirky Cats | 71

ground: getting lost together in Alice's adventures. Dixie was, no doubt, taking notes from the crafty wisdom of that Cheshire Cat. She probably could've given him a few lessons of her own.

— Kathleen Gerard —

Shadow

*I love cats because I enjoy my home; and little
by little, they become its visible soul.*
~Jean Cocteau

We had been without any pets for many years. With our children now out of the house having families of their own, we felt it was time to adopt a kitten, preferably a female. Looking through the glass window at the adoption center of our local PetSmart store, we saw several possible candidates. We made an appointment to meet them, and when the attendant opened the cages, several kittens came bounding out. It seemed like they were so excited to be out of their cages that they were bouncing off the walls — except for one little male tabby who was standing quietly by my wife Cyndy's foot.

She picked him up and cuddled him. He promptly fell asleep in her arms. That's all it took for us to decide that this was the kitten for us!

Popeye was not the ideal candidate for adoption. Most noticeably, his back legs were flayed out to the sides, causing him to walk like a sailor (which is probably why they named him Popeye). His ears were bright red, showing some kind of infection, and when we got him home, we realized there was more. This kitten, as cute as he was, had major medical issues. With his infected ears and his labored breathing, we wondered if he would even survive.

Cyndy held the kitten in her arms and virtually willed the kitten to breathe all weekend. On Monday, we called one of the local

Quirky Cats | 173

veterinary clinics and were told, "Just take him back and tell them you got a defective cat and want another one!" Aghast at their suggestion, we resolved to help this kitten get better.

At his first exam at another veterinary clinic, we were given even worse news. Not only did he have both viral and bacterial infections in both ears, but he also tested positive for feline herpesvirus (FHV), feline calicivirus (FCV), and feline coronavirus (FCoV) — issues that were possibly life-ending. We took him home and treated him with medications and lots of TLC. Over time, he began to get better.

Even with the "swimmer's legs," as the vet called it, he managed to get around all right. We took him to a cat neurologist who diagnosed a neurologic problem where his front and back legs don't always work together because of issues with his spine. He also tested positive for toxoplasmosis. More medications and time brought this little baby more healing, as he wedged himself deeper and deeper into our hearts.

We changed his name from Popeye to Shadow because he would follow me wherever I went around the house. He has been my little shadow ever since.

He not only became a playful kitten, but we were amazed at his intelligence. He made up his own games and taught us how to play with him! At night, we placed a small towel between us on our bed, where he happily slept.

As days turned into weeks, Shadow became more and more verbal. He seemed to pick up and articulate many words from us such as "water," "mama," "out," and his favorite word, "no." My daughter scoffed at our comment that Shadow could talk — right up to the moment when she saw him and said, "Hello, Shadow," and he responded, "Heh-woe." Astounded, my daughter turned to us and said, "He just said hello to me!" As years went by, he developed more words we could understand, and we marveled at how intelligent he must be to try communicating in our language while we could not communicate in his!

We now have three other male cats (originally adopted to keep Shadow company) in the house. Shadow is the alpha cat and periodically checks to see where everyone is. At bedtime, he will search the house, room by room, until he has located each of his three brothers and made sure they are all right. If one of "his people" is either sad or not feeling well, he seems to sense it and will stay by their side, ready to give comfort.

Shadow is eleven years old now. As he gets older, his swimmer's legs and spine issues give him more problems, but he doesn't let that stop him. We have made accommodations for him throughout the house, placing pet stairs here and there so that, even with his weaker legs, he can go where the other cats go.

He still loves to sleep in my arms in the evening while we watch TV and between my wife and me at night, although he periodically gets up to check on the rest of his brothers. Because of his FHV, his throat gets very dry and he must drink water frequently. His latest "trick" is to wake during the night crying "wore-er" (water). We keep small cups at our bedside so all we have to do is reach over, uncap them and hold them out for him to drink. When he is finished, we all go back to sleep.

He is, by far, the smartest cat I've ever seen. And after all these years my Shadow is still my shadow. His latest new word is "home." Although I have been retired thirteen years, I still volunteer two days a week. Whenever I return and open the door, I call out to my wife, "I'm home!" Shadow has picked up on the word "home." To him, it means that "Dad is coming through the door." My wife said it broke her heart the first time she saw Shadow sitting by our front door crying "Home! Home!" as if by saying that word, I would come walking back in.

I have a T-shirt that reads, "My shadow has a tail and four legs." He also has my heart.

— Roger A. Wilber —

George and His Hairy Snake

*Cats do not have to be shown how to have a good time,
for they are unfailing ingenious in that respect.*
~James Mason

My husband dangled an eight-inch, stuffed fabric strip in front of my face. The nondescript, brown object had a furry side but nothing to cause the sparkle of delight in Spence's eyes.

"What is it?" I wondered if he'd remembered the hairball food the vet had recommended for our longhaired black-and-white cat.

Spence waved his arm, flopping the brown object. "It's a hairy snake. George'll love it."

I couldn't imagine George playing with that toy.

Spence knelt and wiggled the strip in front of the four-year-old cat. "See, Georgie. It's a snake."

George sniffed and walked away. The toy didn't have catnip.

Spence left the snake on the floor. "He'll come back."

As if the toy could crawl, the snake magically appeared in different rooms of our Western Pennsylvania log house: beside the bed in the morning, under fern fronds by afternoon, next to the refrigerator at dinnertime. And while we slept during the night, we woke to the sound of George's mournful wail.

His wailing remained a mystery until one day when Spence was

Quirky Cats

gardening, and I'd curled in a chair to read a friend's letter. The wail erupted in the hall.

I glanced over my shoulder.

Gripping the snake's middle in his teeth, George dragged the toy between his legs and plodded down the hall.

George saw me watching and dropped the toy. He plopped onto his butt and gazed in the opposite direction of the snake.

Although Spence thought George sang a joyous song celebrating the snake, I heard the wail as solemn. George's processions seemed like the act of a shaman protecting us and our house.

Under George's rituals, the once-straight strip twisted into a wobbly U shape with a pinched Barbie doll waist. The scruffy toy turned up in the dirty laundry one day. I plucked out the snake and dropped it in the hall for George.

The third time the snake landed in the laundry basket, I realized George snuck it in on purpose. I washed and dried the toy. That night, the wailing had a joyful undertone.

George remained devoted to his hairy snake, dragging it, singing to it, and hiding it for the next ten years.

Gradually, George stopped eating the food in his bowl. We'd had other senior cats who had grown fussy about their wet food, so I planned to buy a different brand at the grocery store. George's limp concerned me more. He hobbled because of an ingrown toenail on his front paw. Spence and I drove George to the vet.

After forty-five-minutes in a crowded waiting room, a vet tech ushered us into the euthanasia room with an exam table, plastic couch, and blue walls decorated by angels between inspiring poems.

White coat flapping, petite Dr. Wolfe rushed in. "Sorry to put you in here. It was the only room available, and I wanted to get you out of the waiting room. I hope you don't mind."

"No. It's peaceful." I hugged George to my chest.

Spence put his hand on my knee.

The vet gently lifted George to the exam table. "He has an ingrown nail? And he's off his food?" She stroked his hair and looked in his mouth. "We'll clip the nail and draw some blood. Then we'll know

Quirky Cats | 77

more." She cuddled George and carried him to the lab.

Spence and I stared at the angels and read the poems about beloved animals until a harried vet tech burst through the door. With her arms outstretched and her hands clutching George at the top of his front legs, she spat her words. "He turned into a monster in there."

George hissed and swung his claws.

"Be careful." She dropped him onto the exam table and left.

Spence and I rushed to our terrified cat. "Poor George." I petted him. "What did they do to you?"

Cradling his precious buddy, Spence carried George to the sofa. "I bet you were brave."

We took turns stroking, cuddling, and talking to the cat in low, soothing tones. "We'll take you home as soon as we can. We love you, George."

The vet returned with her clipboard and the news. "His kidneys shut down. We'll need to keep him in the hospital." Moving the clipboard under one arm, she gathered the docile, purring cat in the other. "If we get an IV in him, he can go home Friday."

That was Wednesday.

Thursday morning, Spence went to visit George. The receptionist shook her head. "You can't go in. George is raising holy hell. They're working to put in the IV. They couldn't get it in yesterday."

Spence raised the dilapidated, hairy snake. "May I leave this for George? It's his favorite toy."

"Of course. It may help him recover faster." She reached for the snake. "I'll make sure he gets it."

That afternoon, the receptionist welcomed me with a smile. "Of course, you may see George. Your visit might help him get better." She led me into a storage room. A cage midway up a stack had a sign that read: BEWARE VICIOUS CAT. Giving me a stool, she opened the cage door. "Be careful. He bites. Get him to eat if you can."

They called this a hospital? Buckets and mops occupied the corner. No other animals were in the room.

Inside the cage, George lay with his chin tucked against his chest and his eyes shut.

"George," I whispered. "Oh, sweetie." I petted him until I spied a comb. Picking it up, I gently combed the long mane around his head—something that soothed him at home. He opened his eyes a little and licked my hand. I stuck a finger in his food and held it under his chin. Combing and dipping, I got him to eat an eighth of the food they'd given him.

"Where's your snake, George? Spence brought it for you this morning. Didn't they give you your snake?"

Shaking and straining every muscle, George struggled to his feet. He tottered a couple of inches to the side and back in the tiny cage, revealing the hairy snake. He'd been lying on it. Too frail to keep standing, George dropped beside the snake, closed his eyes, and fell asleep.

Weak and wobbly, George came home Sunday.

For another year and a half, he picked at his food yet marched with the hairy snake. He filled the house with wails and left the snake in unexpected places. Spence held our tenacious cat while I pinched his skin to stick in a sharp needle for subcutaneous fluids. Each and every day of that time, we rejoiced to have George and his hairy-snake rituals grace our lives.

—Janet Wells—

Adventures in Cat Food

> As anyone who has ever been around a cat for any length of time well knows cats have enormous patience with the limitations of the human kind.
> ~Cleveland Amory

My cat just ate my last sticky note. Why? It's not because the smell was appealing. It wasn't the color (because her favorite color is fish). It's not because she is hungry. She had a big breakfast of gnats at the windowsill less than an hour ago. Why, again, why?

We buy her organic, grain-free, holistic cat food. Nothing but the best for the Queen of Castle Watson. She eats it occasionally, after giving us a "Gee, thanks" look and a yawn of appreciation. More often than not, she pretends to bury it under invisible mounds of earth for a future apocalyptic event. Sometimes, she'll come back for it later, after its putrid aroma has penetrated the entirety of the house, only to knock the bowl to the floor, fish juice and all, because it has sat out just one minute too long for her liking. This then requires that the clean-up crew (usually me) sop up the remnants and begin the entire feeding process again, hoping against all hope that the second batch will somehow make the grade. It usually doesn't.

She often eats intruding moths and spiders. I have seen her snatch flies from the air as a mid-afternoon snack. Crickets are a favorite.

And when really looking for a delicacy, she will tackle a swirling dust bunny from under the bed and inhale it right down. I attribute her eclectic palate to the fact that she was born a wildling in our backyard and survived for a long time on whatever crossed her small path. But a sticky note?

She refuses any human-grade food. Free-range chicken, sans spices? Nope. A little egg, scrambled with fresh salmon? Not a chance. We've even tried "exotic" meat cat foods from other countries, and she will always choose a wayward insect over any of it.

Her food is always delicately placed at her royal paws in a special cat-feeding bowl so as not to disturb her sensitive whiskers. She is not impressed. If it is dry food, she will take it between her tiny teeth, piece by piece, place it on the carpet ever so gingerly, and maybe (just maybe) eat a kibble or two. The rest gets batted about the house in a frenzied game for the resident humans of "Find-the-Kibble-Before-the-Ants-Do."

At the semi-old age of thirteen, she is not overly skinny even though it appears that she is solely sustained by air, water, and dust. She is not starving. She has no allergies or conditions. The vet says she is perfectly fine and not to worry. "She'll eat when she's hungry," he says as she gnaws on his ungloved hand.

But today, she chose to eat my last sticky note, ripping it into bite-sized morsels and flicking the snippets into the air before near-total consumption. And she watched me the entire time, waiting for acknowledgement of her naughtiness and daring me to do something about it. (I did manage to get the sticky part away from her with only minor blood loss.)

I have come to the conclusion that she does this because she knows it annoys me. She does this on purpose because she thinks it's funny, and she enjoys my misery and frustration at buying twenty-nine different cat foods per week, of which only one will be consumed.

So, the simple answer to the question "Why?" is this: She does it because she can… and she enjoys every minute of it!

— Dorenda Crager Watson —

59

If He Only Had a Thumb

There is, incidentally, no way of talking about cats that enables one to come off as a sane person.
~Dan Greenberg

My cat, Boo, thinks he is a human being. We are the only family he has ever known, and I believe Boo models his life and actions after the way we do things. When we eat, he eats. When we watch television, Boo watches with us. When we sleep, he sleeps. Boo knows our activities and schedules and what to expect when, and he acts and reacts accordingly. When I tell people that our cat thinks he's human, they look at me a little strangely. But I know it is true because Boo, in his own way, meets most of the criteria that distinguishes humans from other animals.

I took an anthropology course in college, and the professor who taught the course identified five qualities or attributes that distinguish human beings from other animals. I think Boo must have taken the class, too, because he seems to recognize these characteristics, and he understands that they are important.

The first factor my anthropology professor noted was the expressive communication skills and extensive language abilities that humans possess. Our ability to speak in past, present, and future tenses is regarded as unique, but Boo also vocalizes different sounds for various needs and activities. He has a "meow" for food, another for "I want to go outside," and still another for "I want back inside." He whines in a different way when he wants to be held, and in a totally different manner when he doesn't want to be around people. If you talk to him, he will talk back, and he'll pause between "meows" to let you respond. When you stop talking, he will start meowing again. These "conversations" can last for long periods of time. I realize Boo may not speak in different tenses, and his verbalizations may not have the expressive power of Shakespeare's dialogue, but he can communicate — and he definitely inserts himself into our family conversations.

The second factor my professor identified was the depth and variety of feelings and emotions that human beings express. Maybe other animals are not in touch with their emotions and the feelings of others, but Boo knows when we are sad or feeling low. He jumps into our laps, licks our faces, and tries to improve the situation by making us laugh or smile. If we argue or raise our voices, Boo jumps into the conversation with loud meowing and anguished cries until everyone stops speaking. If we are sick, Boo sleeps cuddled up next to us, instead of in his usual bed. He knows our moods and emotions, and he shows us that he understands. He has empathy, and he gives us unconditional love. I don't know about the depth and variety of his feelings, but Boo certainly has feelings, and he is definitely aware of ours. In fact, in many ways, Boo is more sensitive and aware than many of the Homo sapiens in our family!

The third quality my professor described was the ability of humans to shape an environment to their liking or comfort level. He indicated that animals are powerless to alter their environment and must adapt to their surroundings, or they will perish. Boo, however, knows how to adapt his environment to meet his desired comfort level. If he is cold, he will drag a blanket where he wants it, paw it into a comfortable, bowl-shaped cave, and crawl inside. If he is hot, he will curl up on the cold tile to cool off. He may not be able to install a furnace or air conditioner, but he does shape his environment to his liking.

My professor stated that the fourth distinguishing feature of humans is the ability to walk upright. Human beings are bipedal, which means that they walk on two legs, while most animals are quadrupedal, or four-legged. Boo, however, can walk on his hind legs. If he wants to enter a room that has a closed door, he will stand on his hind legs and push on the door to open it! He may not be able to walk upright for extended periods or play basketball, but he knows that some activities require him to be taller, and he has no trouble extending himself to his full height to accomplish these activities. If he desires a certain scarf or sweater that is lying on top of a tall dresser, he will stand up on his hind legs and use his front paw to swipe down whatever he wants. If that procedure should fail for some reason, he leaps up onto the dresser and continues pursuing his goal. With the proper training, Boo probably could play basketball because he certainly can jump higher than anyone else in our household!

The fifth feature that supposedly makes human beings "human," at least according to my college professor, is our long, opposable thumb. Many primates possess opposable thumbs, but humans can bring their thumbs all the way across their hands to their ring and little fingers. This dexterity helps humans grasp and manipulate objects in ways other animals cannot. I'll admit that Boo doesn't meet the thumb benchmark. He doesn't have a thumb, but he knows he doesn't have one, and he tries hard to compensate for it. Boo will stand at a closed door on his hind legs and reach up with his front paws to try and turn the doorknob. He knows this knob or handle has to be turned to open the door! He also knows that he doesn't have a thumb, so he will incessantly paw at the knob in an attempt to get it to rotate. After a period of time trying, he will cry out about his lack of a thumb with an unmistakable sound that commands any nearby human to open the door.

Even without a thumb, Boo still thinks he is human. He adapts daily to fit in with our family's fluctuating routines and activities. He understands the changing desires and emotions of our family members, and sometimes he's the first to recognize these changes. He is a bona-fide member of our family, and he enriches our lives every day.

None of us has the heart to tell him that he is not a member of the Homo sapiens species, and even if we did, he wouldn't believe us.

—Billie Holladay Skelley—

Chapter 7

Learning to Love the Cat

The Gentleman Cat

When you walk in purpose, you collide with destiny.
~Ralph Buchanan

My neighbor Ted was a grumpy older gentleman. He disliked parties, pets and, apparently, me. If I had girlfriends over, and we quietly sipped wine on the porch until 8:00 p.m., I'd hear about the "racket" I was causing at night. When I crossed paths with him at the mailbox, I'd get lectures about my house needing a good power wash.

But, despite all this, when I got shoulder surgery, Ted mowed my grass all summer, even though I told him I'd hire someone.

"That won't do," Ted told me.

When I got the flu during Christmas, he left homemade soup on my porch.

I had a feeling that, deep down, Ted was a softie.

When summertime came again, his lovely wife, who had long been sick, passed away.

I saw the spring fall away from Ted's step. His lawn, although still passable, wasn't tended with the same care. And he walked to the mailbox with steps so heavy that I could feel the weight of grief pressing down on him.

I knew I had to do something, but my attempts to invite him over for dinner were rebuffed.

"That won't do," he'd say. "I'm miserable company right now."

When I went to see my friend who volunteered at an animal

Learning to Love the Cat

shelter, I got an idea. I would get Ted a cat for company!

I knew I had to be sneaky. Ted wouldn't willing take on a pet. He'd say they were a nuisance and needy.

I told my friend at the shelter all about Ted and how he'd need a very special, non-needy cat. But did such a cat exist? My friend began shrieking with joy.

"Oh, it's going to happen. Finally, we've got a home for Milton!"

Who was Milton, you may ask? A cat that had been returned to the shelter... twice.

Milton was a middle-aged-standoffish-grump-of-a-cat. But also kind of a gentleman... just like Ted.

When I took Milton home with me, I tried to pick him up and cuddle him. Milton craned his neck, looked me in the eyes, and literally frowned.

Next, I tried putting him on my lap. He hopped off but sat near me, two cushions over. When he wanted food, he went to his bowl and meowed once. Once. That's it.

He would follow me from room to room but at a safe distance, never getting under my feet.

And when I went in for a head pet, he ducked but still stayed nearby.

My heart soared; he would be perfect for Ted.

So, I made up my mischievous plan. Holding my breath, I knocked on Ted's door with Milton in my arms, exasperated and itching to get free.

I told Ted that I had adopted Milton, but I might be allergic. I begged him to watch Milton for a day or two, just to give me some relief until I could find him a new home.

Ted grumbled fiercely but finally relented and let Milton in.

Several days later, I called to check in. Ted told me all was well, and I didn't need to "rush" anything. Two weeks later, I went in to check on the pair.

Ted's house had been transformed. A three-tiered cat tree was proudly displayed in the den. A bowl of cat treats rested on the kitchen counter. And Milton was sporting a red bandana around his neck like a little cowboy. I had to place a hand over my mouth to suppress a giggle; it was so darn cute.

Ted greeted me with a frown. Was I there to take Milton back? he asked solemnly. Smiling widely at my successful meddling, I told him that my allergies were too bad for a cat, so I had to figure out something else for Milton.

Ted shrugged. "He's settled in. He may as well stay."

As I headed out, Ted shuffled into the den and sank onto the couch. He called for Milton, patting the cushion next to him. Milton came at once and nestled down a respectable distance from Ted but still close enough to show that he cared.

"That'll do," Ted whispered. And he smiled, just a bit.

—Annette M. Clayton—

I'm a Dog Person

I used to love dogs until I discovered cats.
~Nafisa Joseph

What was that? My dog and I paused in the middle of our walk to look quizzically at each other. Then, we heard it again, barely distinguishable between the sounds of the morning rush hour: the mewling of a tiny kitten.

I glanced across the street at my neighbor's driveway. At first, I didn't notice anything. Then, suddenly, it was as if a small oil spot near one of the cars moved!

I ran back inside with the dog and yelled upstairs to my daughter. Then, I turned around, went back outside, looked both ways, and sprinted across the street. I didn't have any particular plan in mind; I just knew that I had to do something.

Our elderly neighbor had a reputation for feeding feral cats. His wife had begun to care for them years earlier, and he had continued the practice in her memory. It was said that he had thirty or forty cats on his property at one time!

As I got closer to the "oil spot," it started moving again. I knelt down and a tiny kitten squinted up at me. I gently picked her up and went to knock on the neighbor's door. There was no answer.

I returned home and took a closer look at the kitten. She fit in the palm of my hand! Her eyes were barely open; I wasn't sure whether this was because of her young age or an infection.

Learning to Love the Cat

I called my other daughter, who lived nearby. After some discussion, we decided that she would take over the care of the kitten. I jumped in my car and made the hand-off on my way to work.

A visit to the veterinarian provided an antibiotic for the infection. It was also suggested that we get special formula to ensure the kitten receive proper nourishment. The doctor estimated that she was only two weeks old.

Later that day, my daughters found another kitten under the neighbor's front porch. They took him to be cared for with his sister. We began to wonder how many other kittens were in their litter.

Our neighbor returned home the next day. We went over to tell him what had happened. He encouraged us to take as many cats as we wanted and led us to a shed behind the house. We discovered three more kittens huddled together in a corner.

The first two kittens didn't survive; they were too small and weak. The other three began to thrive. We decided to go back for one more look.

We found two black kittens beneath an old, rusted trailer in the backyard. They peered curiously out at us but sat just out of reach. I grabbed a cat carrier and a can of tuna and set about trying to coax them out. Eventually, it worked.

The entire litter took up residence in my daughter's bathroom. They continued to grow, and their health improved. We began to discuss their future.

My daughter's small apartment couldn't accommodate five cats. She suggested that I consider taking one. "No, thanks," I protested. "You know I'm a dog person." My mind was made up.

We spent the next couple of weeks administering eye drops, bottle-feeding formula, and socializing the kittens. Every time I went to help out, one of the black kittens would climb over the others to come to me. He would then curl up on my lap, heave a contented sigh, and fall asleep purring. My resolve began to crumble.

Over time, the kittens continued to grow stronger, and "Theo" continued to grow attached to me. I could no longer deny the inevitable; I took him home.

Learning to Love the Cat

If I were to be honest, I would admit that I almost returned him more than once during our first two weeks together. He clawed at things, raced around like a maniac, and refused to sleep through the night. Something had to change.

As I marked the days and prayed for a new home for Theo, a change did take place. The change was in me. I began to notice how smart Theo was. His silly personality was infectious; I found myself laughing at almost everything he did. I saw the bond that he formed with his dog brother. We became an inseparable "pack" of three.

We spent many days and nights enjoying each other's company. We would toss toys around. The boys would wrestle good-naturedly. I would sit and read with one of them on either side of me. We would fall asleep all curled together.

After two years, our dog, George, left us. Theo mourned with me. In fact, he refused to enter the bedroom for the first two months that George was gone. When he finally did go in, he sniffed around briefly and then turned and looked at me as if to say, "Where is he?"

Although our pack has become smaller, Theo and I continue to find joy and comfort in each other. I can't imagine life without him. And I continue to be grateful for the lessons he's taught me. Through Theo, I've learned to not close myself off to new possibilities. Sometimes our preconceived notions have the potential to stand in the way of our happiness.

—Rebecca Ruballos—

Feeling Fine Feline

You are no longer lonely or lost when you hug your cat.
~Missy Dizick

He came out of nowhere, a black-and-gray tabby cat perched calmly upon the still-warm hood of the lawn tractor. I was accustomed to the neighborhood cats visiting, but this fellow was new. I was sure I'd never seen him before.

When the local cats come around, I don't mind their visits. Their presence helps keep vermin under control around my buildings, especially the chicken house. My own four cats had been unceremoniously tossed out upon the road to fend for themselves before I took them in. They started out in my little barn, scattering to hide among the bales of straw whenever I entered. My heart ached when I saw how terrified and hungry they were. They wouldn't have a chance if a fox or coyote saw them, so I trapped them and brought them into the heated garage. *It's only temporary,* I reassured myself.

Like an idiot, I believed me.

The little mothers had their babies in the shelter of the garage. Shortly after the babies were weaned, I had the adults spayed. Sadly, but knowing it was the best thing to do, when the babies were old enough, I surrendered them to the Humane Society for a better life through adoption. I'd intended to surrender their mothers as well, but they were adults by then, and I was worried they wouldn't be adopted.

I'd sworn that I would never have another cat, and suddenly here

I was with three more in addition to my mother's kitty, another discard. With a sigh, I watched them loll about in comfort in the heated garage because it was only temporary, you know. But when I wasn't looking, as stealthy as mold growth, they took over the entire basement.

Currently, I'm writing this with a cat draped across my arms and two more in the window. They've been here twelve years now, but I'm still adamant about this arrangement being temporary.

And now, all these years later, this new castaway appeared.

"Hi, there," I said to the tabby while raking the last of the leaves as he watched my efforts with what looked like disapproval.

Everyone's a critic.

Arching his back, he strolled regally around on the mower's hood. Then, well, technically, it could be called a meow, but what really came out of his throat was a rough, groaning blast of noise.

A feline air horn.

Giving his back a rub, I noticed that he was so thin that I could see his vertebrae, and his ears were like tattered lace from past battles. He was older than I had thought, but he was a friendly fellow, content to watch from his vantage point. When it came time to fix supper, I gave him a quick cuddle. It was time for him to go home, too.

Later in the evening, when I went out to close the chicken coop for the night, he was still perched upon the mower. He followed along as I locked up and then trotted back to the house with me. I was troubled that he was still there that late but thought he'd surely go home when I went inside.

The next morning was overcast and cold when I went down to release the chickens. To my bitter disappointment, there he was, curled up on the hood of the mower as a light, cold rain began to fall. So much for my hopes that he was local. He was soaked to the skin, and when he saw me, he stood up slowly and stiffly. My heart sank as I looked at the battered, old cat.

"Please don't be a dump! Please," I whispered, caressing him.

He paced along the hood, purring and bellowing his discordant screech, and was ecstatic when I gently scratched him under the chin. The cold rain hadn't affected his sweet personality. My suspicions were confirmed. He didn't act like a barn cat: furtive, slipping silently around, avoiding human contact. Not this fellow. He cheerfully followed me to the coop again and then back to the house.

As a heavy rain began to fall, I couldn't help peering out the windows. Sphinx-like, paws curled beneath him, his eyes squinted against the rain, he remained on the mower. Obviously, the poor fellow had nowhere to go. I was infuriated with whoever had been heartless enough to coldly dispose of him, especially at his age.

With a groan, I stomped downstairs. Opening the door, I went out and carefully picked him up and carried him in. In the garage, I dried him off and gently rubbed his scalloped ears. Stiffly, he followed me around with an odd, swaying bounce. The cold and rain were obviously affecting his arthritis, or he'd had an injury, or it was a combination of both.

When I opened a can of food, he wolfed it down in seconds and then curled up on the blanket in front of the warm radiator. A booming purr began. Poor fellow. He deserved so much better. Had he been a pet, and now that he was older, had someone simply tired of him? Or had someone's aged parent gone into a nursing home or passed away? By dumping him, their problem was solved, but his had only just begun.

The old man, now called Toby, lived with me until a suitable home was found for him. He was placed in an assisted-living facility with the stipulation that he'd be returned to me if his placement should become temporary. But I've got a feeling that Toby will never be homeless again. He's an affectionate old guy, and it seems appropriate that a senior cat with that much love to share should be part of a senior assisted-living environment. He can't get enough attention, and with a population of forty-plus humans, he should easily get his daily allotment of love and pampering.

Animals, like people, can come into our lives for a season and, occasionally, perhaps for a higher purpose. Maybe I was simply a conduit to help an unwanted, old cat on his way to the next, best part of his life.

— Laurel L. Shannon —

The Feral Cat and the Family Dog

The cat has too much spirit to have no heart.
~Ernest Menaul

One fall morning, my husband opened our back door to let out my dog and started muttering something about the darn feral cat. My ears perked up. Living out in the country, I've seen my fair share of feral cats come and go from our fifty acres. No matter how hard I tried, I could never get any of these wild beauties to stick around very long. I assumed it was because of our three giant dogs who roam freely on our land.

I peered anxiously over my cup of coffee. Had Will Feral, Captain Jack Feral, Woody Feralson, or one of my other feral friends returned?

No. This was a brand-new frisky feline to befriend.

My husband tried to shoo away whoever this new inhabitant under the porch was before I could lay eyes on our little guest. It was a rude thing to do. How could I name this mystery cat without a formal introduction first?

However, before I could force my husband to sleep on the couch for being so callous about my deep desire for a cat, the feline was back, poking her head out from under the porch. After getting a look at her fluffy fur, sassy swagger, and mysterious, deep eyes, I knew exactly what her name was.

"I will call her Feral Fawcett," I announced over the groan my

Learning to Love the Cat

husband let out.

I tried to approach Ms. Fawcett slowly, but she responded like a typical diva. I went back inside but started to panic when I remembered my chocolate Lab, Bronco, was out strolling the yard.

I didn't want him to upset our new guest. I quickly learned that my cat celebrity did not like being disturbed while she rested. I held my breath as Bronco walked over to the porch where she was hiding and stuck his nose under to give her a sniff. To my amazement, Ms. Fawcett came out from under the porch and started nuzzling Bronco. I stood at the glass door watching, and as soon as I opened it, she went back into hiding. Feral Fawcett was playing hard-to-get.

The next morning, I let Bronco back outside, and he took off into the field for his morning stroll. I watched as he got smaller and smaller in the distance. Suddenly, something was bobbing up and down alongside him.

I grabbed my feral-cat-spotting binoculars, and sure enough, Feral Fawcett and Bronco were leisurely walking next to each other. Every time he stopped to sniff, she rested her body against his, and he waited patiently for her to catch her breath before continuing their stroll.

Soon, they were inseparable. Every morning, Ms. Fawcett waited with her face pressed against the back door for her breakfast and morning stroll with her honey.

My other two dogs were not nearly as enamored with Feral Fawcett as Bronco was. They didn't care that they were in the presence of greatness. They had no interest in celebrity-cat pawtagraphs or morning walks and instead chased after her.

It was sad to see such a dignified creature run for her life while being chased by a ten-year-old German Shepherd who could easily be outrun by my ninety-year-old grandma with her artificial hip.

Still, she came back to be with Bronco. And their love grew.

**

As winter drew nearer, I started worrying about Feral Fawcett's fate. Living under a porch was not acceptable for someone so refined, but she had no interest in living inside with her boyfriend.

My husband and I decided it would be best to contact a local cat rescue to get Ms. Fawcett some medical care and suitable housing. Bronco unknowingly helped us lure her into a trap, and she was taken away to a foster family.

Bronco waited for her on the back porch for weeks. He searched for her under the porch and cried for his lost love. It was heartbreaking.

Months went by. Bronco continued his morning walks alone but not before searching for his missing girlfriend first. He lost the pep in his step, his head hung low, and his favorite toy (Pearl the potholder) lost her allure.

Life didn't make sense without Feral Fawcett. But what could we do? She was long gone by now. I imagined her with a new family, being carried around on a cat throne and hand-fed fresh sardines all day.

Then, in the middle of winter, the phone rang.

It was the volunteer from the cat rescue. She said Ms. Fawcett was not suitable for rehoming and was my responsibility since I had brought her in. She had been fixed and vaccinated, and now she was being returned to my backyard.

I looked out at the mounds of snow blowing through our open field. The temperature was barely above freezing. A pit formed in my stomach when I thought of the poor cat being released outside in the dead of winter.

Luckily, I had some time. The volunteer told me that Feral Fawcett had escaped the confines of the bathroom and was hiding somewhere in the basement. She would be returned once she could be coaxed out.

My husband was out of town for work, and with all the commotion, it must have slipped my mind to tell him that Bronco's feline companion was returning. Besides, I hardly had time to fill him in when I was busy scouring the Internet for the best feral-cat accommodations.

I came across a website advertising "feral villas," little two-story shelters to keep outdoor cats warm and dry. Disregarding the high price, I immediately purchased the fancy cat house and an outdoor heated bed.

No expense should be spared for my dog's soulmate.

By the time Feral Fawcett was released out back, the feral villa

Learning to Love the Cat

and heated bed were waiting for her by the porch.

As soon as Ms. Fawcett was back "home," I let Bronco outside and waited nervously. What if they didn't remember each other? What if her love for him had disappeared when he aided in her capture months before?

My fears immediately disappeared when I saw her run right up to Bronco and touch her nose to his. I watched as they rolled in the snow together and enjoyed their familiar leisurely walk in the crisp winter air.

Five years later, Feral Fawcett still resides in her feral villa. She still takes her walks with Bronco, and in the summers, they sunbathe together on the porch where their love story began.

This is one love story where I can honestly say they lived happily ever after.

— Kendra Phillips —

Petal's Budding Romance

Life is Beautiful! Cats and love are all that you need.
~Arthur Bridges

"There's a young, stray cat that has been hanging around my mom's house for quite a while now," I explained to the veterinarian I worked for. "The tomcats are around her, and I think she might be going into heat. Would you spay her for me?"

The veterinarian smiled. "I'd be happy to. Just bring her in. We'll spay her and get her shots up to date, no charge. I'll take care of the medical; you take care of finding her a new home."

That day, I scooped up the scrawny, black cat from my mom's house and took her into the vet clinic. She needed a sweet name to match her nature, and by unanimous vote from my co-workers, she was given the name Petal. During her stay at the clinic, we discovered that Petal was a really special cat. Not only was she loving and affectionate, but she was incredibly serene. Nothing seemed to faze her. The steady stream of people with sick and stressed animals bustling in and out of the clinic seemed to have no effect on her at all. *Who wouldn't want this mellow, sweet cat?* I thought. *Finding a home will be so easy!*

What I thought would be a cinch was not. Time after time, phone call after phone call yielded nothing. Clients whom I thought would be a perfect match turned me down. I didn't give up. I knew there was a great home out there somewhere.

Then, the perfect person popped into my head. Wendy had lost her senior cat a while back but still had another cat at home. Perhaps her cat needed a friend. Excitedly, I gave her a call.

It wasn't the reception I was hoping for. "Jill, I don't think so. The two cats I had, Tigger and Trooper, didn't get along. Tigger used to beat up Trooper, and now that Tigger is gone, Trooper is a different cat. Trooper is really happy being the only cat in the house."

For some reason, I knew this was the right home for Petal. I just had to convince Wendy to give it a chance.

"I have an idea," I said. "Take Petal for a trial run. I'll walk you through how to assimilate two cats, and let's see how it pans out. If it doesn't work, Petal comes back to the clinic. You have nothing to lose."

Wendy seemed doubtful. "Well, okay. We'll give it a try. But if this brings any stress to Trooper — if they fight at all — I'll bring her back."

Wendy arrived that afternoon, cat carrier in hand, to take Petal to her home. As I said my goodbyes to Petal, I knew that I wouldn't see her again. I had a great feeling about this, and I knew in my heart that it would turn out wonderfully.

The next day, I answered the phone, and Wendy was on the line.

"Jill, I have to tell you that Petal is just lovely. She's so affectionate and sweet. My husband and I locked her in our office separate from Trooper to give them time apart before slowly letting them meet. When my husband went in to do some work, Petal was all over him. She was lying on the keyboard and climbing up onto his shoulders. My husband fell in love with her."

"That's wonderful!" I exclaimed. "I'm so happy."

"Well, don't be upset, but we didn't follow your instructions. We let Petal and Trooper meet."

At this point, my heart started to beat fast in my chest. I pictured the worst-case scenario: Petal in a corner, cowering before a hissing, angry Trooper. "Oh, no! Please tell me that Petal is okay. Did they fight?"

"Jill, it's okay," Wendy said. "They absolutely love each other."

"Really!"

"Absolutely. At first, Trooper was very scared and cowered when

Learning to Love the Cat

they met. But Petal started rubbing against him, and although he seems a little intimidated by her, there's no aggression at all. In fact, she really wants to be his friend. Trooper seems confused by all this affection from her, but I think it will work out just fine."

I breathed a sigh of relief. It was only the first day, but I was hopeful that the budding friendship between Petal and Trooper would continue to grow.

"Please, Wendy, keep me posted. I'm happy to help however I can."

A month passed. Luckily, I was at reception when Wendy came in.

"Jill, I really wanted to say thank you for talking me into adopting Petal. She and Trooper are the best of friends. He calls for her when she's in another room, and she comes running to see him. They sleep in the same bed, and the playing…! Trooper is twelve years old, and they chase each other around the house. Petal has brought such a great energy into our family, and Trooper acts like a young, happy cat."

Then, Wendy pulled out her phone to show me photos. One showed Trooper and Petal curled around each other sleeping and another of them crouched side by side, looking out a window.

"Oh, Wendy, you made my day," I said. "I'm so happy that Trooper and Petal love each other."

I had to drop by my mom's that evening to tell her about the new romance between Petal and Trooper. It's not every day that you have the privilege of becoming a cat matchmaker.

—Jill Berni—

Mimi Made Me a Cat Lady

*Since each of us is blessed with only one life,
why not live it with a cat?*
~Robert Stearns

"Surprise, Mom!" My youngest son, a college senior, had just burst in the door for his Thanksgiving break. Distracted by the fact that he needed a haircut, and looking around for the dirty laundry that usually accompanied his return home, I didn't immediately notice the pink pet carrier in his right hand. With great ceremony, he placed the carrier on the dining room table and unzipped the top.

I looked into the carrier and understood immediately. It was my turn to babysit his college house cat, Mimi.

I knew the story. Two years earlier, someone had found this skinny kitten wandering the streets in Philadelphia, and they had brought her back to their house at the University of Delaware. The vote among the eight boys was unanimous.

Yes, they would keep her. This loud, ramshackle house filled with lacrosse players and computer geniuses was about to be ruled by a petite black kitten named Mikasa.

I had listened to tales about "Mimi" for two years. That they had had her chipped. That they had gotten her an air tag. That she had once killed a rabbit. That they had once lost track of her and an

Learning to Love the Cat | 203

hour later found her visiting another house of boys across the street. That they kept windows and doors open (screens in) for her so she could look out at the squirrels and birds in their yard, which was her favorite thing to do.

And I also knew that she was universally loved by everyone who met her. A few months earlier, I had even asked my son for a turn to babysit her over the holidays, since it was our last chance.

He smiled and answered stoically, "We'll see."

So, she was ours for a week.

As a dog family, we had no experience with cats. However, the death of our beloved dog Mojo at age twelve three years earlier had left a gaping hole in my heart.

Nevertheless, as a widow and empty nester, I was reticent to enter into the "cat lady" phase of life. I was indeed lonely and missed having a pet. But as a college professor and an avid traveler, I knew having a pet at this phase of my life was not only impractical but fantastically selfish.

And I sure didn't want to be a "cat lady."

But that Sunday, when my son pulled her out of that carrier, I knew I was done for.

Mimi was cute. Petite, black, with a white nose, white paws, and a small nick out of her right ear. Low maintenance, affectionate, fun to play with. A great purrer.

I fell in love fast.

I loved listening to her crunch her little food pellets. Watching her little tongue daintily lap up water. Feeling her purr machine against my chest early in the dark fall mornings, when I would come downstairs to make coffee, and when she was the most affectionate. Hearing her little mews as she tried to talk to me. I even loved that she took over my favorite chair and my favorite throw as her personal domicile.

I loved just watching her exist as this perfect ball of black fluff, with her own daily schedule. I was reminded of a quote I had once read about animals — that when we watch animals, we are released from ego. When I would watch Mimi pad soundlessly through our house, I became transfixed and forgot what I was supposed to be doing.

The week flew by, and as my son packed up his stuff to leave that next Sunday, I joked with him that Mimi and I had discussed it, and she was staying with me. He laughed and gently zipped her into her carrier.

Then, something occurred to me.

"Say, when you guys all graduate in May, where is she going to live?"

He furrowed his brow.

"We're not sure yet."

"Well," I said, hugging him goodbye, "throw my name into the ring for that discussion."

He said he would, and as I watched him drive away, I knew it had happened.

I was a cat lady.

— Mary F. Oves —

The Cat Plan

*God made the cat in order that man might have
the pleasure of caressing the tiger.
~François Joseph Méry*

Because I can seldom resist an opportunity for self-improvement, particularly where it concerns my husband, the plan comes to me quickly. The complaints from him that our cat Mishka avoids and dislikes him are common.

Despite my pointing out to my husband that his movements are abrupt and he often makes a racket, he answers, without fail, "She just doesn't like me." Even an unperceptive, single-celled life form could easily detect his impatience when letting Mishka in or out of the house, which leads to him slamming the door and further deterioration of the relationship.

I am famous in our household for concocting hard-to-follow, intricate schemes. So I am pleased with the simplicity of my corrective approach, which assigns to my husband the nice things I do for Mishka: giving her fresh water, filling her bowl with food, throwing catnip toys around for her to play with, fluffing up the bedding, getting down on hands and knees in the living room and waiting for her to come around to be tickled, jumping up quickly when she stands by the door, jumping up quickly again when she raps at the window to be let back in…

He is pessimistic about anything improving and not keen about the responsibilities being foisted upon him, but I badger him into compliance.

In the two weeks that have now passed, the changes have been remarkable, with a number of firsts — Mishka rubbing against his legs, Mishka asking him for food, Mishka leading him to the living room for playtime. Jarring though it is to witness their relationship, which seems akin to what Mishka and I had two weeks ago, I work furiously to jettison any feelings of jealousy. Killjoy is not a term I want applied to me. I know I'm losing out, though.

Muttering to myself about fickle loyalty, I hear her galloping past me as if she doesn't even see me, her meows shrill and unpleasant to my ears. And when she reaches him, she throws herself stupidly at his feet.

Now that the dark, unintended consequences of my plan have emerged, I am unappreciative of its success, and crabby, with diminished affection for both my husband and Mishka.

Offhandedly, I inform my husband that a new plan is being formulated, one in which I will relieve him of some of his Mishka obligations. I hear him say in a confused tone that he doesn't mind, that he actually enjoys his duties. Quite grumpy now, he says he doesn't want to lose her, and I answer curtly that I'm sure that won't happen, even as I slash his list.

Strategically, I assign him to cleaning the kitty litter, taking her to the vet, being responsible for her during the most inconvenient hours of the day, and so on, until, exhausted by my own machinations, I decide on a midafternoon nap.

They are in the living room together, him doing a crossword and her on his lap, projecting her purr so loudly that I could hear it even before I entered the room. Unable to actually ignore them, at least I don't look over as I lie down on the couch and pull the heavy blanket of misery over me.

When I close my eyes, I hear murmurs of satisfaction and paper rustling as my husband fills in more words. Visions of their joyous life together after I'm gone disturb me.

Yet, I can't help praying — yes, I'm praying now — that someday soon, she will remember me. But then I glance at them together and wonder in my dark heart, *What are the chances…?*

Zero, I think hopelessly, just before I hear the thud of her hitting the carpet and feel the weight of her landing on my feet, and then the slow, familiar, and painful walk up my legs and over my belly.

After settling herself comfortably on top of me, she touches my face tenderly with her paw, and I open my eyes slightly to gaze into hers.

—Gwen Swick—

There's a Problem

When you touch a cat with your spirit, in return they touch your soul with their heart.
~Author Unknown

For those of us involved in the world of cat rescue, the last thing we want to hear is "There's a problem." Occasionally, though, those words can lead to lovely surprises.

The first time I heard them was before I got officially into rescue work — although my first-ever cat was, I realize now, a rescue. I was visiting a horse farm, and the barn kittens were running around.

"Want one?" the barn manager asked. "Tomorrow, we're rounding them up to send to the pound."

"I can't," I said. "I just moved into a house with seven other students. We'd need a meeting to discuss getting a cat."

He didn't answer. He just bent down and scooped up a random kitten. "How about this one?" He held up a tortoiseshell with comical facial markings. "At the pound, they only keep 'em three days, and then they put 'em down." He looked at me pointedly.

I returned to the city with the kitten. Prunella turned out to be a gentle, affectionate, all-around sweetheart.

One night, years later, I let her out after supper. (Everyone let their cats out back then.) Soon after, I heard loud barking. I rushed out to see two big dogs at the base of my neighbor's tree, and Prunella hissing on a branch above them. I chased them off, brought her inside and, to my horror, discovered a huge gash in her thigh.

Learning to Love the Cat | 209

At the emergency-vet clinic, they told me that the dogs had done some real damage. She'd need to be anesthetized and stitched up. I'd have to leave her overnight.

"You said she's fifteen?" the vet asked.

"Yes."

The vet bit her lip. "Hate to say this, but you'd better say your farewells, just in case. Given her age, she might not pull through."

Stunned, I tearfully kissed Prunella goodbye. I barely slept. I couldn't imagine life without her.

Heart pounding, I called the clinic the next morning.

"Prunella needed a lot of stitches, but she made it through," the receptionist said.

"Thank God! Can I come get her?"

"Yes. However," she paused, "there's a problem." Her tone was solemn.

This was my first time hearing those words in relation to an animal. "There is?" My heart was pounding again.

"Yes. The problem is," now I could hear the smile in her voice, "we're all in love with her. We're not sure we want to give her back!"

I chuckled with grateful relief.

Prunella made it to age twenty-two, and not long after, I got involved in cat rescue.

The next time I heard those words was when I was fostering feral kittens for a rescue group. After I'd tamed them, the group sent a young couple over to see them.

"I'm the one who really wants a cat," Anya explained. When Anya and I went up to my spare room to see the kittens, her husband stayed downstairs reading the paper.

"You're sure your husband's okay with this?" I asked. "He's not going to mistreat the kitten?"

"Gosh, no," Anya said. "Roberto's a sweet man. He just doesn't 'get' pets. Never had any growing up."

Anya chose a cuddly gray kitten. Stroking him, she sighed. "I'm hoping, in a few months, Roberto will start enjoying him."

Two days later, I made a follow-up call. "How's the kitten?" I said.

Learning to Love the Cat

"He's fine," Anya replied. "But…" And then that phrase: "There's a problem."

My heart sank. "What's going on?"

She began to giggle. "The problem is that Roberto's been carrying him around ever since we got home. I can't pry the little thing out of his hands!"

"Smitten by a kitten," I said, and we both dissolved in laughter. Phew! Another "problem" that turned out to be anything but.

A couple of months later, I took on the role of foster/adoption coordinator for the rescue group. I returned a call from a woman named Kate. She seemed to have trouble getting out each sentence.

"My cat died. I had him almost… twenty years," she said. "So, I…" Her voice trailed off.

"That's very sad," I said. "I'm sorry."

"Thanks. Petey was… my best friend."

"My first cat lived to be twenty-two, so I get how hard this is for you."

"It really is." She sounded teary.

"So, you're looking to adopt?" I gently prompted.

"Adopt?" She sounded horrified. "It's way too soon. I'm sure I'll need a year before I'm ready."

"Of course. So, what can I help you with?"

"Well, it's lonely. Someone suggested I could… foster?"

"That's great!" I exclaimed. We were always short of foster homes but never short of street cats waiting to be fostered. All us volunteers, including me, had at least one foster in our homes as well as our own cats.

I interviewed Kate. She passed the screening. "I have a young black-and-white foster here called Oreo," I told her. "I can bring him over tomorrow."

"Tomorrow?" She sounded startled. "That's so quick. I…"

I was beginning to lose patience. I had three more calls to make. "Kate, if for any reason it doesn't work out, I'll come get him."

"Okay. Because I don't want to… get stuck with him or anything."

"No worries. He's lovely, so I'm sure he'll get adopted quickly."

I took Oreo to Kate's apartment. I suggested that, as I always did with fosters, she restrict him to the bathroom for a few days until he got

Learning to Love the Cat | 21

used to her. "Some foster cats will dive under a bed immediately," I told her, "and hide for weeks."

We set up Oreo in the bathroom, and Kate fed him treats. "Looks like he'll be fine," I said.

I called her the next afternoon. "How's Oreo doing?"

"Um..." Kate hesitated. And there it was again: "There's a... problem." *Uh-oh,* I thought. *Did he shred the shower curtain? Pee in the tub?* "What is it?"

"He slept on my bed last night."

"He got out of the bathroom?"

"Well, he's so friendly..."

I knew what was coming. "You felt sorry for him?" This had happened before with new foster homes.

"Yes... so I let him out." She sounded contrite.

"It's okay. Luckily, Oreo's a very tame cat."

"Then, he came into the bedroom. He slept on the bed all night."

"You can shut your bedroom door, you know. I'm sorry he bothered you."

"It's not that. I mean, the problem is he slept on my bed."

I was feeling rather stumped. "That's a problem because...?"

"He slept beside me. He purred. It's like he's chosen me."

"Ah." No one told me that "therapist" was part of the coordinator job description, but I was starting to figure it out. "You're falling for Oreo, but you feel like you're betraying Petey?"

"Maybe. See, I never had a cat before Petey."

"And you feel like it's wrong to replace him?"

"I guess."

"Kate, Petey will always have that special place in your heart as your first cat. Oreo isn't replacing him. He'd be... succeeding him, that's all. I'll put him on hold, and you can think about it. No pressure."

Kate adopted Oreo the following week.

Now if only all cat-rescue "problems" could have such lovely resolutions!

— Marie-Lynn Hammond —

Living in Harmony

There is something about the presence of a cat... that seems to take the bite out of being alone.
~Louis J. Camuti

I am not a crazy cat lady. It is true that three black cats share my house with me: Miles, Tiny and Mama Cat. For a time, there were five black cats: one mother and four kittens rescued from a feral life of prowling about our yard. Two went to live with an actual crazy cat lady and one — Mama Cat — had mixed feelings about indoor living and returned to the great outdoors. But considering it was an especially snowy winter, Mama Cat returned. So now, there are three.

There is a crazy cat man. When he sits on the couch, they jump up behind him to purr in his ear and knead his shoulders. When I sit, they look at me like a large, hideous slug has invaded the sofa.

The cats and I had an understanding. We could live in harmony if we ignored each other. I did not feed them. I did not change the litter box. In turn, they did not sleep on my bed, sit on my lap, or show me any affection. Our only conversations consisted of wordless roars of rage on my part when they decided that the furniture needed some claw attention.

I am certain they believed that the cat man chose poorly when he picked a mate. After all, what human ignores the clear signs of meowing cats wrapping around ankles during the morning rush? Suspicions ran high in the feline community that I didn't even know where the cat

Learning to Love the Cat

food was kept! It was a shame that cat man was saddled with what had to be the dumbest human in the world. So sad for poor cat man.

The cats and I continued living parallel lives, joined only by our mutual affection for cat man. All that changed when the company I worked for was swallowed up by an even bigger company. In the corporate musical chairs that followed, I found myself without a chair... or an office... or a job. On Friday evening, the cat man and I stood in the doorway of the guest room. The only guests it saw on a regular basis were three black cats. They lolled on the bed, the chair, the windowsill.

"This could be a great office."

After a guest-bedroom-to-office transformation, the job search began early Monday morning. Things went well for about two hours. Then, there was a soft but unmistakable tap, tap, tap at the door. As with all things cat-related, I ignored it. Tap, tap, tap. Pause. Great! He'd gone away. Tap, tap, tap. I tried to ignore the shadows of a cat trying to push his head under the door. Tap, tap, tap.

"Fine!" I burst out, reaching out to swing open the door.

He stood in the doorway for a moment, considering the changes before prowling in on light feet. He stood where the bed used to be, and, even though I didn't look, I could feel his accusing eyes on me. Then, I heard an odd rattle. I turned my head just in time to see him disappear into the closet, somehow closing the sliding door behind him. I heard rustling among the holiday decorations, boxes of books and winter coats. Finally, he settled, and I went back to work.

A little while later, the closet door rattled open, and he stood next to me.

"M-e-o-w!"

"What?"

He rubbed up against the closed room door.

"Okay, then." I swung open the door and out he strutted, like a Rockefeller having the door to the Plaza held open by the doorman.

Finally, I dove back into a world of resumes, interviews and job boards. I was just about to break for lunch when I heard it again. Tap, tap, tap. I opened the door, and he headed for the closet. I sent one

Learning to Love the Cat

quick email and started to leave when I heard the now-familiar rustle of the closet door. Whatever he was doing in there was quick this time. We walked out for lunch together.

It continued throughout the day, and the next day, and the next. The tapping, the closet… Eventually, he began hanging out on the windowsill, the treadmill, and the top of the filing cabinet. We developed a… relationship. He would give me a heads-up meow when he saw an interesting bird outside the window. I would practice interview questions on him. I took his super slow blink as code for "Yes, you did come off as professional and knowledgeable."

Eventually, job searching became a new remote job, and all three cats began visiting with a soft tap, tap, tap. As any worker huddled in a solitary home office will tell you, the occasional visitor makes the day go faster. An added plus was that I could talk to them if I felt like it. But if I was busy, I could just ignore them completely. This does not work with your mom.

The cats and I have reached a new understanding. We are remote work buddies. Crazy cat man is amused.

—Jodi M. Webb—

Sometimes the Best Revenge Is Living

*An animal's eyes have the power
to speak a great language.
~Martin Buber*

At my husband's lumbermill, a mother cat settled in to have her kittens. We found the litter under a bridge on the mill property one morning just at the beginning of winter. We were living in Clarksville, Tennessee, and both our kids, ages four and two, wanted their "own" kitten.

The litter was small — only two were there when we found them under the bridge. They were healthy, but their mother had run off. We had to take the kittens home or they'd die.

"I don't know if we can take care of two kittens," I said, in a futile attempt to resist the inevitable. Then, one of the kittens turned to me and closed a green, mischievous eye in what appeared to be... a wink. That was the beginning of my relationship with one of the most tenacious cats I have ever known. We called her Coco.

Coco and her sister Crystal were exact opposites. Crystal was a pure-white cat with big blue eyes. She was sweet and affectionate. From the first day we had her, she exhibited a kind of "Thank you for saving me" attitude. She was neat with her litter-box habits, always ate what we put before her, and never fought with her sister.

Coco was dark. As a very young kitten, she looked solid black

Learning to Love the Cat

with an orange stripe down her sides. As she grew older, the colors began to differentiate until she resembled a tortoiseshell cat. And, of course, a tortoiseshell, or "tortie" as our vet called her, she was. Her jade-green eyes shone with an insolent, malevolent glow. That glow should have alerted us to the shape of things to come — that our house would turn on her feline whims.

Coco put up her nose at any food we put down, yowled all night for no reason, clawed at anyone who tried to pet or hold her, and picked fights with Crystal. We marveled at how different two sisters could be.

With time, Crystal mellowed, but not Coco. If you walked past her and she was lounging on a chair, she would wait until you were almost past and then gouge you, the unsuspecting person, with a barbed claw.

She had some other habits that were equally mystifying and even troubling. She loved my hair elastic ties (scrunchies). We'd spayed both cats when they were young, but Coco would treat the scrunchies as if they were her newborns, moving them from place to place and putting them in a neat pile in the corner of a closet or quiet room. When she tired of caring for her "kittens," she would take the scrunchies to the nearest toilet and, one by one, drop them in.

Years went by, but there was no change in Coco. She grew fat and, as they say, sassy, ballooning up to a whopping twenty-four pounds. When my husband and I took her in for a check-up, the vet held her, looked in Coco's green eyes, and said, "Wow! You have the most beautiful eyes I've ever seen!" Then, her gaze took in the rest of the rotund Coco. "But you are really fat!"

"I guess that means she's not going to live much longer?" my husband asked.

"Oh, no!" the vet asserted. "She could live to be twenty-five."

"Oh, no, she's not!" my husband replied — perhaps a bit too quickly.

Despite all Coco's ways, which most people found offensive or even disturbing, there was something about her that touched me. I think we had an almost-mystical relationship. There would be times when I would be feverishly writing, and she would jump up and take a stroll on the keyboard. Rather than think that Coco was demanding attention, to me she was telling me to take a break from work. When

Learning to Love the Cat

she yowled and woke me in the pre-dawn hours, I think she was telling me to use those quiet hours to get some writing done to meet my next deadline. In so many ways, Coco was my biggest taskmaster. Writer's block simply didn't exist in my house; my "tortie" wouldn't allow it.

By the time I had more than 700 magazine and newspaper articles published and had just released my eighth book, Coco was a feline fixture in my office, with her bed by my writing desk. Coco was probably the ripe old age of fourteen when she became seriously sick. My first clue was her change in attitude. Before, she'd acted as if she allowed us to live with her. Now, she followed me from room to room, mewling. She stopped eating. After a few more days, she stopped drinking water. I weighed her, and she had gone from her usual twenty-four pounds down to seventeen. It was time for a stay at the vet's office.

"This tortie's sick, all right," my vet agreed when I brought in Coco. "We'll have to get her on fluids today and see if we can make her eat." The vet's staff got Coco started on intravenous fluids (she immediately pulled out the IV tube with her teeth) and then began force-feeding her with a syringe. After a few more tests, the vet came back with a diagnosis: liver failure.

"People live off their fat when they stop eating," the vet explained. "With cats, that causes their liver to shut down. She may not survive this."

I kept visiting Coco during her week's stay at the vet's. On Friday, the vet allowed me to take Coco home so she could die in peace. Any true animal lover knows how painful this can be. And looking at Coco hurt, too. Her once-glossy fur was matted, and her beautiful green eyes had a glazed, faraway look in them. She had lost so much weight by this time that she looked skeletal.

Unsure what to do at this point, I knew that if I could just get her to eat, Coco would make it. We tried everything from tuna to liver paté. What finally did the trick was when my daughter fed her pepperoni. Coco devoured every bite and mewed for more. We knew that Coco would make it then.

The following week, after a successful check-up with the vet, I was sitting on the sofa watching the news with my tortie next to me.

My husband came in from the mailbox, waving a bill from the vet. "It's right at $800," he said, glowering mildly at Coco. "I don't see how you could have spent that much money on a cat that doesn't even have a sense of appreciation. And she's not even charming, like her sister."

At that moment, I felt Coco's paw by my hand. She opened her paw and curled it around the ends of two of my fingers in as close to what I could call a feline handholding as possible. "Yeah," I agreed, "she's not appreciative at all."

I looked at Coco, and I could have sworn I saw one of her green eyes close in what might have been... a wink.

— T. Jensen Lacey —

A Cat Hater's Tale

*I think having an animal in your life
makes you a better human.*
~Rachael Ray

My husband hated cats. His frequent and vehement declarations left no doubt in anyone's mind. Cats rubbed against him and left hair all over his pant legs. They scratched furniture and people and left deep scars on both. He could show evidence to prove his point.

Also, cats hissed and prowled at all hours. They climbed where they had no business going. They ignored what they did not like.

In short, they were worthless pests, and he wanted no part of them. Dogs were fine. They listened and learned. But cats, never.

When we moved to the country, we raised cattle, grew hay, and planted a small orchard. We chose apple, pear, peach, and cherry trees, plus blackberry and raspberry bushes. They grew and produced well as a result of our tender loving care.

My dad, a master gardener, oversaw our pruning and inspected our trees and plants whenever he visited. His "uh-oh" on one visit surprised us. We thought everything looked good. Our trees showed no signs of stress or disease, had bloomed well, and were beginning to yield that season's fruit.

However, Dad was not looking at the trees' limbs. Instead, he directed our attention to the ground around their trunks. He pointed to numerous, previously unnoticed, small holes near the base of several trees. He said two ominous words: "meadow voles." Although cute little critters, they love to gnaw on the roots and lower trunks of fruit trees. We saw no obvious damage at that point, but Dad had no doubt there would be problems.

"What do we need to do?" I asked.

Dad rubbed his chin in thought and then said, "The simplest solution is to get a cat."

"A cat? Really?" I glanced at my cat-hating husband, who shrugged and, to my surprise, said, "Okay."

Dad continued, "Our mama cat recently had a litter, and I can give you one if you want it." That sealed the deal. We would soon become cat owners.

A few days later, we visited Mom and Dad. Before we returned home, we caught a feisty gray kitten, placed it in a small animal carrier, and took it with us. Its pitiful mews filled the car as we drove away from its mama and the only home it had known. When we arrived and introduced Smokey to her new surroundings, we fed her milk and made a bed for her in the garage. We left the door up so she could explore our yard and orchard. She grew well and quickly found her way around our property.

A couple of weeks later, Dad returned. He had built a tiny house for Smokey, complete with siding, inside paneling, and a carpeted floor. Smokey found the new residence to her liking and moved in. She also spent much of her free time following my husband to check the cattle. She frequently rubbed against my husband's legs, scratched and climbed whatever was around her, and did her share of hissing and prowling.

As spring turned to summer and summer to fall, Smokey continued to shadow my husband as he completed daily chores. One cool evening, my husband zipped on a warm jacket, and he and Smokey headed over the hill behind our house while I prepared dinner. I glanced out the kitchen window a little later just as my husband topped the hill on his return. However, Smokey was nowhere in sight. She was not leading or trailing my husband or chasing any stray creatures in the pasture.

Then, I spied her. My cat-hating husband had tucked Smokey

Learning to Love the Cat

inside the front of his jacket and zipped it high so only Smokey's head peeked out from under his chin. Laughing, I stopped what I was doing and ran out to greet them.

"I thought you hated cats."

"I do, but I was afraid she might get cold." With an embarrassed smile, he continued on to the house where he gently removed that once-hated creature from his jacket and set her down in front of her food bowl before going inside for his own meal.

Meadow vole problem resolved. Cat-hating husband reformed.

—Diana Derringer—

Chapter 8

Meant to Be

Samantha

In the garden of memory, in the palace of dreams...
that is where you and I shall meet.
~Lewis Carroll, Alice Through the Looking Glass

I got home from my second chemotherapy treatment feeling wiped out. Moments after reclining on the sofa, I drifted into a state of twilight — not quite asleep, yet not fully awake. Bobcat, my burly, affectionate feline, jumped onto my lap. I put my hand on his back, and before falling into a deep slumber, I saw a lucid image in my mind of myself holding a small, fluffy cat. I instinctively knew the cat was female. Her coat was ginger-colored with shades of orange and fawn. Startled by the vivid image, I opened my eyes.

Who was the cat in my daydream? I didn't dwell on it for long; nausea distracted me. It was time for some meds.

A few weeks following the vision of the fluffy cat, I crawled into bed, relieved to have my third chemotherapy treatment behind me. Bobcat was lightly snoring as he slept next to me. Fatigue suddenly hit hard. I turned off the bedside lamp and was out like a light.

In the middle of the night, I awoke from a dream in which I observed myself with the fluffy ginger cat again. I was grinning and holding her close to my chest, feeling blissful. It was as though she was my cat, although I'd never had a cat like her before. I wondered if chemotherapy was causing an overactive imagination.

Meant to Be

***

Bobcat had been diabetic for about nine months. Although overweight, he seemed content and displayed no signs of distress since the diagnosis. Then, a couple of weeks following that third chemo treatment, Bobcat became listless and stopped eating. A friend drove us to the vet who, after an exam and blood work, delivered the grave news that his body was shutting down.

Losing Bobcat was the last thing on my mind. I thought we'd have at least a few more years together despite the diabetes. I couldn't imagine getting through my remaining treatments and the long road to healing without him. Three days following the vet appointment, my sweet Bobcat passed peacefully in my arms in the cottage we shared. I'd had cats in my household since I was twenty-six. For the first time in thirty-three years, I was without feline companionship.

Gearing up for surgery was a distraction from losing Bobcat. After weeks of anticipation, the big day arrived and went by in a flash. One minute, I was being prepped, and the next thing I recall was waking in recovery with my surgeon by my side, assuring me that the surgery went well.

During my hospital stay, the fluffy ginger cat showed up in dreams despite constant interruptions from medical staff. The dreams were the same. I was holding her, feeling happy, and sensing she was my cat. And although thoughts of Bobcat consumed me, the cat from my dreams also popped into my conscious mind.

After three days in the hospital, I was released and eager to get back home. My heart ached at the thought of not being greeted by Bobcat. My mom kept me company until I needed to get to bed for the night. I awoke the next morning reaching for Bobcat. Within moments, I snapped back to reality — he was gone.

That night, I had a lucid dream about a Persian cat that was in my life for only three years before she passed of cancer. I had a strong connection with Bella and her passing was painful, but that was eight

Meant to Be

years ago. I wondered why I was suddenly dreaming of her and not Bobcat, who was fresh on my mind.

***

Six weeks had passed since surgery. I was getting stronger and encouraged about getting my life back on track. I was able to take brief walks, my appetite was increasing, and I had more stamina. I spent time journaling, reading, and listening to podcasts.

The cat from my dreams continued to pop into my waking thoughts. She reminded me of Bella, and thinking of her helped ease the sadness of missing Bobcat. I would imagine the ginger cat sitting on the sofa by my side and started thinking that it would be nice to have a girl kitty again.

One afternoon, I jotted down a list of suitable names for a female cat. With the heaviness of losing Bobcat lifting, I was emotionally ready, but I still had to go through two remaining rounds of chemo and wasn't sure if I would be able to focus my attention on a new cat yet. But, I thought, it wouldn't hurt to put out the word.

On a Saturday morning, I texted a friend, Ann Marie, who volunteered at the local animal shelter, and asked her to be on the lookout. I was almost ready.

That afternoon, on her volunteer shift, Ann Marie met a cat that had recently been relinquished to the shelter. She sent me a text message: "If you like Persian cats, you'll love Annie." She included a link to the online news publication where Annie was featured as "Pet of the Week."

I had that feeling in my gut you get when something big is about to happen. I clicked on the link. The image took my breath away. There she was: the fluffy ginger cat.

I met Annie at the shelter the following Wednesday. She was perched upon a cabinet, looking down at me as I was walked into the room. I sat on a towel placed on the floor and motioned for Annie to come down. She hopped from the cabinet to the floor, sashayed over to me, and placed her paw on my hand. Tears welled in my eyes. I felt an instant connection with this cat who had appeared in my dreams for the past several months. We looked at each other.

"Well, hello there!"

Annie replied with a purr and a meow.

My application to adopt Annie was approved on the spot, but my final chemo treatment was a couple of days away. I explained to the shelter volunteer that I would need a few weeks following chemo to regain strength before I could bring Annie home and asked if the adoption could wait. The volunteer explained that Annie was relinquished to the shelter with bladder stones that required removal. She was recovering from surgery and would not be ready to be released for a couple of weeks, anyway. The volunteer said that Annie could be kept at the shelter for as long as I needed, and I could visit her in the meantime. It was a perfect arrangement.

That April, four years ago, I completed the adoption agreement, giving Annie a new name in the process. I'll never understand why this precious cat, only a year and a half old, was relinquished to the shelter. But the Universe stepped in and perfectly orchestrated our encounter, knowing we were meant for each other.

I was given a preview of what was to come through the recurring dreams. Then, with impeccable timing, Samantha came home with me and settled into her new life with a new name in a cottage by the sea as though we'd been together forever.

— Pamela K. Knudsen —

Unexpected Love

*My cat came out of nowhere and
became my everything.*
~Author Unknown

Like all good love stories, this happened when I least expected it. It was during my junior year of college, when my roommates and I had a terrible mouse problem. We saw droppings everywhere and movements out of the corner of our eyes. We thought it couldn't get any worse until my roommate woke up with a mouse stuck in her hair.

We tried everything: basic traps, humane traps, rat poison, house bombing, taping holes… The infestation was unbearable. It got to the point where most of us weren't sleeping in our house.

After weeks away, I was telling my friend about the situation, and she mentioned that whenever she had a mouse, she'd borrow a cat. "Mice hate the smell of cats, and when they know they are around, they will steer clear."

Since I was newly twenty-one, many of my friends hadn't begun "parenthood," and there was no one to borrow from. So, I did what any young person would do when they need a fast solution: I went on Craigslist, where I found listings for hundreds of cats.

Being a horror-film fan, I opted for a black cat and messaged a few people on the site, saying I was looking for a cat as fast as possible. Within an hour, I had a response from a woman who worked at a pet rescue.

As I walked inside her home, she had a big smile on her face. "I

Meant to Be

have three to choose from, but I have the perfect one for you."

I saw three little black furballs all snuggled together, just barely eight weeks old. I picked up a beautiful kitten, who had bright green eyes and looked like he was ready to take out some mice.

"That one's nice, but he's not like this other one," the woman said.

As she handed me what looked to be the runt, I tried not to look at him with disgust. His eyes were gooped together, and his ears were black on the inside.

"Looks like he's fighting some ear mites," she giggled. "And don't mind his eyes. I just got flowers, and I'm pretty sure he's allergic."

Do you know the feeling when someone believes they know better and are pushing something on you that you are uninterested in? And you can't tell whether they are playing you or they truly know better?

As I tried not to make a face, I pulled him close to my neck, and he nuzzled. Immediately, I felt him purring. Before I knew it, we had made a connection, and I felt he was the one. I had been intending to merely borrow a mouser, but I had suddenly become a cat owner.

"I told you," she said when she realized it was a perfect fit. "He really, really loves people and is very affectionate. I've never seen one like him before."

From then on, it was a true mother-son bond. He was so tiny, but every day he walked up and down three flights of stairs to greet me as I came in from class. Every evening, he snuggled on my chest and slept soundly through the night. He loved being cuddled and picked up. Before I knew it, I was a cat person. Everyone knew he was obsessed with me as he followed me everywhere. So, I named him Sombra, the Spanish translation for being my shadow.

Within a few weeks, every mouse disappeared, and our house was once again livable. It turns out that Sombra truly was allergic to flowers, so his eyes cleared up, and the ear mites went away, too. I had fallen in love with a cute little cat, and now ten years later that black fur has gone gray, and he is snuggling his nose in my arm and trying to sit on my keyboard as I write this.

— Amber Curtis —

The Story of Poppy

*Blessed are those who love cats,
for they shall never be lonely.
~Author Unknown*

I was a surrogate father for my next-door neighbor's children after she divorced her husband. The kids liked to knock on my door and then run and hide. I would open the door and say, "Who's that knocking on my door?" They would jump out and gleefully shout, "It's us, Artie!" We would then go on little adventures together.

One day, I was sitting on my couch and heard a bang on the door. I got up, opened the door, and was about to say my line when I heard a meow. I looked down and saw an orange cat looking up at me. He walked into my living room like he owned the place, jumped up on my couch, curled himself into a ball, and promptly went to sleep. I couldn't believe it. I didn't want to disturb him, so I just sat down on my couch and continued to listen to music. About two hours later, he got up, went to the door and meowed, so I let him out. I thought it was rather unusual, but things were about to get even more unusual.

Two days later, the same thing happened. This time, he stayed for about three hours. Then, he left, and I did not see him for another three days. Then, it happened again. This time, he spent the whole day with me. At one point, he even climbed up on my lap and slept. He had no collar, but he looked well-fed, so I knew he belonged to somebody. But I was beginning to fall in love with this little guy. He left at nightfall, and I did not see him again for a few days.

Meanwhile, I started asking all my neighbors about this cat. They all had seen him, but nobody knew to whom he belonged. One afternoon, as he was sleeping on my couch yet again, I saw the neighbor who lives behind me for the first time. I asked him if he knew anything about an orange cat.

"Yes! I have an orange cat. Why? Do you know where he is?"

"Yes, he's sleeping on my couch! He shows up every couple of days literally knocking on my door to come in. He hangs out with me for a few hours and then leaves."

My neighbor apologized profusely. He came over and picked up his cat. He explained that he and his wife had just had a new baby, and Patrick (the cat's name, which I misheard as Poppy) was very verbal and would wake up their child. So, they put him outside.

About three hours later, Patrick was back. My neighbor was still working in the yard, so I told him that we should just leave it at that. If he did not see the cat, not to worry, because he was visiting me. And if I didn't see him, I knew he was back home. And that's how it started. Slowly but surely, Patrick — whom I was now calling Poppy — was spending more and more time with me. Eventually, he started to stay overnight. Then, he would be with me for days at a time.

It reached the point where the only time he went to his original owner was when he had to go to the veterinarian for his annual shots and check-up. Poppy's original owners still wanted that responsibility, but after three years, I was fully adopted by Poppy. Amazingly, Poppy would come when I called him, which is unusual. If I said, "Poppy, kiss," he would run over to me and rub his cheek against my lips. This little guy was my son!

A few years later, I met a woman whom I would eventually marry. Jeannie fell in love with Poppy, and he took to her as strongly as he had to me. He used to like to sleep between us. Sometimes, he would spoon with Jeannie, sometimes with me, but always making physical contact with one or both of us.

Poppy had come into my life when he was about two years old. Thirteen years later, he became very sick and began to lose weight rapidly. The veterinarian could not find anything wrong. He stopped eating. Even when I tempted him with a special treat, he wouldn't be able to keep it down.

When I found him digging a hole in his litter box and lying down in it, I knew it was time to help him across the rainbow bridge. He was so horribly thin. Jeannie and I took him to the veterinarian, and as she prepared the injection to put him to sleep, Jeannie and I sang the song I had been singing to him for most of his life, to the tune of "My Darling Clementine":

Oh, our Poppy
Oh, our Poppy
Oh, our little Poppy boy
Mommy loves you and Daddy loves you
You're our little Poppy boy

And, on that final note, he sighed contentedly and went off to the next phase of his life.

— Artie DeMonte —

Formula for the Perfect Number of Cats

When I look into the eyes of an animal, I do not see an animal. I see a living being. I see a friend. I feel a soul.
~A.D. Williams

"No, no. Three cats are enough! You know the formula," my husband stated for the hundredth time.

There he was again with his handy-dandy, human-to-cat formula. According to Jon's Theory of Household Cats, the highest number of cats a family should have is one more than the number of people in the house. Since it was just Jon and me, that meant three cats should be sufficient. He'd lived by that mathematical cat equation for years.

"But she sits outside all day looking into the house like she wants in," I pleaded. "You don't see it while you're at work, but I open the window to feel the breeze, and she sings! She lets out these long, mournful meows, serenading our cats all day long."

My husband shook his head, laughing at the image.

"It's like she's looking through the window and singing that song from *The Little Mermaid*. 'Wish I could beeee part of that wooooorld,'" I added in an out-of-tune, sing-songy voice.

"I'll think about it."

As soon as he said that, I knew the cat was as good as ours.

Meant to Be | 233

This was no ordinary cat. A few months before, the neighborhood mascot, a gray tomcat named, appropriately, Tommy, had passed away. He'd lived outside his entire life and had the battle scars to prove it: ripped ears, cataract-covered eyes, and a slow, devil-may-care walk. He was at least twenty-one years old and beloved by everyone on the street who fed him and invited him into their garages for the winter.

So, when another cat with Tommy's gray, faded tabby patterning started showing up six months after Tommy's death, frequenting the same houses, it was like a resurrection. The new cat was a young adult, old enough to be wary of humans. We named her Tammy in Tommy's honor, and after a few months of offering food and treats, we gained her trust enough that she'd let us scratch her ears.

For months, Tammy roamed the yards throughout the neighborhood but eventually took a shine to one house: ours. When Jon left for work, Tammy sharpened her claws on our catalpa tree. When I went out to check for the mail, I'd find her on the porch. When I opened a window, she'd lie in the mulch under that window. And the whole time she sang and sang and sang.

Weeks went by, and hardly a day passed when Jon and I didn't have a conversation about Tammy. It was hard to ignore her — she was right outside, and she was loud.

"Babe," I said, "this cat has stood outside our house every day for months literally asking to be a part of our family. She chose us. Who are we to tell her no?"

My husband's eyes welled with a single tear, but that was all it took.

"Okay, let's make a plan for catching her."

We booked an appointment at the vet for a few days out and acquired a humane cat trap. And tuna.

It didn't take Tammy long to notice that her food that day was a tuna delicacy. She was so delighted that she didn't think twice about going into the trap. That was when we realized...

"Hey, um," Jon began, stifling a laugh. "It looks like Tammy is actually a Timmy."

We'd been calling him Tammy for so many months that Tammy was the name he answered to, so the name stuck. It worked out alright for the boy named Sue, we reasoned.

For someone who didn't want a fourth cat, Jon eats his words every day. When Jon sits in his recliner, Tammy jumps in his lap. If Alabama football is on TV, Tammy watches as dutifully as if he'd matriculated there himself. When Jon reads in bed at night, Tammy is at his feet. If given the choice of which of us to curl up beside, he'll choose my husband every time.

"Hey, now! I'm the one who got you adopted, remember? Jon was going to leave you outside!" I'll teasingly say as I scratch his ears and try to coax him to my lap.

Our family of two humans and four cats was complete — until it wasn't.

About ten months after we adopted Tammy, now in the middle of the pandemic, another cat showed up on our porch. It was a brown tabby with white socks, a white chest, and a white spot between his yellow-green eyes. His talent wasn't in singing but in racing. When I went out to get the mail, he'd race me back to the front door and try to slip between my legs into the house.

"He's making his wishes known, babe," I said to Jon after the second day the cat insisted on coming into the house. "He's demanding to be let in. It was all I could do to keep him out while I ran inside."

"Alright, let's call the vet," he said without argument or resignation.

A week later, TinyCat was officially brought inside and made part of the family. (TinyCat's name proved to be another misnomer on our part. He scarfed down food at such an alarming rate that he's now twenty pounds.)

"And then there were five," I laughed to Jon. "So much for your perfect cat formula. You didn't even fight me this time."

"I figured if he wanted in the house so badly, it was only a matter of time."

Cats have an innate wisdom that people sometimes have trouble sensing. Cats know where they want to make their home and who they want to care for them. You can put the tastiest food out on your porch, but if the cat has decided to make another house its home, it'll eat your food — they are hungry opportunists, after all — and go where they want to be.

    The wisdom of cats has no respect for formulas or reasoning. You don't choose the cat. The cat chooses you.

    And once you've been chosen, it's only a matter of time.

— Mandy Shunnarah —

A Cat Named Zubenelgenubi

Looking at cats, like looking at clouds, stars or the ocean, makes it difficult to believe there is nothing miraculous in this world.
~Leonard Michaels

It was March, and an astronomer's dream was coming true in the early spring skies. The planets Venus and Jupiter were in close conjunction with the moon, two brilliant gems hanging from a crescent necklace. A week of clear, dry, dark skies promised great photography. My husband, Tom, was getting set up on the flattened apron of the driveway. The list of materials included two tripods, a chair and table, lenses, filters, a red-light flashlight, and a buoyant air of anticipation. He would be out every night for the next seven days. Hours each night. Photos by the hundreds.

Every part of this scenario is one I have experienced before. Tom is a dedicated amateur astronomer. He has logged hours monitoring various stars. He built his own telescope, a big one, designed to observe deep-sky objects like galaxies and nebulae. He is never happier than when he is looking at the sky, and little distracts him from the task at hand. But he did not count on a sapphire-eyed ball of white fluff coming out to watch the stars with him.

Several neighbors had commented on the stray kitten that had been skirting yards and driveways for a month. I had seen the cat once

Meant to Be | 237

when a friend was trying to entice the creature to her porch with food and kind words. This woman is a true cat whisperer, so I was sure the stray would soon be in friendly hands and a warm house. I was wrong. That cat was having none of it. While the creature was frequently seen, often admired and occasionally fed, no one could get near her.

The only person not particularly concerned about the kitten was my husband. He had his stars to keep him occupied. But there is one thing that both astronomers and stray cats have in common: They both love the night.

That first night, Tom was checking photos and adjusting settings when he became aware that he was being observed. The elusive kitten, the one who wouldn't let anyone within twenty feet of it, was standing at Tom's feet, looking up in the direction of Venus and Jupiter.

Tom gave the cat an offhand greeting and asked if she liked star gazing. She mewed in assent and returned her eyes to the sky. So did Tom.

The second night, she joined him again and rubbed against his legs. When he reached down to pet her, she rolled on her back and let him rub her tummy. That was first contact. By the third night, we were offering her food.

Soon, the cat was showing up early for her night of astrophotography. She was enjoying a square meal and getting attention as well as instruction in astronomy. Around this time, we learned that our neighbor Dale had been trying to trap the kitten. He had put a deposit down on an appointment at the local clinic to get her spayed, but the cat was no longer coming to get the food in his humane trap.

Whoops!

I went to Dale's house and delivered my mea culpa for foiling his plan and asked if it was his intention to adopt the cat.

"No," he said, "we have two cats and don't want a third. I'm just tired of seeing more stray cats everywhere. I'll have it spayed and then either take it to the shelter or let it loose." And then there was that pause as the light dawned. "Unless you want it."

"Yes," I said, "we definitely want the cat."

We did not feed the cat that night. Sure enough, it went to the ready meal offered in the trap. Dale took the cat to the vet the next day, and we picked it up that afternoon, paying the bills and reimbursing Dale for his surgery deposit. Unfortunately, spaying was the smallest problem facing our star-gazing cat.

The life of strays is not easy. Sometime in the weeks when this little girl was on her own, a predator of unknown type had almost gotten her. There were two bites on her back, near her tail. She had gotten away, but the bites had sent germs deep under her skin. The wounds had healed over, trapping the infection inside where they began to fester. Our kitten was in trouble.

The vet had done the spaying and then opened both wounds, draining them of their poison. While the spaying, done under sterile conditions, would heal without problem, the open wounds would need to heal from the inside out, which would take weeks. During this time, our semi-feral cat would need to be kept indoors and given both oral medication and topical antibiotic cream applied to her open sores twice daily.

It seemed daunting, but I had not counted on the bond that Tom and the kitty had forged in the night. Tom could hold the kitten, soothing her, while I administered the medicine. Instead of a fight, all we got was a rumbling purr. The cat also took immediately to the litter box, assumed the soft bed we bought was hers, and was happy to eat whatever food we offered. She was, from the first, at home. Her home.

She was also a beauty. The white body, dark lilac markings on the ears, paws and tail, and the plaintive voice all spoke to some Siamese DNA. And then there were those brilliant, almond-shaped, blue eyes. What she did not have was a name.

The weekend after we brought the kitty home, we went out to dinner with friends. Tom enjoyed telling the story of how the unapproachable cat had decided to enjoy a little astronomy and now was living her best life. Our friends asked me what we called her, and I deferred to Tom.

"It's his cat. He's got to name her."

All eyes turned to my husband.

"Well, one of my favorite stars is the alpha star in Libra. It has an

Arabic name: Zubenelgenubi. But that seems a little long."

There was a pause, followed by laughter. Every person at that table knew that our cat now had a name. A long name, true, but the right name for our stargazer. A cat who chose an astronomer for her best friend.

We call her Zubee (rhymes with ruby). Her sores healed, and she is fiercely healthy. When she is not patrolling the house, she can be found on the top level of a cat tree set up by windows that look out at the stars. At night, she will curl up next to Tom, and the two of them will dream about swirling galaxies, cloudy nebulae, and moons and planets colliding in the sky. I know she is dreaming of these things because the tip of her tail twitches in a cosmic and mysterious way.

—Louise Butler—

Going Through Hell? Keep Going!

Explaining a miracle doesn't make it any less of a miracle.
~Athan Fletcher, The Swordsman and The Priestess

"Don't tell Mom, but there's a cat with one eye missing hanging around the shed." It was my daughter, Lianna, calling to give me the heads-up. We both knew that my wife was a pushover for lost cats who always seemed to find their way to our home in the woods.

"See if you can shoo it away," I told her. "Maybe it will leave and go back home."

But, when I got home from work, this little calico with only one eye was still hanging around. He was certainly friendly enough, but the last thing we needed was another cat.

As my wife pulled up in the driveway shortly afterward, Lianna and I were loving up this little lost soul, petting him on the swing that hung beneath our upstairs deck. Fortunately, my wife was in agreement this time. We had enough cats already; there was no room at the inn.

When we tried to wrap up for the evening and send him on his merry way, his demands for our attention grew more frantic. It was already fairly brisk out this late November evening, and the temperature was dropping quickly. It had been drizzling on and off all day, leaving him pretty damp and muddy, too. That's when I realized he was

Meant to Be

shivering, nearly convulsing even, from the cold. Something inside me told me that he was in distress and wouldn't survive the night if we left him outside.

"Just for the night," I decided. "We'll bring him in overnight, and then we will send him on his way tomorrow morning." Once we had him inside, however, where we could see him better, we realized that his situation was, in fact, dire.

The next morning we took him to the vet and learned that his jaw had been shattered. And, in fact, he wasn't missing an eye; it was just swollen completely shut. Something, or someone, had badly brutalized him. It was doubtful that he was going to make it. His mouth hung open, and he drooled profusely on the right side, so much so that my wife fashioned a bandana for him to wear to mop up all the saliva.

We brought him home, and this poor cat just lay on his side and didn't get up for nearly a week. My wife has always excelled at hospice care, so she spoon-fed him with a little, rubber-coated baby spoon as we tried to keep him comfortable for what were likely to be his last days. At least his final days would be spent feeling loved, warm and well-fed.

My wife named him Winston because Winston Churchill famously said, "If you're going through hell, keep going!" and that's what she kept telling him to do. Miraculously, Winston started to come around. He only weighed about four-and-a-half pounds when we found him, and the vet said he might not ever get bigger. However, Winston proved him wrong, eating his way all the way up to twenty-one pounds!

He's been an integral part of our family now for seven years, and he is the sweetest, gentlest guy you could ever meet. And he's our constant reminder that, if you ever find yourself going through hell, keep going!

—Jon M. Ketcham—

Eight Lives to Go

> Cats know more than we think and think
> more than we know.
> ~H.P. Lovecraft

"I think that's everything," Bubba said. "Honey, is there anything else that needs to go on the U-Haul?"

I stepped out onto the back deck to see the truck fully loaded from top to bottom. My husband and his brother had played the adult version of Jenga for hours to perfect it. "I'm not sure anything else could fit!"

"Good! That's the goal!"

He shook hands with Brandon and Kayla, the young couple he had known for years, and handed them the keys. "Are you sure y'all don't mind keeping the outside cats?"

"Are you kidding?!" Kayla exclaimed. "I'm so excited about it."

"Super excited. So, uh, how many?" Brandon asked

Bubba laughed. "Five. There's Bames, Thomas, Marshall Lee, Karen, and Chester," he said. "They are outside cats for real. You won't ever have to worry about mice, B." Chester emphasized the point by jumping off the deck.

"Awesome."

"Once the sun goes down, they'll start coming back up to the porch to sleep. They never miss out on breakfast. I left their food out back for you," I said. We gave out a few more instructions before getting everyone loaded up for the last time.

Meant to Be | 243

"Y'all drive safe and let us know when you make it to Missouri!"

"We sure will. Enjoy the house. It's beautiful out here, but I won't miss this heat," I said, and we all laughed. July in Mississippi is no joke.

Bubba jumped into the driver's seat of the U-Haul with our twelve-year-old and two Chihuahuas riding shotgun next to him. I secured the three house cats — Pawl, Little Punkin, and Moww Kitty — in the backseat of our Cavalier for the 500-mile trip. And then with his sister, nephew, and our Border Collie pulling up the rear in his old truck, we were a sight for sure as we headed toward our new life.

Our ride was uneventful minus the couple of actual cat fights I had to break up. But I got creative and put a barrier between the cats around thirty miles in. We stopped at a dollar store to get better supplies, and Bubba, my technical genius, perfected it. Soon, we were back on the road.

We pushed forward as long as we could, only being able to travel 50–60 miles per hour the whole time. We stopped to eat and stretch our legs before continuing. Finally, we gave in and pulled up to the motel with our troops to catch some sleep. We quietly made our way to our room with our three adults, two children, two Chihuahuas, one Border Collie, and three cats. We were ninjas as we took the dogs out to do their business in the dark. And we all slept in that tiny, two-bed motel room until the next morning.

When morning came, I was glad to get loaded up and back on the road. I was anxious to see our grown children and granddaughters. My children had graciously agreed to meet us at the new house and help unload the trucks. I knew no one was looking forward to it, but we were all excited to be reunited after a couple of months apart.

There was a buzz of activity when we pulled up to the house that late morning. The Missouri heat was already proving itself, but we had trucks to unload and animals to get inside. We put all the animals in the basement level to get acclimated, be safe, and stay out of the way as the trucks were unloaded and the rooms began to fill with boxes. I stepped outside to check on the progress and bring water out to all the guys unloading. Rylan, my twenty-one-year-old, asked, "Mom, you brought the cats in?"

"Yes. They're all inside. They rode with me, and I put them in the basement with the dogs. You guys are good."

"No, I don't know that we are. I think I just found a cat."

"What! Where?"

"It's in the truck. I thought it was a stuffed animal when I first saw it," he said, still in the U-Haul, walking toward me.

"Oh, my gosh. Is it… alive? Who is it?"

"I'm actually not sure. It won't move."

I hollered for Bubba, who came rushing back out. We told him what was going on, and he and Rylan went into the back of the U-Haul. They moved some boxes, a lamp, and my old side table until Bubba could reach in and pull out a black cat.

"Marshall Lee? Is that you?"

Indeed, it was. Marshall had decided at some point that she didn't want to stay in Mississippi after all. She wanted to try and be a city cat. But how? She had stowed away in the back of our 26-foot, Jenga-packed U-Haul. By our calculations, she was in there a minimum of twenty-nine hours. She had no water or food. It was not air-conditioned, and there were no windows. The inside temperature had to be over 120 degrees. We had stopped at least four times, and even when my husband had opened the back of the U-Haul to check that nothing had shifted she had made no sound.

That poor cat stayed with our boxes and furniture while we slept in an air-conditioned motel room. Even after we arrived in Missouri, when the truck door was opened and items were being removed, she had made no sound.

Miraculously, Marshall Lee was alive and well. She was dehydrated and hungry but otherwise unharmed. Within a couple of hours, Marshall was right at home, inside this time!

Today, she is enjoying life as a housecat. No more outdoor living and chasing mice for her. In her retirement, she's pampered, fat, and living her best life. We think she's earned it.

— Angie Blackledge —

He'll Stand on Your Shoulders

Are we really sure the purring is coming from the kitty and not from our very own hearts?
~Emme Woodhull-Bäche

I was a corporate sales trainer, and a large part of my job involved riding with the sales reps in the field while they called on their clients. One day, I was with Jeff, a promising new salesman. We were working in the Gainesville, Florida area and were wrapping up a presentation to a veterinarian. We were leaving when Jeff remembered something he wanted to ask and returned to the doctor's office.

I stood by the receptionist's desk, chatting with the staff, when I noticed a beautiful, longhaired gray tabby cat in a cage close by. The cat was rubbing against the bars of the cage closest to me and purring loudly. I put my fingers inside the bars to pet him and noticed how very soft his fur was. Then, because of the physical touch, his purr machine went into overdrive!

"Nice cat!" I commented to the receptionist.

She smiled and said, "That's Sparky! Everybody loves him. The staff wants to keep him as the 'clinic cat,' but we already have one, so the doctor said we need to find him another home."

My ears perked up at hearing that. My wife loves cats, especially tabbies. Trouble, her beloved gray, longhaired tabby, had died a month

Meant to Be

ago, and she was still mourning.

But she'd said she didn't want another cat.

"You can take him out if you'd like. He's super-friendly."

I was very tempted, but my wife's words rang in my head. "I don't want another cat for a while!"

No, I will resist taking this cat out of the cage! He's very cute, very friendly, but Grace said she didn't want another.

"He'll stand on your shoulders!" *Uh oh.*

In sales, you always want to point out the advantages of the item you are offering. But there's the "zinger"! That's the real point that drives the buyer into a positive buying mood. It can be something major or something minor. But there's always something that makes the difference.

And she had just found mine.

"He'll stand on your shoulders!"

I don't know why, but that really appealed to me. I imagined myself wandering around our house with Sparky perched by my head.

I opened the cage door, and Sparky leapt into my arms. He was so soft, and purring away. He rubbed my face with his face. I scratched his ears, and he nestled deeper into my arms.

And now, the crowning moment! I lifted him up and onto my shoulders…

And he tumbled onto the floor!

I scooped him up, and he seemed to be okay and rather forgiving. I started to lift him up for another attempt…

And Jeff came out of the doctor's office and announced we had to rush to avoid being late for our next appointment! Reluctantly, I gave Sparky a quick hug, put him back in his cage, and closed the door. Both he and the receptionist seemed disappointed.

As Jeff and I raced to his next appointment, I considered the possibility of adopting Sparky. I am not a big fan of cats. I prefer dogs. But since Grace favors felines, we have always had cats. In fact, I rejoiced at her proclamation of not wanting another cat, hoping it might open the possibility of a pooch joining the family.

"He'll stand on your shoulders…"

I tried calling Grace to ask if she might be interested in Sparky. But after repeated calls, I decided she was likely in another long-lasting meeting at work.

Several hours later, Jeff and I returned to our office. I tried calling Grace again. No answer.

"He'll stand on your shoulders!"

I looked at my watch. I had an important meeting that evening near home. The veterinarian's office was nearly a one-hour drive from our office. From there, it was almost a two-hour drive home. Add a half-hour to shower and change clothes and another half-hour drive to the meeting, and I would arrive exactly on time. This was my last assignment in this area for a long time, so a decision needed to be made now!

"He'll stand on your shoulders!"

The veterinarian's staff cheered when I called and said I'd be returning to take him home. The receptionist said they were disappointed that he didn't leave with me, but she felt in her heart that Sparky and I had hit it off and I might return for him. I arranged for them to give him all his shots and a deworming before I arrived.

I ran into the veterinarian's office because bad traffic had held me up. I paid my bill, and all the staff came up to congratulate me and give Sparky a final hug. They quickly told me the friendly cat's story. He had been a barn cat for a dairyman named Mr. Sparkman. He ventured too close to a bad-tempered cow, received a nasty kick and became lame. Mr. Sparkman brought in the cat and asked that he not only be treated but also rehomed. And he was named in honor of his benefactor.

Sparky was placed in a closed box, and I put the box on the passenger front seat and headed home.

For an hour, I talked with the enclosed cat to keep him calm, but he seemed fine. I talked, and he purred.

However, he stopped purring and began meowing. The meowing became louder and more urgent, and I had no idea why his attitude had changed.

I was looking for a safe place to pull over, and then the meowing stopped — and a sharp, pungent smell filled my car.

Apparently, the deworming and his shots had given him a terrible case of diarrhea. He had bravely held on as long as possible but had finally lost his intestinal battle.

I rolled down the windows.

I got home and decided to skip my meeting. I called the participants and gave them my apologies.

I carried the still-closed box into the bathroom and ran a warm bath in the tub. I collected rags and old towels, several shampoos and some baby powder. When I opened the box, I saw how terrible the situation was. The cat was literally coated head to tail.

I don't know who was more miserable, but we both suffered.

Sparky was a trooper! He allowed me to wash and rinse him over and over. He was patient while I drained the tub and refilled it to bathe him in clean water. I toweled him off, coated him in baby powder, and placed him in a cat carrier while I scrubbed the tub.

When I returned to the very moist cat, the terrible smell was still present. Back to the bathtub and more scrubbing.

Then, Grace came into the house, and she fell in love with our new cat. I said, "Let me show you his trick!" and I put him on my shoulders.

It's a good thing that cats land on their feet because he again crashed to the floor!

It's been fourteen years, and he's never stood on my shoulders.

That receptionist was a heck of a salesperson!

— Chip Kirkpatrick —

Lucky Break

*Have faith in your intuition and listen
to your gut feeling.
~Ann Cotton*

Our house had been too quiet since our older cat passed the prior August, so in April we went to the animal shelter on a quest for two cats. We'd hoped for siblings or a bonded pair because I'd experienced firsthand managing two cats who did not like each other. At. All. It was time for some peace.

Unfortunately, the shelter only had individual kitties up for adoption, not pairs, so we began circling the large room, meeting many, many cats, trying to decide how to know which ones we'd like to know better. With so many cats to choose from, we were at a loss for how we'd know how to find "our" cats.

Then, we spied Brownie, a hugely rotund tiger who had a special spark. We began to think that maybe we should just pay attention to the cats and let the choosing happen organically. We met Brownie alone in a larger room, and his first act was to jump in my lap, throw both arms around my neck in a very endearing kitty hug, and affectionately head-butt me. Then, he did the same to my husband. Deal sealed. He was sweet and funny, and we knew we'd be taking all twenty pounds of him home.

We met with a few other kitties, all lovely, I'm sure, but none felt quite right — until the volunteer brought in Tiny, an aptly named slip of solid gray fur. She was a mess. Her eyes were weepy, with perpetual brown stains at the corners. Then, there was the drool. Pearls of it beaded along her chin, dripping incessantly. She didn't care. She tilted her head, squinted at me, jumped in my lap, curled into a warm comma, and began a purr that had no end.

I looked helplessly at my husband and my drool-dampened pant legs and said, "This is the moistest cat I've ever met. Who else is going to take her home?" We agreed that Tiny would come home with us after her spaying surgery the following week.

Since they were adopted individually, we had no idea how they'd do together. We just had to hope that the portly, outgoing tiger and the miniature moisture-factory would manage to get along. It was a leap of faith, as so much is. Brownie came home with us that day. He settled in easily and quickly owned our house and hearts.

Soon enough, it was time to pick up Tiny. We had her tucked into a carrier, careful of her new stitches, and sat with the shelter folks to go over her adoption.

The volunteer read Tiny's paperwork, shuffled the pages, re-read them, and then looked at us quizzically. "You adopted Brownie, too? Last week?"

We affirmed this, and she shook her head, bemused. "Well, this is weird. Tiny's paperwork says that she and Brownie had been living together and were brought to the shelter as a pair. Did you know that already?"

We definitely did not.

"I'm surprised that we didn't adopt them out together. Normally, we would for cats that are already bonded. Well, be sure to keep her isolated in a separate room for a few days because of her stitches and also to get them re-acclimated to each other."

We installed Tiny in the downstairs bathroom where I sat with her as frequently as possible. It's an old house, and nothing is square, which meant the bathroom door had a triangular gap at the bottom. Brownie took advantage of this and constantly stuck his paws in the space, trying to reach her. With this obstacle, it was increasingly difficult to enter and exit the room while keeping him away from Tiny.

Meant to Be | 251

After a day, Brownie's persistence paid off, and he managed to slip inside. The two cats stood nose to nose, and I would swear that if they had cartoon dialogue bubbles above their heads, they would have read:

Brownie: "About time you got here!"

Tiny: "We did it!"

They settled right in to a life together and with us. She slept perpendicular to him, face pressed into the pillow of his generous belly.

I have absolutely no idea how they managed it, but these two had plotted for us to adopt them both, and their reunion scheme worked flawlessly.

And the incessant moistness that made us adopt Tiny because no one else could possibly want a ceaselessly drooling cat? What a lucky break that was! That little girl never drooled again.

— Christine Grecsek —

The Cat Who Adopted Us

*If you really want to get along with somebody,
let them be themselves.*
~Willie Nelson

On a recent November evening, I stepped out onto the porch as usual and told the dog to make it quick, which of course, he never does. I turned slightly, intending to sit down on the wicker settee, when I saw a brown-and-white tabby cat stretched out on the cushion, staring up at me with the brightest sea-green eyes I'd ever seen.

"Who are you?" I asked. The cat continued to stare at me and began to bathe himself. I didn't know what would happen when the dog came back up on the porch, so to prevent an altercation, I walked down the stairs into the yard, picked up my dog, and carried him into the house. Out of the corner of my eye, I saw the cat watching us. Fortunately, the dog was oblivious.

The next morning, before I let out the dog, I stuck my head out the door and looked at the settee. No sign of the cat. Two nights later, I found the cat napping on the settee again. This time, I gingerly walked over to the cat and slowly offered him my hand to sniff, which he did. Then he stretched out his neck and offered me a spot to massage as though I was his personal masseuse. *Friendly guy,* I thought.

A few days later, I heard our dog barking his brains out in the

Meant to Be | 253

backyard and looking up into a big elm tree. I walked over to see what the commotion was about, expecting to see a squirrel. Sitting on a wide and sturdy branch was the cat, peering down at the dog.

I called to my husband to help me get the cat down while I banished the dog inside the house. The cat began making his way down the tree into my husband's arms and down onto the ground. He sauntered away, his tail waving upright, telling us thanks and goodbye, I supposed.

I soon discovered that the cat was visiting most of my neighbors. Some were setting out food for him, and one had built him a protected bed in her carport. I saw photos of the cat one neighbor had posted on social media, asking if anyone knew who he belonged to.

It turned out the cat belonged to a neighbor five blocks away, and my husband knew him. The man came over to retrieve his cat, and as we stood on the front lawn chatting, the cat walked up and meowed at the man. He was pretty happy to see his cat because he had been MIA for two weeks. He took him home and fed him, and we all figured that was the end of that.

Except it wasn't. The next day, the cat showed up on our back porch again. My husband called the owner, who came and retrieved the cat again. The same thing happened the next day and the day after that. The cat kept showing up at our home. Then, in early December, the temperature plummeted.

One evening, we had gone to a friend's home for a holiday party, and when we returned home, we found the cat sitting in the middle of the street in front of our driveway. He finally moved and followed us into the garage.

We knew that the cat's owner was out of town, and we couldn't leave the cat outside in thirty-degree weather. Somehow, he seemed to know it. He followed us into the enclosed breezeway that connected the garage to the main part of the house. We made a bed for him and set up a space heater, food, and water. He seemed content with his new arrangement, although he did try to sneak inside the house when we opened the door.

The next morning, we let him out of the breezeway to run around the neighborhood. Before the sun set, he showed up at our back door, and we let him into the breezeway. That time, when we opened the door into the main part of the house, the cat successfully made it into the kitchen where first he encountered the dog, whom he'd already met, and then our cat.

At first, the cats' tails blew up like bottle brushes, followed by loud meowing and circling one another. Finally, our cat backed down and let the visitor investigate our home. He drank out of the communal water bowl, ate our cat's dry food, and curled up where our cat likes to sleep. In one fell swoop, he moved in, and surprisingly, our cat was okay with it. They played together, napped together, dined together, and generally kept each other company. Until then, we hadn't realized that our cat wanted a feline buddy.

When the owner got back into town, my husband told him that we'd been caring for his cat and urged him to come over and take him home. He also suggested that he keep him inside, something the owner said he couldn't do because he was mostly an outdoor cat. Other than the shed, the cat lived outdoors.

The cat continued to show up at our house, and my husband kept calling the owner, who finally told my husband that it was obvious that the cat wanted to live with us, and that he was now ours.

I felt bad for the man. He lamented that he'd never had a cat abandon him before, especially one that he'd raised from a tiny kitten.

What could we do? We'd been chosen, and when you've been chosen, you take it seriously. That day, we took the cat to the town veterinarian, had his records transferred, updated his shots, and visited a pet store to get him a collar.

Next, we needed to give him a name.

He had proven himself to be in charge of his destiny, a cat who made his own decisions. He was also a bit of a wild child who was not going to be hemmed in. We named him after a famous musician who was born and raised just five miles from our house, a musician who is considered one of the greatest country artists of all time: Willie Nelson.

From the start, our Willie made it clear that he would forge his own path and set his own rules, just like his namesake. He gets his freedom as long as he comes home every night. There are foxes and coyotes, birds of prey, and poisonous snakes where we live, and we want to keep him safe without boxing him in. He comes and goes as he likes, naps on a warm bed inside, has plenty to eat, and a safe place to live where he doesn't have to sleep with one eye open for predators.

He chose to adopt us for a reason. We're not sure why, but it doesn't really matter. We're grateful that he picked us, and I'm pretty sure the dog and our other cat are, too.

—Jeffree Wyn Itrich—

A Perfect Match

Cats are bundles of love, wrapped in a fur coat.
~L.M. Montgomery

"Oh, you're soooo handsome! She is just going to LOVE you!" I froze in terror. It was the voice of our building's "resident matchmaker," and she was coming toward my office.

I started looking for a way to escape. My matchmaking colleague seemed to have a knack for pairing up the most incompatible people you could imagine, and her well-meaning attempts at introducing me to Mr. Right had all gone horribly wrong.

I considered rushing out the door, telling her that I was off to cover a story. But I had been waiting for an important phone call, and this was in the olden times before every reporter had a cell phone. I stared at my old desk phone, willing it to ring, but it remained mockingly silent.

"You're such a cutie!" the matchmaker's voice crooned just outside my door. "So gorgeous! You're just perfect for her!"

Oh, no. I'd been on dates with guys who were "perfect for me" before. The last one had thrown a full-on temper tantrum when I'd said that *Deep Space Nine* was my least favourite *Star Trek* series.

Maybe I could pretend to be on the phone? Climb out the window? Curl up in a fetal position under my desk and hope she didn't see me?

By now, however, it was too late to do anything. The door to the office swung open, and there stood the resident matchmaker.

Meant to Be | 257

"There you are!" she squealed. "I have someone to introduce you to!"

But instead of ushering in another reluctant Romeo, she held out a tiny grey tabby.

She said her husband had found him wandering all alone in the woods. Some awful person must have dumped him there. And she wondered if I might like a kitten.

It was love at first sight.

His name was Tiberius, and he was my faithful companion and live-in therapist for thirteen good years, through four moves and several terrible boyfriends.

I guess even the most misguided matchmakers get it right sometimes!

— Wendy Joyce Patterson —

Chapter 9

My Very Good, Very Bad Cat

82

My Betrayal

Some people say that cats are sneaky, evil, and cruel. True, and they have many other fine qualities as well.
~Missy Dizick

Every time I looked into his eyes, I saw my betrayal. He seemed to be saying, "How could you do this to me?" I felt like the worst parent ever. I would hold him close to my chest while telling him how sorry I was. Tears would sting my eyes as he looked up at me. I would carry him from room to room cuddled in my arms.

It wasn't that I hadn't tried to get him help. I had immediately taken him to see Dr. Jones, who saw nothing on the X-ray or in his examination that explained why TT could not walk normally.

What had happened? Well, to my shame, I wasn't looking where I was going and I had stepped on his paw. He yelped so loud that I thought I had crushed him. I quickly picked him up and rocked him back and forth while saying soothing things. I carried him for the rest of the day.

When Tiger Tummy didn't get better, I took him back to the veterinarian. Dr. Jones said again that he saw nothing. But TT continued to limp along on three legs with his injured paw up in the air.

This went on for more than two weeks. I didn't know what to do. I carried him to eat, to the litter box, and to the couch to sit on my lap. I felt awful.

One night, I had friends over for dinner. My guests happened to be TT's favorite visitors to our home. I went in the kitchen to get something to drink for my friends. TT ran over to them, rolled on his back, and played fetch with them.

When I walked into the living room, I saw TT just as he saw me. Sure enough, he began limping again. I was so ashamed. I had told my guests about the horrible, devastating situation and guilt that I felt.

My guests started laughing. "Why are you laughing?" I asked. How could they laugh at a hurt animal, let alone my Tiger Tummy?

"He's fooling you. He was just running and playing fetch with us," said one of my guests.

I looked at TT and said, "Busted. That is not nice. Game over."

TT looked at me. His eyes revealed that he knew he had been caught. He put his paw down and never limped again.

— Elizabeth Brown —

83

The Jumper

> *In ancient times cats were worshipped as gods;*
> *they have not forgotten this.*
> ~Terry Pratchett

I could hear mournful meowing through my kitchen window as I sipped my morning coffee. The mewing sent a chill up my spine, so I went out to investigate. I knew it couldn't be one of our cats because they were all indoor-only cats.

I searched, but I still couldn't see the distressed cat, although her calls were louder in our backyard where we had very tall pine trees. I ran back into the house and grabbed a pair of binoculars.

Finally, I spotted a brown tabby about forty feet up in one of our ponderosa pines. It was Anya, one of our cats. Somehow, she had escaped, and now she seemed to be stranded.

I called her name. I rattled a food dish. I even offered her a filet of halibut that was supposed to be our dinner that night. Anya seemed paralyzed with fear. She'd never climbed up a tree before, let alone down one.

The hours crawled by slowly.

When my ten-year-old daughter Ari arrived home from school, I told her about Anya's predicament. Because of the intense bond that Ari and Anya shared, I thought that Anya might respond better to Ari. Ari called out to her many times. Anya meowed back, but her anxiety kept her frozen in place. When my daughter burst into tears, I broke down and called the fire department.

Soon enough, a red firetruck turned into our court. I had never been so happy to see anyone in my life. Three firefighters walked up our driveway, chatting with one another as if this was a social call. I explained the situation again.

They surveyed the stately evergreen. The oldest of the three said, "I don't think our ladder can get close enough, so that's that."

"What are you saying?" I was so confused.

"Ma'am, we're not going to climb your tree. We don't risk our lives for cats."

Then, the rookie said, "Don't worry, ma'am. We've never seen a cat skeleton in a tree before." His comment elicited laughter from the other two.

I wanted to show them my children's books that depicted brave and caring firefighters who rescued children's cats from trees and rooftops. The three left as quickly as they had arrived. Ari's tears started up again.

Our poor Anya spent the night in that tree with no food and no water. I promised Ari that, by hook or by crook, Anya would be down before she got home from school. I told her that I'd climb the tree myself if we couldn't find anyone else to do it. My husband shot me a look that said, "Are you crazy?"

I called six veterinary practices and four rescue organizations for advice. All told me to call the fire department. I guess we had all read the same children's books. My husband and I brainstormed possible ideas. Who could climb our tree and emancipate our cat?

My husband said, "What about a tree service?" Interesting idea, I said. I called at least twelve tree services before finding a man who was willing to rescue our runaway feline. It would cost $150. I told him I didn't care how much it cost! My husband visibly flinched.

Within thirty minutes of calling, a tall, lanky man with weather-beaten skin knocked on our door. Pete looked like he could play the Marlboro Man in a cigarette ad. He strapped on leg spikes and a leather belt while he recounted his past rescue missions.

He then shared with us the three categories of cat climbers: sitters, greeters, and runners. "The sitters stay put. They patiently wait for their savior. The greeters make the climber's job easier because they

My Very Good, Very Bad Cat

actually crawl toward the climber. The runners are the most challenging because they bolt out of fear, usually higher up the tree."

We'd get a discount if Anya was a greeter.

Pete shinnied up the tree with grace and speed. Dangling from his belt was a rope and a soft cloth bag that would securely hold Anya on his way down. Soon, he was eye-to-eye with our little fugitive. Pete carefully reached out, and Anya bolted upward.

"Oh, man, she's a runner," Pete called down to us. He wiped his brow, took a deep breath, and climbed higher up the tree, which was nearly eighty feet tall. As the two neared the crown, the tree began to sway precariously.

I felt as if icy water was flowing through my veins. My husband began rubbing my back. I could feel his chilled fingers through my shirt. We were both filled with a sense of foreboding. I loved Anya, but I did not want to be responsible for risking a man's life. Perhaps the firefighters had been right.

When Pete and Anya were as high as they could go, Pete tied himself to the tree. I was holding my breath. "I'm reaching out to her now. Okay, I've got her," Pete announced. Then, we all watched in horror as a flash of fur hurled through the air.

"Oh, my God," Pete shouted, "she jumped!"

We watched as the tree branches broke Anya's fall for the first fifty feet, but she then plummeted to the ground for the last thirty feet. She looked like a flying squirrel. Anya landed on her feet, dazed but alert. I carefully scooped her up and kissed her little black nose.

Pete felt horrible and told us we didn't owe him a thing. I wasn't going to let him walk away empty-handed, so we compromised on $75. Pete said that he was going to have to add a new category to his list of kitty tree-climbers: jumpers.

We rushed Anya to the vet. She was bruised and had suffered a hairline fracture of her collarbone but was otherwise okay.

Ari was thrilled to find Anya resting on her bed when she arrived home. I told her the story of Pete's attempted rescue and how bad he'd felt when Anya jumped. She said she'd write him a thank-you note.

She then turned her attention back to Anya. "Listen, Little Miss.

Do you have any idea how much worry you caused me? I don't know how I would go on if something terrible had happened to you." Anya began to purr. "There will be consequences for your behavior. No TV for a whole week!"

Anya did her best to look repentant even as Ari rewarded her with spoonfuls of our leftover halibut.

— Victoria Lorrekovich-Miller —

Klepto-Kitty

*Even if you have just destroyed a Ming vase,
purr. Usually all will be forgiven.*
~Lenny Rubenstein

My middle-school-aged children named the male, bob-tailed kitten, Clinger, after the comic character in the television series, M*A*S*H. The starved-for-affection rescue kitty clung to everyone, demanding a lap or shoulder to ride upon. He also had a fetish for stray socks and my younger children's Beanie Babies, which he'd carry off to undisclosed locations.

One evening, six months after Clinger joined our family, an ear-splitting yowl sounded from somewhere upstairs. We all ran up the stairs and found that Clinger had given birth to three kittens in the back of my sewing-room closet. Who knew?

A few months later, in late November, our family relocated to a mountain home in Whitefish, Montana. Preferring to be outdoors but unable to maneuver outside in the heavy snow, Clinger stepped up her nesting instincts. She seemed possessed by the laundry basket, littering the stairs nightly with a trail of towels, socks and kids' clothing. When I reprimanded her for pulling items from the basket, she'd run and jump on the piano keys and then walk her way slowly down the scale as if in defiance.

When spring arrived, I was relieved to send her outside—that is, until I discovered a white crew sock and a full-sized, blue linen tablecloth on the back deck of our patio. Neither belonged to us.

A day later, an expensive men's golf jacket appeared as well as two men's golf shirts with the tags still attached. Although I'd only recently become acquainted with the neighbor below us, I had driven by a house above us whose owner drove a black convertible with the top down. I figured he must have left the items in his car. While deciding on my game plan to return the items, our cat added a wool sweater and a blue teddy bear to her stash.

With the Radio Flyer wagon loaded with stolen goods, my three youngest children and I started up the hill, ringing doorbells. Our explanation that our kleptomaniac cat had dragged home their belongings and stockpiled them on our back porch was met with looks of amazement, then laughter. Eventually, every article made it back into the hands of its owner.

Clinger's drive to drag home clothing finally subsided after she delivered her second litter of kittens, but not before she raided one neighbor's garage sale, bringing home a fox-fur collar.

— Barb Miller —

Norman Bates

Cats are independent, by which I mean smart.
~Dave Barry

We'd promised a cat to my six-year-old when we moved cross-country. Belle had always wanted one. My husband Scott and I thought it might magically help her and her brother adjust.

As soon as we moved into a house, I took Belle to a local shelter. There was no shortage of cats. She moved down the wall of cages and stopped in front of one where an older cat snarled and hissed.

"Don't touch that cat!" the shelter worker said, hurrying to Belle's side. I followed. "It's feral," she said. "We found her with her kittens alongside the highway."

"Are those her kittens in there?" asked Belle.

I peered in. At the back of the cage, I could see patches of black-and-white fuzz inside the folds of an old blanket. The woman put on a long, heavy glove and reached into the cage. The mama cat growled but backed away. Then the woman withdrew the smallest kitten I'd ever seen. Its paws looked misshapen and far too big for it.

"He has extra toes," she said. "He's a tuxedo kitty with mitten paws." She handed the black-and-white kitten to Belle.

My heart sank. The kitten's fur looked unhealthy, not fuzzy but spiky. It looked too small to survive, and I didn't know if it could walk on those big mitten paws.

Belle clutched it to her chest, whispering, "I want this one, Mom."

"I don't know," I said, looking at the woman for help. "Is it even big enough to leave its mother?"

"Yes! He's a strong little guy, and he'll be a good mouse hunter."

In the car on the way home, Belle tried to hold him, but he wiggled away.

"I'm naming him Oreo," she said. "I had to take him, Mom. No one else would have!"

At home, the kitten was so tiny that he couldn't get into the litter box. But when Belle sat him inside, he knew what to do.

"He's smart," she said. "He can already use a litter box!"

Our little house backed up to the woods and miles of trees. Scott and I had already decided to keep the cat inside. We didn't want him to get lost or hurt. Belle wanted to carry Oreo everywhere, but he didn't like to be held or even touched. He seemed happiest exploring on his own. Despite his struggles getting in and out of the litter box, his size didn't hold him back. Plus, he grew quickly.

Oreo foraged for food on his own. Preferring to gnaw his way through a package of bread or bagels, he'd ignore his bowl of cat food. If Belle or her big brother, Oliver, left their bedrooms at night, he chased them. They learned to run from him because, when he caught them, he dug his nails in and hung on. Scott and I often had to detach that fierce kitten from their pajama-clad legs at night.

Even the kids' new friends were chased around in the house by the cat. They learned to put socks on their arms to protect themselves. He'd leap at them, and dig in all his nails, and hang on. Those extra toes had extra nails in them, and I worried about all the scratches.

Oreo didn't climb on the furniture or counters like most cats. He liked being on the floor. Nobody could touch him with their hands. He'd bite or scratch like a bandit and run off to hide, peeking around corners or from under furniture. At night, I could hear his nails catching on the carpet as he raced around doing zoomie laps.

"Mom!" Belle learned to call from the safety of her bedroom. "Protect me from the cat so I can go to the bathroom!"

"Dad!" Oliver would shout from the doorway. "Will you make sure the cat doesn't get us until we get to the couch?" And he'd run with his friends to hop onto the safety of the furniture.

Somehow, the sweet name Oreo had been replaced with simply "The Cat."

Twice, I found a mouse left by my bedroom door in the morning. I didn't even realize we had them.

"We live in the woods now," Scott said. "I guess that's part of it."

One night, I'd left our bedroom door open, and the cat kept racing into the room, nails snagging as he went.

"Saffi, put him outside," said Scott, rolling over. "I don't think he's the kind of cat you can keep inside."

"I don't want him to get hurt," I said, refusing.

"I don't think anything would dare hurt him," said Scott, pulling a blanket over his head.

Somehow, we fell asleep, but in the dark of night, a strange voice woke me. It sounded like it said, "Out." I thought I was dreaming.

"Out. Out. Ouuuuut," it said, deep and guttural.

I opened my eyes. The cat stood against the side of the bed, his face nearly against mine. "Out," he growled. I sat up with my heart hammering.

"Scott! Did you hear that?"

"I told you to put him out."

"He said 'out'! That cat said 'out'! Did you hear that?"

"That's what it sounded like," Scott said.

Half-fearful, I hopped out of bed and opened the sliding glass door in our bedroom. The cat ran out. Between him talking and my worry that something would happen to him, I had trouble sleeping.

At some point, far before our morning alarms went off, I heard a meow through the glass door. When I opened it, the cat strutted in. In the dim light, I could see a small army of mice on the patio outside. They weren't moving. I closed the door fast.

"Scott! You have to clean off the patio!"

He groaned.

"I mean it. The cat was busy last night."

Scott got up to look.

"Good gravy! I thought Oreo was supposed to be a sweet, magical cat to help the kids adjust."

"Well, he talks," I said. "He seems more like a Norman Bates to me than a sweet little Oreo."

"Like from the movie *Psycho*? Well, he is a serial killer. That's a lot of mice out there!"

The name stuck. There was nothing sweet or fluffy about Norman, but he was magical. He could talk. For many years, he kept the mouse population under control and tolerated our presence as long as we never put our hands near him.

— S.R. Karfelt —

The Bandit and the Burglar

A cat is more intelligent than people believe and can be taught any crime.
~Mark Twain

It was a nice Florida evening. I had the windows open and there was a gentle breeze blowing through the screen door. I finished feeding my cat, Charley. He took a couple of bites, turned up his nose, and proceeded to follow me around the kitchen, meowing. He was much more interested in what I was cooking for my own supper. So, as usual, I put aside a little bit of the cooked hamburger for him. As it was cooling off, I put the finishing touches on my homemade soft tacos: shredded lettuce, tomatoes, sour cream, salsa, and hamburger. I put the plate on a TV tray in the living room.

I walked back into the kitchen to see if Charley's hamburger had cooled off. Just as I fed it to him, a loud scratching noise at the front door caught my attention. I went to investigate and there, hanging on the screen, was the biggest raccoon I had ever seen. I yelled, trying to scare it off. The raccoon ignored me and kept wrapping one paw around the handle on the screen door. He was trying to open the latch and get in.

That little bandit wore a black mask like Zorro over his eyes. Did he think it would make him harder to identify in a line-up? How fitting — he was there to steal my supper, the little rascal.

My Very Good, Very Bad Cat

Several minutes later, I got braver, grabbed a broom, and started waving it at the door, yelling, "Shoo, get out of here!" Nothing fazed this raccoon. He wouldn't budge. Charley just sat there, taking it all in.

At this point, I got on the phone and called animal control. As I explained my dilemma to the officer, my back was initially turned away from the plate of food. But then I turned around and discovered that Charley had jumped up on the TV tray and was chowing down on my supper. I yelled, "Charley, get down from there!"

It was too late. He had already eaten the hamburger off the top of the tacos.

I turned back and the creature hanging on my screen door had disappeared. I was still on the phone with animal control so the officer heard the whole story. He laughed and said, "Hey, the raccoon was in on it. He distracted you while the cat stole your food. They planned it together." We had a good laugh, and he said I should call him if the raccoon came back.

So, Charley had an accomplice, and the two of them pulled off this caper together. I had to admit it: I had been outfoxed by a masked bandit and a cat burglar.

— Sandy Wright —

Our Last Cat, and That's Final

A kitten is, in the animal world, what a rosebud is in the garden.
~Robert Southey

"Our last cat, and that's final." That's what we said when we adopted Tucker, an adult stray like most of the nineteen cats we had before him. When he passed after a drawn-out illness five years later, we reaffirmed that he had been our final cat. We had grieved too many times.

Besides, now in our mid-seventies, my wife was recovering from a broken pelvis and wrist, and I had recently gone through shoulder surgery. Physical therapy ate up our days.

A month passed. My wife said, "I miss a cat."

I said, "What about our vow?"

She said, "I like to snuggle."

"I can snuggle."

"You don't purr."

I said, "Remember hairballs? And kitty litter."

She said, "So, you're too busy?" She glanced at the crossword puzzle on my lap.

Ouch.

She said, "We can compromise."

"How do you compromise owning a cat? Time-share like a condo?"

"No, Grumpy." She had discovered that the local cat-rescue organization held "Pet the Cats" afternoons on Sundays. "We pet and play with them for an hour, then go home. It's good therapy for the cats and people."

"Huh. And you believe we will go home without a cat?"

"Of course." Her expression was so innocent — like the shining face of a child promising not to eat a cookie when her mother left the room.

At the storefront shelter, there were four adult cats. Wary, but gentle and grateful for attention, they would be quiet snuggle pillows. On the floor, a dozen kittens tore around like a mob in a Mel Brooks movie. They tumbled in fur-for-alls, climbed our legs, chased our fingers and, after a few strokes, fell asleep on our laps. "This little one's tongue sticks out when he sleeps," Carol said. "So cute! It's been a long time since we had a kitten."

His name is Fritz, and he is absolutely the last cat ever. I had her write it down.

After a period of adjustment — about six minutes — those few ounces of orange-and-white puff reorganized our lives. An older cat would have settled into sunny spots to contemplate his nine lives. Instead, Little Fritz follows us from room to room, his ears at permanent attention as if asking, "What are we going to do now? Huh? Huh? I can chase a paper ball or a string. I can bat the thread dangling from your sewing needle or swipe that cursor on your screen. Wanna play hide and seek again? You run and hide, and I'll find you! Huh? Huh? Ooh, shoelaces!"

Fritz keeps us active and exhausted. He does the running, but we walk, bend and throw the stuffed mice and squeaky things. We grunt and groan, but the activity limbers up our stiff joints.

Fritz loves being inside boxes and bags. Once, I made the mistake of pulling him while he was in a box. He rolled around inside and then leaned over the edge to swat the trail of cat toys on the floor. I tied a string to the box for easier pulling. Now, every day, he hops inside and stares up expectantly, like a pharaoh in his chariot. Onward, Lightning!

My Very Good, Very Bad Cat

There's no Lightning, but old Dobbin drags him around the house. "It's good exercise," my wife says.

I dusted off my tools to build him a couple of platforms with holes and hiding spots. The saw and drill buzzed. I cut and stapled carpet over his new gyms. Carol said, "More creative than crosswords."

Next, I made him a tunnel from a folded piece of cardboard. Ecstasy! He crouched at one end, his butt quivering. As I cocked my arm to toss his red bird, he rattled through the tunnel, burst out the other end, and pounced. Then, we retrieved the toy and played the game in the other direction. Back and forth through the tunnel and down the hallway. I panted, but Fritz's butt waggled for longer, faster throws. He wanted to have his limits challenged. I had forgotten about doing that. We tossed foam balls around corners, and Fritz skidded sideways after them. "Get it, Fritz! Get it!" Carol whooped and applauded at this cat rodeo.

As he grew, the tunnel had to be raised and wooden support frames added to keep it from collapsing when he leaped on top. I lengthened it to six feet and told Carol that I was thinking about using plywood because the cardboard was getting beat up. Maybe I would even add a side tunnel… My wife smiled.

Every night, Fritz carries the red bird to bed with us. We have a lively half-hour of tumbling and tossing. He charges into my legs, and I startle. Carol reminds me that you sleep better if you have a little activity before dropping off. "Is that so?" I mutter as I toss the bird out the door.

Another mistake! New game. He uses my stomach for a launch pad to pounce on it and bring it back. Carol thinks my "oof!" is very funny. He drops the bird on my chest, as if he's saying, "Again! Again!" When we are all properly tired, he carries the bird under the blanket to sleep. As he pushes deeper under the covers, he burrows into Carol's backside. She yelps.

"Sleep tight," I whisper.

Fritz's obsession with getting into things caused him some trouble recently. Carol's physical therapist was visiting and seemed pleased at her progress. "You must be staying active," she commented. We rolled

My Very Good, Very Bad Cat

our eyes. On cue, Fritz attempted to crawl into a boutique paper bag with hemp handles. But he tried to enter through a handle, and it snagged on his shoulders. It began crackling and following him.

There was a sudden explosion of paper and cat. He streaked along the top of the couch with the bag handle around his head and the bag flapping on his back. The monster chased him as he leaped onto the kitchen counter to escape — scattering mail, utensils and cookies.

I ran after him, and Carol and the therapist joined the rescue posse. We circled the kitchen island, grabbing empty air as Fritz leaped from counter to counter, with the bag whipping like a flag. Then, he raced into the bedroom. We heard sounds of crashing objects. Just as the rescue team reached the bedroom, he shot back out, dodged six grasping hands, and tore up the stairs. We climbed toward the sounds of claws skittering on wood floors, thumping and tearing paper.

At the head of the stairs, we found our warrior, the bag ripped to shreds and gone, but the handle still hung around his neck like a medallion. He stared down at us as if to say, "What's next, eh?"

The therapist said, "Have you considered getting him a playmate?"

— Garrett Bauman —

Tempting Fate

Cats, as you know, are quite impervious to threats.
~Connie Willis

My cat, Poke, was not a fan of cold weather. He would go to considerable lengths to make sure that his environment was warm and cozy.

This didn't pose a problem most of the year. He knew where to find patches of sunlight throughout the day. We knew we'd find him curled up in the kitchen in the mornings, and on an old sofa in the den in the afternoons. You only had to know where the sun was to find the cat. Poke had his routine down pat and rarely deviated from it.

Winter, however, was different. We got maybe ten hours of daylight total, and the sun lay so low in the sky that it afforded far fewer opportunities to bask in a patch of sunlight. And then, there were days when the sun never appeared at all.

During one particular stretch of bad weather — it was late January or maybe early February — a hard freeze set in, and the skies stayed overcast for days on end. It was flat-out miserable, and nobody enjoyed it, least of all Poke. He moped around the house, and even when he went outdoors, he didn't stay long. It was just too darn cold.

Heating oil prices were at a premium that winter, and in an effort to economize I set the thermostat low and used a pair of space heaters. You can figure for yourself where Poke spent the bulk of his time: parked right in front of a space heater.

My Very Good, Very Bad Cat

"What a surprise!" I would declare on coming into the den and finding Poke all but draped over the heater. "Who would have thought to find you here! How about you give somebody else a chance once in a while, huh?" Poke never budged. I don't think he was entirely oblivious to the sarcasm. He just didn't care.

If it came down to a matter of him being cold or me being cold, I knew exactly how that was going to shake out. I could have had an icicle dripping from the tip of my nose, and Poke wouldn't have moved so much as a millimeter. He was all about me, me, me!

"You better take care, Poke," I warned him. "You better remember who's in charge here! One of these days, I'm going to go out and replace you with a dog!" Nothing. Poke didn't even lift his head. He figured my threat was idle and wasn't afraid to call my bluff.

A couple of days later, I noticed that it felt warmer in the house. I figured maybe the outside temperature was finally starting to climb. Turns out I was wrong. It was every bit as cold as before, but somebody had turned up the thermostat. When I consulted the digital readout, it was seventy-two degrees! I was beside myself. I was burning heating oil at a rate that would land me in debtors' prison before the week was out. I might as well have been shoveling pallet loads of cash into the furnace.

I immediately confronted my wife. She denied having anything to do with it. "Well, if it wasn't you, who was it then?" She directed a pointed glance over at Poke, stretched out — where else? — in front of the space heater. I started to protest, but the more I thought about it, the more plausible it seemed.

Poke had only to jump onto the top of the bookcase, a feat he was easily capable of, to access the thermostat. But was he really that devious, that underhanded, that selfish, to attempt such a thing? That was a question that answered itself. Of course, he was!

Whether it actually was Poke who did the dirty deed, I suppose I'll never know. He never denied it. But he never admitted it, either. He didn't act guilty — but then, neither did my wife. Poke had both motive and opportunity, that much was certain. So, I took the precaution of moving the bookcase. Unless Poke somehow miraculously grew a set

My Very Good, Very Bad Cat

of wings, he wouldn't be able to adjust the thermostat anymore. I kept a close eye on him, just the same.

When spring finally rolled around, no one was more overjoyed than Poke — unless, of course, it was me. I could finally shed the sweater and the bulky flannel shirt and stop worrying about the price of fuel oil. But I never moved the bookcase back to its original position. I don't believe in tempting fate.

— Thomas Canfield —

The Reign of King Louis

If I had a dollar for every time my cat made me smile,
I would be the world's richest person by now.
~Ernest Hemingway

I am cleaning the cat box. It is not something I like doing. But I am doing it anyway, and as I clean it, I see the speckles of twenty-dollar bills sprinkled like confetti throughout the box.

The cat box is the domain of King Louis. He is a regal cat, hence the name. He is yellow with long streaks of brown, a mane that looks like a crown, and a curlicue tail, which he uses to gently sweep your face when he passes by on the back of the couch.

King Louis adopted us two years ago after he sauntered into our house through the doggie door and plopped down on Sammy's corduroy cushion. Sammy is our twelve-year-old, cranky Dachshund. He did not appreciate it when Louis homesteaded on his bed and said so. But King Louis was unimpressed with Sammy's protestations and gave him a dismissive swipe with his paw, sans claws. And that was that.

Upon adopting our family, Louis made it clear that his principal bedfellow and confidant was to be Ayla, our daughter. They became inseparable. Besides sleeping with Ayla, Louis sat on her lap when she was eating dinner, watching TV, or doing her homework. He even insisted on riding in the car when she was being dropped off at school.

That is, until now. And here's why.

As graduation from high school approached, congratulatory cards from friends and family poured in for Ayla, most of which contained money, primarily in twenty-dollar bills.

Since Louis has a bad habit of eating things not intended for that purpose, such as shoelaces, dryer sheets, artificial flowers, and toilet paper, he viewed the money as a treat expressly meant for him.

And he ate the twenty-dollar bills that Ayla left in a basket on the floor of her bedroom.

About $200 worth.

For his part, King Louis did not recognize the severity of what he had done and fully expected things in the household to continue the way they had always been.

Ayla did not share this view.

"Dad!" she lamented, clearly distraught. "What kind of a pet eats your graduation presents?"

"King Louis, apparently," I calmly offered, "particularly when they are left on the floor of the bedroom that he shares with you."

"He had no right to do that!" she exclaimed, unable to see the role she had played in the demise of her Andrew Jacksons.

And, from that decisive moment on, King Louis was banned from Ayla's bedroom, her lap, and the car rides to school.

King Louis did not understand his banishment and complained about it in the only way he could. Mournful meows and baneful bellows filled our home.

And then, after three days, something strange happened.

I had seen King Louis and Sammy make their morning foray into the backyard through the doggy door and thought little of it when Sammy returned alone. King Louis often spent the mornings lounging on the patio, taking in the sun, and chasing away the occasional squirrel that blundered into his backyard.

But, around noon, I became concerned when he had not come back inside. I assembled a search party of one to look for him.

Nothing. Nowhere. King Louis had abdicated his throne and flown the coop, something he had never done before.

And then my phone rang.

"Uh, this is Principal Leonard," the voice said with officiousness. "We have a little situation here."

"Is Ayla okay?" I asked nervously.

"Oh, yes, she's fine, just fine," he remarked with a reassuring chuckle. "It's just that we've never had anything quite like this happen before."

I was there in minutes, standing in the front office, where I found the principal.

"Follow me," he implored. "Ayla's waiting in my office."

I was shocked, amazed and relieved by what I saw. There was my daughter, sitting on a couch, with Mr. Entitled, His Highness, King Louis curled in her lap, purring like a jet engine.

"Dad! Look! Louis came looking for me!"

"What? Why? How?" I stammered.

"He must have known where I was from all the times he rode along when you dropped me off at school."

"Apparently," the principal interjected, "your cat waltzed into the cafeteria like he owned the place, jumped on a table, and much to the enjoyment of the students he nonchalantly strode from one table to the next until he found Ayla."

"Poor Louis. He was upset because I haven't been paying any attention to him, so he did the only thing he could think of: He came here looking for me," said Ayla.

Perhaps in return for the fine performance turned in by King Louis, the principal gave Ayla the afternoon off, whereupon we returned home and King Louis was rightfully restored to his soft pillow throne in Ayla's room.

And, to Ayla's great surprise, our family and friends were so moved by the story of King Louis, his culinary transgression and ultimate redemption, that they re-contributed to Ayla's graduation.

But, this time, it was different. No twenties this time. No, no, no. Only hard plastic, King Louis-proof gift cards.

— Dave Bachmann —

Chapter 10
Opening Hearts

Remembering Sir Lancelot

When we lose one blessing, another is often most unexpectedly given in its place.
~C.S. Lewis

"Would you like to come in?" I asked, surprised at myself for inviting him in. It wasn't the first time that I'd seen Lance hanging out at my front door. This time, my isolation trumped my fear of what Lance might do once inside.

I privately thought of Lance as Sir Lancelot, like the legendary knight who loved Queen Guinevere, his king's wife. But his owner, my neighbor Linda, referred to him as just Lance. You could hear the affection in her voice whenever she talked about him, unaware he was cheating on her with me.

Linda was a forty-something, never-married career woman with no children. She probably didn't have a clue that her beloved would show up at my place when she was at work or away somewhere. Back then, I was a single woman in my early forties similar to Linda. Unlike my neighbor in the adjoining condo, though, I was blessed with an adult son named Zach who had grown up and moved out. Plus, I had experienced the sting of divorce followed six years later by an engagement that ended a mere eleven days before our big church wedding.

Thankfully, throwing myself into my career as a local TV reporter

Opening Hearts | 285

and working long hours soothed my wounded ego. Entering the "no-time-for-a-social-life zone" also protected me from getting hurt again.

Or so I thought, until Lance's first visit, followed by more covert meetings. In my defense, it was his dogged insistence and incessant meowing that ultimately clinched the deal. The strange thing is, I was even more wary of cats than male humans back then, and Lance was a large, orange feline. Still, I let him in.

My phobia about animals originated in childhood, since my late mother was terrified of anything with fur and four legs. Growing up in a household without pets, except for an occasional goldfish, led to me naturally embracing the label, "Not an animal lover," like Mom.

In college, I tried to befriend a freezing cat by giving him shelter in the warm home where I lived with several roommates. Unfortunately, not knowing much about cats, I ended up getting clawed pretty badly. The frightened cat had to be rehomed, solidifying the fear of animals that Mom had instilled in me.

This changed when I married my ex-husband who owned a Cocker Spaniel named Max. With my then spouse working long hours as a small business owner, I forged a strong bond with Max.

My son Zach was a little boy at the time, and Max grew incredibly protective of both of us. When the marriage ended, the only possession I fought to keep through the court system was Max. Sadly, because I wasn't his original owner, I lost custody of him. It was heartbreaking, but life goes on.

Through the following years, friends and neighbors expounded on the virtues of their faithful canines. As a television reporter, I personally covered a local story about a St. Bernard who rescued a family during a housefire. The friendly dog's saliva dripped from his mouth, soaking the leg of my dress slacks, while I was interviewing his grateful master. The huge hound had successfully pushed a clothes dryer out of his way to open a door to get upstairs and awaken the sleeping family after he smelled the fire.

There are accounts of heroic cats as well, although not as many. I certainly never reported on one. But Lance saved me. He came in that afternoon to spend time with a broken woman who was afraid to let

Opening Hearts

her heart feel again.

    He usually showed up when I was at my lowest point. The cat must have been on a divine assignment because only God knew how rejected and lonely I truly felt. Lance's visits weren't frequent because he would only come over when Linda was gone, but he brought hope with him. He was an excellent listener, too, and I could tell him all about my troubles, confident of his discretion. Each time he popped in, my wounded heart healed a bit more.

    For some reason, though, I sensed that I shouldn't tell Linda about her cat's clandestine visits. In a way, Lance was her whole world, and I was afraid that she might resent his affection for me. After all, my neighbor and I were cordial, but we maintained healthy boundaries that led to harmonious condo dwelling.

    After almost a decade of living next door, Linda packed all her possessions and moved out one night, telling no one. Later, I heard a rumor that she had lost her position and relocated to a large city seventy-five miles away for a new job. I was shocked by the way she left and devasted that Lance was gone. I'm pretty sure that Linda wasn't aware of my feelings for him, though. If she had been, maybe she would have let me say goodbye to my furry knight in ginger-striped armor.

    I mourned for Lance the way I did when I lost Max. It's the kind of grief that anyone who has ever lost a pet can probably relate to. Ironically, though, my cat didn't die, similar to the way my dog didn't die. They never belonged to me. Still, my heart hurt for a long time whenever anything reminded of the lovable tabby who had become my secret companion.

    I don't believe it's a coincidence that, not long after Lance moved away, I met the love of my life, Larry Claypool. Larry and I have been married more than two decades now. He's a really good man, but he has bad allergies so we can't have any pets.

    Besides, people who know me well would likely tell you that I'm not a cat lover. But I did love a cat once and miss him still. His name was Sir Lancelot, a feline friend who taught me that letting your heart love again can be worth the risk.

— Christina Ryan Claypool —

Baby Steps

For me, cats are the role model for being alive.
~Haruki Murakami

Another second-grade teacher poked her head into my classroom. "Hey, I was on recess duty today, and your new kid is refusing to come in again."

It was Thomas's third day at our school, and it was the third day he'd hidden under the slide during recess and refused to come inside when it was time.

The first two days, his foster mom had come to pick him up. But today, I headed outside to coax him in. As expected, I found him under the slide, looking like a scared animal.

"Thomas, it's okay," I said. "Come inside."

He stared at me with wide eyes, and my heart broke for him. His foster mom had told me a bit about his past, and I couldn't blame him for being scared. "He won't let any of us touch him," she told me. "He hardly speaks, and the only one he likes is our cat, Sophia."

In the end, I couldn't get Thomas inside, and his foster mom picked him up for the third time. We agreed to keep him inside during recess for a while, hoping it would help him adjust, although I wasn't sure that anything would help this poor boy.

After that tough day at school, I headed home. As I started making dinner, my male cat, Tigger, brushed against my legs. I bent to pet him.

"Hey, Bud! How are you? Where's your little sister?"

I asked the question, but I already knew the answer. Annie, the

288 | Opening Hearts

female cat we'd had for a few weeks, was hiding, just like she always was. She was a shy cat, and when I tried to push her to socialize, she got aggressive.

She was a beautiful kitty, and I loved her. It made me sad that she wanted nothing to do with me. I wanted to help her feel comfortable in our home, but I didn't know how. All our other cats had been friendly from the start.

I had a friend who worked as a vet tech, so I called her for advice. She told me to go slowly and give her space and lots of treats.

Although it was hard, I resisted the urge to try to force her to be close to me. I left a few treats just outside her favorite hiding place, hoping to draw her out. My friend warned me that it would take time, and I'd need to be patient.

The next day at school, I told Thomas that he'd be staying in the classroom during recess. To my surprise, he looked relieved. I felt apprehensive. I wanted to help Thomas, but I didn't know how.

Days went by, and each twenty-minute recess period felt much longer. At first, I tried talking to Thomas, but he just shrugged and refused to look at me. In the short time he'd been in my classroom, I'd discovered that he was smart and was usually the first to finish his work, so he had nothing to do during recess. I'd encourage him to choose a book from the shelf, but he'd just shrug.

"I don't know what to do for him," I confided to a co-worker. "He wants nothing to do with me or anyone else. He's the same way with his foster family. Completely closed off. He's like the human version of our new cat."

My co-worker eyed me. "What are you doing to get the cat to trust you? Maybe the same thing will work with Thomas."

"You might be onto something," I said.

Annie and I had been making progress, a little at a time. I'd been continuing to give her space and leave treats in strategic locations. She wasn't curling up in my lap or anything, but she had been coming out of her hiding place more often. I felt hopeful about the baby steps she'd taken.

As I was grading papers one day, I noticed that Thomas had drawn

Opening Hearts

a cat on the back of his paper. He was a talented artist.

The next day, when his classmates headed to the playground, Thomas returned to our classroom and found a new sketchbook and a set of colored pencils on his desk. As I worked on the computer, I snuck glances at him. It was the first time that I saw him smile.

The day after that, I found a little present on my desk. It was a drawing of an orange cat with the words "My cat Sophia" written on it.

That night, I sat near Annie's hiding place, trying to get her used to my presence, and Tigger curled up in my lap. I talked to him about the progress we were making, both at home and at school.

Annie poked her head out several times, but she never hissed at me. More baby steps.

The next day, I left a photo of Tigger on Thomas's desk. He sketched him and left it on mine. I hung the drawing on my filing cabinet, where I kept all the things my students had made for me.

The little presents continued. I found drawings of Tigger wearing hats, playing with toys, and snuggled up with an orange cat named Sophia.

One day, I left Thomas a note, explaining that I had another cat named Annie, but I didn't have a picture of her. He came in for recess, read the note, and then said, "Why?"

The sound of his voice caught me off guard. He hardly ever spoke and never at recess when it was just the two of us. I looked up and found him staring right at me. "Why don't you have a picture of her?" It was the most words he'd spoken in the weeks he'd been in my classroom.

"She's afraid of me," I said quietly. "I would never hurt her, but she still doesn't trust me. She hides in my laundry room, so I can't take her picture."

He nodded. "That's sad."

The next day, I found a note asking what color Annie was. "She's black," I said. Later, I found a drawing of Tigger, Sophia, and a small black cat sitting on a washing machine. Beneath the drawing were the words, "She likes you. Just keep being nice."

It seemed like good advice for both home and school.

Opening Hearts

So, I kept being nice. I sat in the laundry room, murmuring to Tigger and leaving trails of treats. One day, Annie came out and brushed against my foot. Weeks later, she let me pet her for the first time. I felt like I'd won the lottery.

"Thank you for trusting me," I said quietly. "And thank you for your help with Thomas."

Thomas was eventually adopted by his foster family and gradually became a new kid. He was still quiet, but he no longer looked like a scared animal. He made a few friends, and one day he asked if he could go outside for recess. "I'll come back in," he assured me.

I smiled. "What about my cat drawings?"

"I'll make them at home." He hugged me and then ran outside.

I'd won the jackpot twice.

— Diane Stark —

Neighborhood Glue

Cats choose us. We don't own them.
~Kristen Cast

Jonathan and I met the butt-end of Eeyore first. We'd gone inside for hot cider, and when we returned to our porch, we found a large gray-and-white cat upended inside one of our just-carved jack-o'-lanterns.

"Is he stuck?" I yelped.

Jonathan bent down and studied the feline. "No," he reported. "He's eating the pumpkin guts."

Thus began the strangest relationship I've ever had with a cat. We knew his name was Eeyore because it was on his collar tag, and we learned that he belonged to a couple over on the next street.

The next time we saw Eeyore he was dragging a bath towel across the yard in the direction of his owners' house. I rescued the towel and this time I jotted down the phone number on his tag. I had a feeling I'd need it.

Plenty of cats have a habit of pilfering laundry; I've seen all the viral videos. Eeyore's compulsion to pull towels and socks off people's laundry lines to deposit on his owners' doorstep like so many dead mice would become both his tragic flaw and his saving grace. It would endear him to an entire neighborhood who forgave him even as they fumed about their missing pants.

A few weeks after the towel incident, I splashed out to get the mail in the rain and found him sounding his barbaric "Yawp!" while dragging my Columbia sweater down the street. Unfortunately, it had been left hanging on a low clothes rack in the rain. I ran inside for my coat and emerged just in time to see him disappearing around the corner. I found my sweater outside his owners' house in a muddy gutter, chewed.

I called his owners' number. "Eeyore's stealing our laundry," I told the woman on the phone.

"Dammit!" she responded. "That cat's going to cost me a fortune in dry cleaning!"

Shortly thereafter, she kicked him out. He appeared to be skinny but undeterred when we found him on our doorstep one cold November day bearing the top half of a neighbor's scarecrow. An hour later, he brought a green Victoria's Secret bra in my size. For his finale, he yowled his way down the steps of the A-frame across from us and offered up a stuffed turtle decorated with the Grateful Dead logo and reeking of pot.

"Let's just feed him," Jonathan said and set down a bowl of food while our three indoor kitties looked on. So began a twelve-year relationship with this cat, who became our adopted toddler's first friend and our neighborhood ambassador. It's impossible not to get to know the people living around you when you're constantly apologizing for the theft of their T-shirts, kids' soccer socks, and dozens of gardening gloves, inexplicably left-handed. We had merely stepped in to help when the felonious feline became homeless, but now he was our problem.

Finally, as the cat's apparent owners, we set a box out on our front steps and wrote EEYORE across it. Neighbors walked over to gather their items and stopped to chat. We became the kind of street with annual block parties and lists of everyone's phone numbers in case of earthquakes or ice storms. We looked out for each other's kids and cats and dogs and chickens. We traded stories about how Eeyore leapt from the street to the mailman's shoulder and scared the poor guy half to death, and how the cat stole a new neighbor's leather driving glove — only the left one — right off the hood of his car.

And then Eeyore disappeared.

We'd gone on vacation and returned to a distraught pet sitter. "He vanished," the woman said. "I haven't seen him for days."

We looked in garages and sheds, under porches, and under our house. Nothing. At last, my daughter and I spotted him with someone's work glove in his mouth, yowling as he made his way to the tiny white house behind us.

We'd focused our neighborly goodwill on our own street; we barely knew the people on the next street over. But Eeyore got around.

We met him at the door of the white house. A woman in her eighties greeted us in coat and hat. "Oh, good, you found my cat," she said. "Now I can go for my swim at the Y."

My daughter and I traded a look. "Your cat?" I said finally. "But he's…"

The woman scooped up Eeyore, who draped himself around her shoulders like a shawl. "He just showed up one day and dropped someone's shorts on my doormat. I washed them." She reached for a pair of black running shorts. "Do you recognize these?"

I did. They were mine.

"Isn't he wonderful?" she said to my seven-year-old daughter, who'd remained strangely silent during our exchange. "He fills a hole in my heart."

"He's actually our cat," I began, but my child stopped me.

"It's okay," she said, looking up at the older woman through kind, brown eyes. "You can have him."

I watched, bewildered, as the woman, Sally, shut Eeyore inside her house. She bid us goodbye and got into her car, and my daughter and I walked back to our house.

"Why did you do that?" I asked.

She reached for my hand. "Sally needs Eeyore more than we do."

And Sally needed us, we discovered. At eighty-eight, she lived alone; her grown children didn't often visit. We went over to see Eeyore and brought homemade cookies, soup and bread. In return, Sally told us stories about her time as a teacher in Guam and displayed Eeyore's latest booty — usually underwear directly from our clothesline.

When Sally required surgery and a month of convalescence at the nursing home down the road, we chopped up the beef livers she insisted upon and fed them to Eeyore along with a dose of gabapentin

Opening Hearts

for his elderly joints. My daughter walked him on a harness into the nursing home to the delight of residents and staff, and he curled up on Sally's hospital bed and purred like a freight train.

"If I die before him, you'll take care of him, right?" she said when she turned ninety-two. "He's such a good kitty." She kept him inside all the time now; he lay on the top of her couch and gazed outside, contemplating his glory days.

I held my breath against the litter box's stench and assured her of continued beef liver and love. As it turned out, Eeyore did pass away before her at twenty-plus years old.

Sally begged me to write an obituary and post it online. Now, if you search for hers, it's vanished into the newspaper archives. But my tribute to Eeyore lives on at everloved.com. You can read it and see photos of Sally with her cat, and for disbelievers, photos of Eeyore with his cache of left-handed gloves, beside the black pants he stole and that my husband washed and kept as pajamas, and strolling with a man's white sock in his mouth.

Years later, all any neighbor has to say at our annual block party is "Eeyore," and the rest of us nod wisely and chuckle, remembering the large gray-and-white cat who ate pumpkin guts, terrorized the mailman, stole our panties, and brought us all together.

— Melissa Hart —

Becoming a Cat Person

*Any conditioned cat-hater can be won over
by any cat who chooses to make the effort.*
~Paul Corey, Do Cats Think?

I never considered myself a cat person. Or a dog person, for that matter. It's not that I'm heartless or cruel, or that I dislike animals. It's just that I was raised in a pet-free home where animals were viewed as an extra chore or expenditure.

So, in the fall of 2019, when the opportunity to own a cat fell into my lap, I wasn't all that excited about it.

The call came from a relative whose next-door neighbor had died in a tragic accident, leaving behind what was described as "a young, sweet cat named Kai." As a busy mother of three, my initial reaction was to say, "I'm sorry, but I can't help."

But I couldn't stop thinking about that cat, and the tragic loss of its owner. He had died helping someone on a busy highway, and that tugged at my heartstrings even more. Sometimes, we make sacrifices for the greater good, even if those sacrifices come with a cost.

The kids were excited about the possibility of a cat. So, I purchased a cat carrier and went to meet my relative, who then gave me a key to the neighbor's home.

I don't know what I expected… Well, actually I do. I expected a small, adorable kitten to come up and greet me excitedly when I came through the door. But that is not what happened. There was no cat in sight, and being in this stranger's home, especially after such a recent death, felt strange, like a violation.

I searched and searched but no cat. Then, as I was about to leave, this enormous fur ball came sprinting out of the closet and ran toward me!

The cat certainly was cute, but not at all small or young.

Kai, this huge, floofy, thirteen-pound cat, looked wise beyond her years, and she was certainly suspicious of me. It was almost as though she knew I was not the normal kind of cat person she was used to.

It took nearly an hour to coax her into the carrier, and she meowed unhappily the whole ride home. I'd spent the day before getting her space ready — a litter box, food bowl, and water-filter fountain — and they were set up for her in our small, spare bathroom.

As soon as I opened the cat carrier, Kai, this wild, fluffy beast, darted into a corner of the bathroom and refused to come closer. It wasn't until later, after I'd left the room, that she slinked out of her corner, took a small bite of food, and used the facilities.

I thought that it might take a couple of days for her to adjust, but no matter how hard the kids or I tried to urge her out of the room to explore and socialize, she wouldn't. She stayed curled in her corner most of the day, and she appeared to be sad.

I knew that animals could love and feel emotion, but I didn't realize that she was grieving. There was a sadness in her eyes, as though she knew that her owner, and the home she'd known before, were gone.

At night, I couldn't sleep. I worried about her. Would she be happy here? Had I made a mistake? If I were more of a cat person, would she sense it and ease into her new life here with us?

A week after Kai moved in, I waited until the kids went to bed, and then I went to the bathroom and picked her up in my arms. I carried her to my bedroom and sat her down on my bed. Instantly, she leapt off and darted back to her hidey-hole in the bathroom.

Every day for the next week, I followed this same routine: putting the kids to bed, scooping her into my arms, and carrying her to my room while saying soothing words in an attempt to make her feel more comfortable.

It wasn't until the second week that she sat on the bed for longer than a few seconds.

I tried not to make a big deal out of it, watching her from the corner of my eye. She scooted in closer, tiptoeing over to me, but as soon as I reached out to stroke her fur, she jumped and ran back to her safe place.

It took about a month, but finally she would sit at the end of the bed for an hour or so, just watching me read or work quietly. We had a peaceful agreement. I won't bother you if you don't bother me.

All that changed a couple of months later when there was a break in our nightly routine. I'd become wickedly ill with a stomach virus, and I'd delegated the feeding and litter-box-scooping duties to the kids for the day. That night, I did not go to retrieve her. Instead, I fell asleep early, curled over in my bed, clutching my aching belly.

Around 2:00 in the morning, I woke with a start. In the dark room, I could hear the heavy breathing of an animal, and then I felt the vibrations of her purring body beside me.

When I opened my eyes, I was shocked to see Kai lying right up against my stomach, curled into me like I was a spoon. Carefully, I stuck an arm out to cuddle her, and the purring grew even louder.

It shocked me. This creature, who was so frightened and sad herself, could obviously sense that it was me who needed her this time.

Over the next few nights, I recovered easily. Kai never left my side when I was sick except to eat or use the litter box. She snuggled in closer and closer each night, purring with joy and finally looking calm and relaxed in our home.

Over the next couple of years, Kai became a central part of our household, growing into a social, happy cat. Now, she hangs out in all our rooms and spends her days slowly climbing cat trees and chasing catnip-filled birds and mice.

Recently, we adopted a new cat from the shelter: a friend for Kai named Willoughby. At first, they were leery of each other, but it didn't take long for Kai to ease her into the family. They've become best friends, chasing each other around the house and cuddling up during naptimes.

Kai is busy now with her best cat friend and her own daily routines of playing and snacking, but one part of our day has never changed.

Every night, as the sun goes low and I tuck the kids into their beds, she comes to my room. Sometimes, she has trouble jumping on the bed now that she is getting older and is not as spry. But she lets me lift her into the bed, and I always pull her close to me.

I hope that somewhere out there, Kai's previous owner knows that, not only am I taking good care of his sweet cat, but she's also taking care of me. For a while, I joked that "I'm not a cat person. I'm a 'Kai person.'" But I don't think that's true anymore.

I think the love of a cat — or any animal — is essential to all of us. I know that she has certainly made a huge difference in my life, and I hope that others will give a pet a chance, even if they don't think of themselves as "pet people."

— Carissa Ann Lynch —

One More Surprise

The cat does not offer services. The cat offers itself.
~William S. Burroughs

Every weekday, I would walk the kids a mile to school for drop-off and pick-up. Kerwin would patiently lie in wait under the bushes. As soon as I walked by, she'd pounce on my feet, scaring me every time.

She also liked to lurk under my bed, hidden by the dust ruffle. I'd innocently lean over to straighten up the sheets and out would jump a cat, landing on my bare foot with her claws extended, just enough for me to feel it but not enough to hurt. It's a wonder I never had a heart attack.

Getting a kitten hadn't been my idea. When we told the kids we would be moving from the United States to England, I wasn't sure how to sell it.

"They have hedgehogs in England," I said. "And no mosquitos. Isn't that wonderful?"

My seven-year-old was unimpressed. "Can we get a kitten?"

Can we get a kitten? Of course, we can get a kitten. Parents feeling guilty about moving you away from everything you know and love will agree to anything but a pony. And so, a little black ball of fluff with a white M on her forehead joined our family soon after we arrived in England.

Kerwin didn't just attack us. She was a neighborhood favorite and she would jump out at anyone. More than once, we heard the

Opening Hearts

postman yelp as the black ninja kitty launched her sneak attack from under the hedge. Schoolchildren would stop on the sidewalk to chat and stroke her smooth fur.

When Kerwin was three years old, it was time for us to move again, this time to Japan. Of course, Kerwin would travel with us. But this turned out to be more complicated than we expected.

I talked to a neighbor who lived three doors down from us. "Would you be willing to help us get Kerwin to Japan? I know it's a lot to ask. We have to spend a month in the States, and she can't come with us. So, you'd have to take her in for a month or two until we get settled and then take her to the vet for preflight checks. A pet-transport company can pick her up and manage her through the complicated quarantine on both ends."

My neighbor, a vet tech, looked at me thoughtfully. "Yes, I'd be willing, but have you thought seriously about what Kerwin would prefer? I know you love her, and she loves you, but she also loves this neighborhood. Cats are very territorial, and they hate moving. My kids already know and love Kerwin, too. I'm happy to take her into my own family and spare her the trauma."

We thought about it, cried about it, and finally decided that if Kerwin had a vote, she'd probably choose to stay in England. We enjoyed one last cuddle and flew away. Over time and many more moves, we lost touch with everyone in our British neighborhood.

Many years later, we visited the area during a family vacation. Memories came flooding back as we walked through the town. Here was the school, the grocery store, and the park where we played. As we walked into our old neighborhood, one of the kids mentioned Kerwin.

"Wouldn't it be awesome if we saw Kerwin?"

"Would she even still be around?" We did the math. If she was still alive, Kerwin would be sixteen years old.

As we turned onto our former street, we saw a group of teenagers blocking the sidewalk. They were bent over and focused on something. As we got close, we could see a black cat in their midst.

Could it be? We waited for the teens to move on and then approached the cat, who was ready to receive a new group of admirers. There were bits of white around her muzzle, but, most importantly, we saw the white M. My daughter dropped cross-legged to the sidewalk, and an elderly Kerwin crawled into her lap.

Sometimes, pets wander into and out of our lives, and sometimes we wander in and out of theirs. When we least expect it, they leap out of hiding and pounce on our hearts, creating bonds that span time and oceans.

—Mary DeVries—

Puffy

The cat, it is well to remember, remains the friend of man because it pleases him to do so and not because he must.
~Carl Van Vechten

It was early days in our marriage, and I agreed to move to London, one of the world's largest cities, because my husband was offered a great job opportunity. The move went smoothly. But then we were there, two people in a city of almost nine million. That made me feel both connected and very alone.

I was from a small town, so the noises of the city kept me up during my first night. I wondered if I would ever adapt to the hustle and bustle, but I couldn't help but feel gleeful when I looked out our living room window at the London Eye and all of London's beautiful lights. Clearly, the city was awake, too. What a privilege to live in this exciting place!

I looked directly across the street into another apartment window and saw an enormous puff ball of a cat staring back at me. This made me happy and also calmed me down and I was able to sleep after that.

When I awoke the next day, the first thing I did was look out the window. Disappointed I couldn't find my friend (my first London friend!), I wondered if I had made up the whole thing.

I was still waiting for a work visa, so I stayed home when my husband left for his new job. As soon as the door shut behind him, I felt so alone. I tackled each moving box and tried to make this unfamiliar place feel like a home. After I completed that task, I went off to explore our neighbourhood.

On my way out, I made sure to look at the building where my friend had made an appearance the night before. Happily, I saw his back pressed against the window, a big, squashed fur ball. I hadn't made him up.

We promptly settled into our new city life, marriage, and work. I hadn't expected it, but city life truly suited us. We were extraordinarily happy. My cat friend, whom I affectionately called Puffy, often made appearances in his window. Somehow, he was always there at the perfect time, right when I needed him. I had strategically placed an armchair next to the window so I could look out and see him. With only a narrow street separating us, it was possible to hang out together, each in our respective places.

I'd secured a teaching job and when I worked on my reports late into the evening, Puffy would stay up with me. He would watch me clean our apartment every weekend. He was always particularly excited if I cleaned windows, patting his paws on his window to mimic me. If I skipped them, he would snub me as he pouted and turned his back.

When I woke up early and sat with a cup of tea and a book, Puffy would also keep me company, only leaving his window when I left mine. Our friendship, which was only known to us, was admittedly odd, but it still made me happy and made me feel more at home in the city.

My husband first found out about Puffy when a heat wave hit that summer. "You want me to walk across the road, go to the third floor of the building across from us, knock on their door, and ask how their cat is doing?" he asked, puzzled.

I explained that I hadn't seen Puffy in a week, and I feared the heat might have affected his health. I pleaded with my husband, but he seemed adamant that I had lost the plot. Looking out the window, wondering if I was game enough to go myself and enquire about Puffy, my puff ball of a cat slowly came to lie down by the windowsill. He looked absolutely exhausted from the heat, but he was there.

On a particularly bad morning when nothing seemed to go right,

I got the fright of my life. My husband had a health scare, which led me to call the ambulance. Feeling absolutely powerless and scared, I looked out the window, defeated as I waited for the ambulance to arrive. I saw Puffy pacing up and down rapidly, clearly matching my nervous energy. A couple of long days and doctors' appointments later, it was declared that my husband had a lung puncture, the worry of it also puncturing my heart. My husband was on bed rest for a while and formed his own friendship with Puffy, who kept him company from across the road. It seemed I had not lost the plot after all.

Our time in London ended prematurely. With a new job opportunity and adventure calling us, we made the brave decision to move across the world to New Zealand. During the days leading up to the move, I was a nervous wreck. I had many sleepless nights during which Puffy always looked over at me, seemingly confused and with his little head tilted sideways. *What a wonderfully perceptive cat,* I thought.

On our last day in our flat, I didn't even think to look out the window for Puffy, my mind too occupied with the move. Moving out our few belongings, a deep clean, a flat inspection, and the return of our keys had left me feeling exhausted before our long journey even started. Already feeling nostalgic for London, my heart ached, wondering how we could leave all this behind. We had had such a magical time in this city; I couldn't imagine living elsewhere. We anxiously waited for our taxi to take us to Heathrow Airport.

Only when it arrived did I remember, impulsively running across the road and looking up at Puffy's window. He was indeed there, waiting to send us off.

— Marie-Eve Bernier —

Baby Nurse

Who hath a better friend than a cat?
~William Hardwin

"You know, Vikings would give their new brides a kitten to see if they would be good mothers," I teased my then-boyfriend. He laughed. As a hobby, Derek does Viking reenactments. We both knew that was just an Internet myth, but it still fit the scenario we found ourselves in. We were on our way home from the movies with my family on Father's Day in 2017 and had unexpectedly become parents to our "furst" baby: an abandoned, newborn kitten.

My younger sister had found it at work and waited to see if the mother would return. (She did not.) She couldn't keep it because she was too busy with college, so she brought it with her to see if our older sister could take it. But my older sister had just had a baby, so her husband put the kibosh on them having a newborn kitten.

I looked at Derek. Our eyes met, and he nodded. "We can take it," I said.

Relieved, my sister handed me the cardboard box. I cradled it in my arms and peered inside. A tiny gray tabby with a white face and paws mewed and crawled blindly on a pink blanket.

"I don't know if it's a boy or girl, but I named it Oliver," my sister explained as she gave us the kitten bottle, nipples, and formula.

The next day, we took the kitten to the vet and confirmed that our new wriggling ball of fur was indeed an Oliver.

The next few weeks were exhausting but also exhilarating. We prepared the formula and fed him every few hours, including through the night. We wiped his bottom to make him go to the bathroom, like a mother cat would. Since we didn't have a heating pad, we filled a plastic bottle with hot water and put it under the blanket in the box to keep him warm.

As tired as we were, there was so much joy, too. Little things felt like a triumph.

"His eyes are starting to open!"

"Look, he's taking his first steps!"

"Do you think he's ready to transition to solid food?"

He never seemed to get full. Even though I fed him the specified amounts, it was never enough. He would mew and claw at the bottle for more.

The months went by in a flash. The next thing I knew, the soft, tiny kitten that once fit in the palm of my hand had grown into a giant, fluffy cat who covered my entire chest when he snuggled on my lap.

He was a jealous kitty. He did not like sharing me with my other cats and often batted Derek away if he and I were snuggling together. He was 100 percent a mama's boy.

Even if it's just an online myth, Derek must have been impressed with my kitten-raising skills because, a couple of years later, my Viking asked me to be his wife. The next thing we knew, we bought our first house together and found out I was pregnant.

As my tummy grew, I would look down at Oliver on my slowly disappearing lap. Did he feel the baby's little kicks? Could he smell her? Did he understand what was happening, or did he just sense a change was coming but didn't know what it was?

On my last day of work before maternity leave, I was lying in bed, slowly waking up. Derek had just left for work. Oliver hopped up on the bed for his morning snuggles, something we did every day. I was reaching down to give him a pat when I felt a small pop and then a gush of wetness in my pants.

"Oh, no, no, no," I stammered, clumsily rolling out of bed, more fluid trickling out as I did. Oliver watched me, confused. I felt a flicker

Opening Hearts | 307

of guilt; how could I make him understand why I had pushed him away so suddenly?

Unfortunately, there wasn't time. I called Derek. Luckily, he wasn't too far away yet. While I waited for him to drive back, I called labor and delivery and let them know we were coming in.

We rushed to the hospital, and ten hours after my water broke, our baby girl, Zee, was born.

Between the surreal moments of holding my daughter for the first time and realizing that I was finally a mother, I thought of my first baby, Oliver. Was he okay? Was he wondering why I had left in such a hurry and where I was now? Would he be jealous of the baby?

We made sure to introduce the cats to her slowly. Between trips to the hospital and home, Derek left a baby blanket on the couch for the cats to smell. When we brought our daughter home, the other two didn't seem too interested, but Oliver was quite curious. He took long sniffs and looked very intently at her.

Breastfeeding was draining, both literally and figuratively. Zee proved to be just as voracious an eater as Oliver. I was told that "cluster feeding" was normal and should only last a day or two. Not Zee. She ate every hour for months. And if I set her down to do dishes, go to the bathroom, or, heaven forbid, eat food myself, she would cry.

As I carried her around the house, exhausted, trying to comfort her, Oliver would follow me around, curiously looking at me and Zee. I felt a prick of guilt that I barely spent any time with him, but Zee was so time-consuming in those early months.

Again, though, there were triumphs amongst the exhaustion.

"She just smiled, like a real smile!"

"Look at her lift her head. She's so strong!"

"Quick, she's rolling over!"

One day, months later, I put her in the bouncer in the living room to make myself some tea. I stepped around the corner to the kitchen, and within moments, Zee was squeaking.

"What're you squeakin' about now, Squeaker?" I said as I turned back into the living room and then stopped mid-step.

Oliver was sitting before Zee with his head bowed, and she was gleefully kicking her chubby baby legs, her little feet patting him on the head. He rubbed his chin on her toes, and she squealed in delight. I intervened when she grabbed hold of his fluffy fur, but he patiently waited for me to untangle him. No scratching or hissing whatsoever. Just pure, gentle love.

He's been her little buddy ever since. He always sits next to her and lets her pat him. He checks on her when she's in the playpen or highchair. He was right beside her as she learned to crawl, almost as if he was trying to show her how to do it. When he sees her coming down the hall, he heads her way, with his big, fluffy tail straight up in the air, purring away.

They have such a special bond now, and it warms my heart to watch them together, knowing my "furst" baby loves my first baby.

— Rebecca Fischer-Smith —

Mom's Farewell Wish

*When I am feeling low, all I have to do is watch
my cat, and my courage returns.*
~Charles Bukowski

"Take care of Boo Boo," my mom haltingly whispered to me from her hospital bed. She was having a moment of lucidity the day before she passed away at the age of eighty-six.

Those were the last words my mom spoke, and I inherited Boo Boo. Mom had fed the stray tuxedo cat twice a day ever since discovering her seven years prior in her Florida courtyard. After Boo Boo had a litter of five on her doorstep, Mom quickly had her spayed. She diligently found homes for the kitties after they were weaned and routinely left her garage door cracked open so Boo Boo could access a safe haven, complete with a cozy cat bed. But like a typical carefree outdoor cat, Boo Boo spent most of her time roaming the neighborhood, avoiding dogs and chasing lizards.

When Mom's health started to fail, I traveled from Connecticut to help her, including feeding Boo Boo every day. One evening, when we returned home from a late-night trip to the emergency room after Mom fell and hit her head, we found Boo Boo meowing and waiting for us at the front door. She seemed to know something was gravely wrong.

After a few months of steady decline, Mom passed away peacefully under hospice care. The day after, I tearfully went into the garage to retrieve a box to ship clothes to the funeral home in Maryland where

310 | Opening Hearts

our family cemetery plot is located. Much to my surprise, I found Boo Boo lying in the corner, whimpering and bleeding from a gaping wound on her back.

I needed to enlist the aid of a neighbor to help me put Boo Boo in a pet carrier to take her to the veterinarian. Until then, I had never picked her up or even petted her since she didn't really let anyone, other than Mom, get that close to her.

It was touch-and-go for several days. The vet concluded that Boo Boo must have been bitten by another animal, probably a raccoon. After surgery and several medications, she was finally ready to return home.

"She's such a sweet cat. You really should try keeping her inside," the young, fresh-faced vet said as she held Boo Boo next to me. Before I could reply, Boo Boo wiggled out of her arms and crawled onto my lap, rubbing her head against my hands and purring. And my grieving heart melted.

Little did the vet know, I had already asked neighbors and friends to help me find Boo Boo a home since adding her to my growing list of responsibilities seemed overwhelming during my season of personal sorrow. A family friend even warned me against taking in Boo Boo due to the inherent challenge of getting a life-long outdoor cat to adjust to new indoor routines like using a litter box and not eating houseplants.

But when I recalled Mom's final plea, I knew I had to give it a try.

After returning to my mother's place from the vet, I carefully opened the door of Boo Boo's carrier in the den. She immediately jumped onto the sofa, settled down, and began to purr. Right away, she became my little shadow, following me everywhere, even into the bathroom when I brushed my teeth. I think she enjoyed hearing her purrs echo off the walls of the walk-in shower.

She seemed to transition to indoor life seamlessly, never once sitting at the front door pining for her old haunts, as I had feared. She purred even when I wasn't petting her or talking to her.

Boo Boo was my brave companion as I sorted through every closet and drawer in Mom's three-bedroom condo. At night, when I had trouble sleeping from the emotional strain, I joined Boo Boo on her sofa, stroking her back while she purred to her heart's content. I

Opening Hearts

had never fully realized how deeply soothing and calming the presence of a purring cat could be until then. Even now, when I read, which is usually a solitary endeavor, Boo Boo curls up beside me to remind me that I'm not alone.

By the time I was able to move back home to Connecticut, I thought of Boo Boo as my cat. And her comforting presence proved to be a ray of sunshine in another dark time, because the following year I tragically lost my longtime beau to brain cancer. Then, when I became a full-time remote worker due to the pandemic a short while later, it seemed fortuitous that I had a feline home-office assistant to keep me company.

Through many of the unexpected curves on my life's path, I've observed the way that Boo Boo resiliently adjusts to change, like moving to a new locale. I recall that she quickly accepted her new surroundings by finding her favorite spot near the living room window to lounge in the afternoon sunbeams.

Even now, at age sixteen, she has quietly adapted to her slightly diminished ability to jump as high as she once did and has found another way to get onto my bed by stepping onto the nearby storage ottoman first. She also routinely finds moments of small joy — like when she expectantly turns upside down for tummy rubs — which always make me smile. Her appreciation for each day, expressed by her constant purring, reminds me to be grateful for the simple things in life.

The pastor who officiated at Mom's funeral highlighted Mom's farewell wish for Boo Boo's care during her memorial service, since it embodied Mom's selfless nature and her inclination to focus on the wellbeing of others, be they people or pets. I'm convinced that Mom's request for me to look after Boo Boo was a precious gift from her — because Boo Boo is still taking great care of me.

— Kay L. Campbell —

Foster Fail

*Having a cat will bless you with the
happiest days of your life.*
~Seanan McGuire

Seven foster cats have come into our home and left again. Every time it happens, we are sad — sometimes more than others. (My husband and I cried when a pair of ginger-coloured brothers named Ralph and Raymond left.) Even so, we know that saying goodbye is part of the foster experience. We provide respite, and then wish them well and move on, eager to see who we can help next.

Now, we are welcoming Bruce. Despite being described to us as a "healthy senior," he staggers out of his travel crate, a grumpy look on his graying face as he sneezes, gurgles and slides about on our slippery wooden floor. He accepts a couple of pats, takes a drink, finds the box we've set up for him and crawls in. We don't see him again for the rest of the day. The next day, he pops out periodically to grab a snack and check us out before disappearing again. What we do see makes us concerned.

"He's a wreck," I say to my husband. "No one is going to adopt this cat." Howard does not disagree.

Over the next few weeks, Bruce grows stronger and healthier. He comes out to say hello when we are in our basement family room and eventually makes it upstairs for the evening to spend time on someone's lap. A round of antibiotics fixes the sneezing, and his strange gurgle

Opening Hearts | 313

eventually resolves into a steady purr. But he's still older, with a wonky back end, an eye that keeps running, and a funny way of eating that makes me think his mouth hurts. And we learn he has kidney disease, which means a special diet and hard decisions down the road when his health deteriorates further.

How long does the Humane Society keep a cat? And who makes the decision? I'm not sure I want to know the answer.

The Humane Society asks for pictures. I send a couple, and the response is quick. Please try again. Grumpy is not a good look for a cat looking for a new home. I feel the pressure. Bruce is not at the Humane Society where someone can hear his purr and see his cheerful personality. He's depending on me to tell his story.

Bruce now greets us in the morning, looking for pats from both of us. He makes a point of being around if we are sitting nearby. He purrs almost constantly, a gentle hum in the background as we go about our day. He comes out to meet our friends. One night, a strange cat appears at the window. Bruce is quick to defend us, howling, pacing and scratching at the glass.

Eventually, we settle on a picture, and it's posted. I check the website. Bruce is on a page with five other older cats. Among the pictures of sleek, sharp seniours, he's the outlier. He's thin, with a rough coat. He looks stern. He looks old. Discouraged, I check out the featured pet of the week. It's a cat named Felix who has been looking for his forever home for 244 days. The number is sobering.

"Well, he stands out, doesn't he?" It's my husband, checking the website for himself. He sounds pleased. I return to the page where Bruce's picture is posted. This time, I see it differently. The other cats all look eerily similar: pleasant-faced and playful. Bruce looks unique. His story makes him sound a bit quirky. If someone is looking for something different, he's the guy.

My gut clenches. What have I done? What if someone is asking to adopt him right now as I stare at the screen? How long until I receive the email? *Bruce has a new home. Please, bring him back.*

These past few weeks, I'd started asking myself if it was fair to put Bruce through another change. I thought about the courage required for any animal to re-adjust, to cope with loss and learn to trust again. Now, I realise I'm the one who can't do it—adjust to an empty lap, a silent entrance, no laughing as I watch Bruce and my husband go through their bedtime routine.

The adoption clerk congratulates us on being Foster Failures. Apparently, it's a well-recognized phenomenon.

—Deb Stark—

The Kitten Who Never Grew

Some people come into our lives and quickly go.
Some stay for a while, leave footprints on our hearts,
and we are never, ever the same.
~Flavia Weedn, *Forever*

The veterinarian stared at the odd creature, with its large head and bony torso, hunched on the examining table. "How old did you say this kitten was?"

"Just over nine months." I rested my hands protectively on Kai's body. "He's a purebred Burmese."

The vet carefully moved him to the weigh scale. Kai let out a loud meow of protest. "He should be at least eight pounds." The vet frowned. "He weighs barely three."

He continued to examine Kai. "I've heard about this," he said finally, "but I've never seen it before. This kitten is a dwarf."

"A dwarf?"

"When the Burmese breed was being developed, there were some instances of dwarf cats. But I read that the dwarfism gene had been eliminated decades ago."

We exchanged a look. "I guess not," I said.

In keeping with the terrible luck that I'd been having in every part of my life, it seemed I'd gotten the one dwarf gene still floating around in the Burmese DNA pool.

Opening Hearts

Normally, I'd never have bought an expensive purebred. Not only was I unemployed at the time, but I knew there were thousands of non-purebreds out there needing homes.

In fact, I'd adopted a couple myself not long before purchasing Kai, after my first cat, an affectionate tortoiseshell named Prunella, had died at twenty-two. I'd rescued her from a barn when she was a kitten, and I was devastated. Four months after she died, I went to our local shelter and picked out Pippin, a sweet, rust-brown adult tabby.

"Can we get Pippin a kitten friend?" my eight-year-old niece asked eagerly. She and her mom — my sister — had recently moved in with me, and my niece had never had a kitten. As it happened, someone had just abandoned five kittens at my regular vet's office. He'd examined them, vaccinated them, and offered one to us free. We chose a fluffy, tabby-and-white cat and called her Bijou.

Bijou was a delight — until she started having seizures two months later. She'd shake, lose control of her bladder and bowels, and tumble off the couch or bed. Afterward, she'd be dazed and wobbly. My vet was shocked; all her littermates were fine. It appeared to be a brain tumour. I made the sad decision to have Bijou euthanized, and my niece was inconsolable.

This was just the latest in a string of major heartbreaks for me. In the previous two years, I'd lost the man and the job I loved, and Prunella had died. Then, Bijou died. I felt stuck and grieving in an endless tunnel of loss.

Soon after, I saw an ad for Burmese kittens, "home-raised, guaranteed free from congenital defects." No more brain tumours, I thought; no more upset little niece. The breeder had only two left. I fell so hard for the runt, a champagne-colored kitten with huge, soulful eyes, that I forgot to ask what her guarantee meant.

Kai was odd from the beginning: fussy about food, didn't want to play, preferred to snuggle with Pippin or on a human shoulder. But we adored him anyway.

Then, at just over three months, he stopped growing. My vet was mystified. There was nothing obviously wrong with Kai; his heart and lungs appeared fine. But he still wouldn't eat much, and I had to feed him by hand. Desperate, I took him to other vets, who also pronounced themselves mystified, until I found that one vet who knew about dwarfism.

"He's been tested for viruses?" he asked.

I nodded. "All negative."

The vet sighed. "I'm sorry. I don't know what can be done."

I called Kai's breeder.

She was stunned. "I've been breeding for ten years. I've never bred a dwarf before!"

"What about your guarantee?" I said.

"It means if a kitten dies under a year old, I'll replace it."

My heart sank.

Sometimes, Kai was so listless that I'd rush him to the animal clinic, where he'd be diagnosed as dehydrated and given subcutaneous fluids. The third time this happened, my vet said gently, "You know, nature doesn't intend for animals like this to live. It's only your love that's keeping him going."

By then, I'd started taking Kai with me whenever I could because I worried so much about him, and he complained with piteous meows whenever I tried to pry him off my shoulder. At one party, a woman stared into his mesmerizing, green-gold eyes and declared, "This cat is an old soul."

Shortly after his first birthday, I found Kai lying on the floor, alive but unmoving. Distraught, I wrapped him in a towel, put him on the car seat beside me, and headed for the nearest emergency vet hospital. With my ongoing bad luck, it was Saturday, and my regular vet was closed.

I drove with my right hand on his frail body, and I glanced at him at every red light. His eyes were half-closed and cloudy with mucus. "Kai," I sobbed, "you can go. It's okay! I don't want you suffering."

At one red light, I looked over. Miraculously, his eyes were wide open, clear, and beaming pure, powerful love right at me. He was rallying!

"Kai!" I cried, thrilled. "Hang in there, Kai!"

The light changed. A moment later, I glanced over. He was gone.

I realized then that he hadn't been rallying. He was saying goodbye.

I wept for the next month. I wept for everything: my lost love, my lost job, my three lost cats, even my traumatic, dysfunctional childhood. But all that crying felt cleansing — and somehow healing.

I called Kai's breeder again.

"He did make it to a year," she said, "but barely, so I'll honor my guarantee. I have kittens available, totally different bloodlines from Kai."

Still, I hesitated. How could any cat replace my magical, difficult, old-soul dwarf? Besides, did I really want to chance another animal from this woman?

When I discussed this with my vet, he said, "Take Jess, our vet tech, with you. She has two Burmese and is super knowledgeable about the breed. But," he added, "if you get one, pick the biggest kitten — no more runts!"

At the breeder's, Jess looked over every cat and kitten. "They're all terrific," she whispered. "You were just extremely unlucky with Kai."

We watched the kittens playing. The cat carrier I'd brought just in case was on the floor, the door open. At one point, the biggest of the litter walked in, sat down, and looked at me as if to say, "I'm your man. Let's go."

I had the strongest feeling that Kai was orchestrating it all.

I took that kitten home, and Moki turned out to be my feline soulmate — super-smart, funny, loyal, affectionate, and sensitive. If I was crying, he'd rush over to me and whimper until I stopped. He slept under the covers with me every night and rode on my shoulder during the day. Moki made it to fifteen, pretty good for a purebred.

So, I'll always be grateful to my little heartbreaker, Kai. Without him, my darling Moki would never have graced my life and finally brought me joy again.

— Marie-Lynn Hammond —

She'll Wait for Me

*Our perfect companions never have
fewer than four feet.
~Colette*

As the steam from my morning cappuccino scented the air, I pulled back the floral curtains above my kitchen sink and welcomed the warm hues of sunrise. But there, on my patio, sat an unexpected visitor: a brown-and-gray-striped tabby cat. She stared at me as if she'd been waiting for me.

I eased open the window and whispered, "Hello, pretty kitty. Where did you come from? New to the neighborhood?" She looked at me out of the corners of her green eyes while licking her paw, as if she was assessing my intentions. I told her, "I've got a piece of turkey for you."

I retrieved the meat from the refrigerator, approached the patio door, and clicked the latch. She startled at the sound, darting away, scaling the ivy and disappearing over the fence.

The next morning, we did the same dance, but she did not leave the yard when I clicked the latch. I placed the turkey slice on the ground and backed away, leaving the door open. The rail-thin, tiger-striped tabby inched toward me, low and slow like a tiger stalking prey.

"Aren't you hungry?" I whispered. "Come closer. I'm your friend."

She attacked the meat like it was a mouse and bolted away with it dangling from her jaws. She took it to the farthest corner of the yard

Opening Hearts

and devoured it.

I told our twenty-year-old son Nick about our mysterious visitor. Despite his autism and difficulty interacting with people, he was eager to connect with her. He said, "I want to see her. I think she will like me." When she returned, Nick opened the door and called out, "Come here, kitty. I have a treat for you."

To my astonishment, she walked straight up to him and ate the meat he'd placed on the patio. Nick timidly reached out his hand, and she allowed him to pet the top of her head. A spark ignited in Nick—a connection I'd never witnessed before.

Each day, they made progress. Eventually, she ventured into the house, drank water from a bowl, and nudged Nick's hand if he stopped petting her. Then one day, when he rubbed under her chin, she began to purr. It was as if the soothing vibration transferred between them and brought healing to both of them.

He talked to her about his problems at school, and I once heard him complain about me. "Mom gives me too many chores." I was glad he had a friend who listened without judgment.

We assumed she was a stray because she had no collar and was so thin. A vet visit confirmed that she had no identification chip and was generally healthy. Nick begged, "Can we keep her? Please?"

Since we had just been calling her "Pretty Kitty," I asked Nick to give her a proper name. Then, as if she knew we were talking about her, she sat down on her rear haunches, put her front paws straight out in front of her, and held her chin high. Nick said, "She is sitting like an Egyptian sphinx. I think she is telling us her name is Egypt."

She became ours—or perhaps we became hers. Egypt claimed territories throughout the house, but her favorite place was on Nick's lap. She also liked to curl up in a tight ball of fur on top of any clothes that Nick left on his bedroom floor. She preferred him over me, which made Nick proud and boosted his self-esteem. "She always picks me, Mom."

During the next few years, Egypt and Nick forged an unbreakable bond. She showed her devotion to him by putting live lizards into his size 14 shoes. She placed her paws over the shoe opening, and as the

Opening Hearts

lizard tried to escape, she pushed it back down, playing a feline form of Whack-a-Mole. Nick laughed until he cried, and she would strut around the room, proud of her mischief. Their relationship transformed Nick, making him more confident and independent.

A few years later, Nick faced a pivotal choice: an opportunity to attend a two-year special-education college that was about two hours away from home. He wanted to go but thought that he would miss Egypt too much. However, after visiting the campus, he decided to enroll, embracing this new chapter. During his time away, I called often, and Nick talked to Egypt through the speaker phone. Each time she heard his voice, she stopped what she was doing, fixed her gaze on the phone, and cocked her head to the side, as if she understood him. Their bond transcended distance.

Toward the end of his second year at school, I noticed that she seemed lethargic and was losing weight, so I took her to the vet. He said she was very ill and that I should prepare to let her go. I wondered if I should tell Nick because I knew he'd be upset, but I didn't want to deny him the opportunity to say goodbye. She was getting worse, so I gently told him the sad news that she might not be here when he came home for his semester break. He surprised me with his certainty as he declared. "Don't worry, Mom. She'll wait for me."

I did everything in my power to keep her comfortable and prolong her life. She spent a lot of time in my lap, and I'd often show her the calendar, pointing out the circled date when Nick would be home. "Please, wait for him, just twenty more days… ten more days… five more days… tomorrow."

She waited. When he came home, she could no longer jump onto his lap, so Nick curled up on the floor next to her. A few days later, her breathing was labored, and she stopped drinking water, so we talked about helping her go to "Kitty Heaven." Nick agreed that he did not want her to suffer. He cradled her in his lap as we drove to the veterinarian's office. Later, he said his tearful goodbyes, whispering final secrets into her ear.

On the way home, he sat in silence, staring out the car window as tears spilled down his face. I offered comfort. "She loved you so much,

Nick. You brought her into our home and gave her a wonderful life."

He wiped away his tears and tenderly confided, "I will miss her every day, and she will miss me, but we'll both be okay because I will see her again in heaven."

Through my own tears, I replied, "I hope she can be patient."

He steadied his voice, sat up straighter, and declared, "Don't worry, Mom. She'll wait for me."

— Nancy C. Anderson —

I Know She Loves Me

*I have felt cats rubbing their faces against mine and
touching my cheek with claws carefully sheathed.
These things, to me, are expressions of love.*
~James Herriot

I see stories and videos about people who dislike cats. They say that cats are heartless, have no soul, no loyalty, and no concern for their owners. Cats are aloof, fickle creatures who don't know how to love a person the same way a dog does.

To that, I say that person has never been patient enough to win the love of a cat. To look into their eyes as they purr, warmth billowing out from their little eyes straight from their soul. As they gently grab your hand, claws nowhere in sight, pulling it to their body to obtain some of the tender, loving scritches that they desire.

There's a particular warmth in the way that cats share their love, and it isn't always one that is easily read. My cat, Castiel, is a fantastic example of this.

Castiel is a twelve-year-old cat whom I've had since she was six weeks old. I found her abandoned in a wet cardboard box in a parking lot when I left work one day, and I knew the moment I heard her wailing that she would be coming home with me.

She's certainly a character, one who always begs for food and will eat cardboard when she doesn't get it. She's round, definitely overweight despite multiple attempts and measures to get her to lose weight.

She doesn't show love like one might expect from a cat. She rarely

Opening Hearts

cuddles with me, maybe once every couple of months if I'm lucky. She only accepts pets on her head and occasionally a belly rub, if the mood suits her. She hates being picked up and has a sixth sense for knowing when I'm approaching her to pick her up instead of just passing by.

But I know that she loves me.

I know it from the way that she follows me from room to room, never sitting on me or right next to me but an arm's length away, snoozing happily in a sunbeam while I work on a craft.

I know it from the way that she looks at me when I scratch her chin in just the right spot, her eyes squinted and blissed out from the affection. She's quite the purring machine.

I know it from how, when I'm crying, she'll come over and roll on her back, showing off her belly in offering to make sure I know that she's there for me.

I know it from how, whenever it's time for dinner, she'll sit so prim and proper next to her bowl, with quiet chirps and mews requesting her wet food as she waits patiently.

I know it from the times when I have to pick her up despite her displeasure, and her claws never come out while she's trying to push me away. Even though she hates it, she never lashes out to hurt.

I know it from how she desperately reaches for my hand when we're in the car on the way to the vet, her paw extending out from her carrier, and crying loudly until my fingers are resting against her toepads. Then, she is silent, just holding on.

I know it when she takes a treat from my fingers, her teeth so delicately making sure she's only grabbing the treat and not accidentally hurting my hand.

I know that even though she does not love me in the way that most people would assume, or desire, she loves me the way that she wants to love me.

And I wouldn't have it any other way.

— Stephanie Luevano-Powell —

Meet Our Contributors

Kristi Adams enjoys sharing her stories in numerous publications, including nineteen titles in the *Chicken Soup for the Soul* series. She and her husband make their home wherever the Air Force sends them, while their feline menace, Tiki, tags along and wreaks havoc every chance he gets. Learn more at kristiadamsmedia.com.

Carol Gentry Allen lives in Greer, SC. She is a Christian women's speaker and loves helping women be the best they can be. She is a published author and loves writing. Carol is also known as the Christian comedian, Miz Molly.

Nancy C. Anderson is the award-winning author of *Avoiding the Greener Grass Syndrome* and a contributing writer to thirty other books, including five titles in the *Chicken Soup for the Soul* series. She lives in Orange County, CA and recently celebrated her forty-sixth wedding anniversary. Learn more at NancyCAnderson.com.

Dave Bachmann is a retired teacher who worked with special needs students in Arizona for thirty-nine years. He now resides in California with his wife Jay, a retired kindergarten teacher, along with their Retriever Atti, writing stories and poems for children and grown-ups.

Garrett Bauman has published twenty pieces in the *Chicken Soup for the Soul* series and other works in *Yankee*, *The New York Times*, *Sierra* and many books and magazines. He and his wife have four children, four grandchildren and one orange ball of mayhem and mischief. He's a retired college professor.

This is **Jill Berni's** fifth story published in the *Chicken Soup for the Soul* series. She enjoys reading, writing and spending time with family and friends. She plans to write more short stories in the future.

Marie-Eve Bernier is a Québécoise living in New Zealand. She has published internationally in print and online. She loves reading and spending time in nature.

Barbara A. Besteni is a writer, spiritual seeker, former rock star, and animal lover. After thirty-five years of writing, copyediting, and producing content for local, national, and international television news, she retired from the corporate world to pursue her passion for writing.

Angie Blackledge received her passion for storytelling in 1983 as a young child with a blank spiral notebook and black pen. As an adult, she's written ten novels, two poetry books, and a series of homeschooling resources. When not writing she's the loving matriarch of her beautifully large, blended family in Missouri.

Elizabeth Brown is a retired school librarian. She enjoys cooking — especially chicken soup with matzo balls — in addition to volunteering and cataloging. Cats are her favorite pet, but she loves all animals and wildlife. She has published three preschool books and one adult book of short stories.

Louise Butler is a retired educator and author with advanced degrees in administration and economics. Her latest book, *I Shall Wear Ivory and Jet*, has led to numerous speaking engagements where she talks about the First Ladies of the United States. Butler enjoys good books, great friends and mediocre golf.

A pickleball enthusiast, **Kay L. Campbell** also enjoys mystery novels and social art. Her published works include a children's coloring/activity book, many devotionals and several greeting cards. This is her third story to be selected in the *Chicken Soup for the Soul* series. She resides in southern Connecticut with two tuxedo cats.

Thomas Canfield was born and raised in Connecticut and is all too familiar with long winters. He moved to Florida and then, to escape the sweltering heat, to the mountains of North Carolina. On a recent camping trip, he spotted the elusive Eastern Hellbender, a rare treat he hopes to repeat sometime in the near future.

Eva Carter is a frequent contributor to the *Chicken Soup for the Soul* series — publishing forty-eight stories so far. She enjoys writing, taking dancing classes, traveling and going out to dinner with her husband Larry and friends. She and Larry live in Dallas, TX with their two cats.

Christina Ryan Claypool is a former TV producer/reporter and author of the inspiring *Secrets of the Pastor's Wife: A Novel*. She has been featured on CBN's *The 700 Club* and *Joyce Meyer Ministries* TV show. Christina adores overcoming-the-odds true stories and anything that glitters. Learn more at christinaryanclaypool.com.

Annette M. Clayton has a master's degree in writing for children and young adults and has authored thirty books. In her spare time, she also enjoys hiking. Annette resides in a quiet Maryland town with her husband and twin daughters. Learn more at AnnetteMClayton.com.

James R. Coffey is a graduate of the University of Florida with degrees in psychology and anthropology. He is a life-long musician and multimedia writer whose work has appeared in numerous publications including *Journal of Compressed Creative Arts*, *AntipodeanSF*, *Red Cap Publishing* anthology, *History Defined*, and the *Chicken Soup for the Soul* series.

Laurie Spilovoy Cover resides in Tennessee, where she and her family live on an off-grid homestead with their nine cats. Most days you can find Laurie writing, vlogging, cooking, gardening, or thrifting for vintage decor. She has a wonderful husband and three ambitious young men.

Tracy Crump dispenses hope in her award-winning book, *Health, Healing, and Wholeness: Devotions of Hope in the Midst of Illness*. She has been published in a variety of publications, and her newsletter, "The Write Life," includes story callouts. Tracy's blog ministers to caregivers—our unsung heroes. Learn more at TracyCrump.com.

Amber Curtis resides in South Florida with her fiancé Calvin and their two newly adopted cats from Candy's Cats. She is blessed God gave her Sombra to help discover the companionship of a cat. Writing this story was therapeutic and she hopes anyone grieving can find comfort in this book, which celebrates the impact of cats.

This is **John Danko's** second story published in the *Chicken Soup for the Soul* series. His first story about his father appeared in *Chicken Soup for the Soul: Angels and the Miraculous*. John started his writing journey later in life but hopes to continue now that he's semi-retired. He enjoys all sorts of outdoor adventures throughout the year in Michigan.

Elton A. Dean is an educator, author, and retired soldier. He has published two children's books, *A Yeti Like Freddie: Talking to Kids About Autism* and *Brandon Sets Sail: A Story About Sharing Success*. His seven-year-old son co-authored the latter.

Artie DeMonte is a retired psychiatric social worker and musician/songwriter. In 2003, his late mother Rosalie asked Artie if he would "punch up" her novel and give it literary color. *The Wooden Spoon* was self-published on October 26, 2009. Artie is married to his beloved Jean.

Mary Grant Dempsey is a retired teacher and former owner of an independent bookshop. Her writing has appeared in newspapers, magazines, and eight titles in the *Chicken Soup for the Soul* series. She worked as a freelance writer for a local newspaper and has published a book of her short stories. Mary resides in Macon, GA.

Diana Derringer, author of *Beyond Bethlehem and Calvary* and caregiver for her husband, shares hope and joy through more than 1,300 devotions, articles, dramas, Bible studies, and poems in seventy-plus publications. She also writes international radio and television programs. Enjoy Words, Wit, and Wisdom at dianaderringer.com.

Lindsay Detwiler is a *USA Today* bestselling author of romance and thriller novels, including *The Widow Next Door* with HarperCollins. She is a high school teacher and lives with her husband, her cats, and her Great Dane Edmund. Email her at lindsayanndetwiler@gmail.com.

Mary DeVries has lived on three continents, in four countries, fifteen cities, and seven U.S. states. Along the way she has raised three children and remained married to the handsome guy she met at college freshman registration. She loves to write about anything and everything. Email her at marydj03@gmail.com.

Pamela Dunaj received scholarships from, and studied at, Parsons School of Design and New York University, both in New York City. She has been published before and won an award for her writing in 2011. Though she is originally from the East Coast and adores the ocean, she has happily resided in beautiful Colorado for many years.

Rita Durrett has been in education for over thirty-nine years. She is a mother and grandmother who, as she says, "belongs to a cat named Mousey and two big attack dogs that might lick an intruder to death but wouldn't bite unless someone gets between them and their food."

Ellen Fannon is an award-winning author, a retired veterinarian, a former missionary, and a church pianist/organist. She has published eight novels, and numerous stories and devotions. Visit Ellen's website, "Good for a Laugh," and sign up to follow her weekly blog at ellenfannonauthor.com.

Glenda Ferguson, who lives in Southern Indiana, received her education degrees from College of the Ozarks and Indiana University. Glenda writes devotionals for animal lovers called *All God's Creatures*. Speckles lived for fifteen years and is missed every day by Glenda, Tim, and Scrappy.

Rebecca Fischer-Smith is a writer and rancher from the Sierra Nevada foothills. Along with three cats, she has many cows and horses with her family. She is happily married with two children.

Manley Fisher is a retired educator who thoroughly enjoyed teaching English as a Second Language students. He is learning to play guitar, speak Dutch and French, and his bizarre sense of humor inspires his writing. He also enjoys woodworking and laughing and chatting with friends over coffee.

Betsy S. Franz is a freelance writer and photographer specializing in nature, wildlife, the environment and both humorous and inspirational human-interest topics. You can visit her online at betsyfranz.com; facebook.com/thenaturelady/; or at instagram.com/backyarder_1/.

Meet Our Contributors

Kathleen Gerard's writing has been widely published and anthologized. She is the author of three novels: *In Transit, Cold Comfort* and *The Thing Is*. Learn more at kathleengerard.blogspot.com.

Julia Gousseva teaches college-level writing courses and loves helping students find their voices. Her work has appeared in *Highlights for Children* and several titles in the *Chicken Soup for the Soul* series. She lives in the American Southwest with her family.

Robert Grayson, an award-winning former daily newspaper reporter, writes books for young adults. Among his books are one on animal actors and one on animals in the military. He also writes magazine articles on professional sports stars. He and his wife have a fervent passion for rescuing and helping kittens and cats.

Christine Grecsek is a writer, singer, and songwriter who works in nonprofit arts administration. Her short fiction has been published in regional magazines and won several awards. A heartfelt ode to peanut butter won her family a mixed case of gourmet nut butters. Sadly, none of them contained peanuts.

Marie-Lynn Hammond is happiest being with animals or being creative. A writer, editor, singer-songwriter and visual artist, she's rescued one dog, two horses, and countless cats and kittens. Recently she co-wrote a young-adult novel, *Moon Storm Rising*, under the pen name Kayden Quinn. Learn more at marielynnhammond.com.

Heather Harshman is an estate planning attorney (licensed in California, Oregon and Washington) a writer, and mother of two little ones. In between work and being a mom, she enjoys bicycling, traveling, gardening, and camping with her family.

Oregon-based author and journalist **Melissa Hart** is the author, most recently, of *Down Syndrome Out Loud: 20+ True Stories about Disability and Determination*. Her work has appeared in *Smithsonian, Nat Geo Kids, The New York Times*, and numerous other publications. She has five cats, six chickens, and a very patient Terrier.

Heather Hartmann resides in O'Fallon, MO with her husband, two sons, and two cats. This will be her second publication in the *Chicken Soup for the Soul* series. Heather has also had several fiction pieces published in a locally produced anthology by Saturday Writers, a Chapter of the Missouri Writers Guild.

Jill Haymaker is an author of clean western contemporary romances set in the Rocky Mountains of her home states of Colorado and Montana. She is currently working on novel number 33. This is her tenth story published in the *Chicken Soup for the Soul* series. Email her at jillhaymaker@aol.com.

Laurie Heard has been writing for many years but has rarely shared her prose. In the last several years she has shared some of her pieces with family and friends. With the reactions she has received, she plans to continue to write stories that will uplift, inspire and perhaps tickle a heart or two along the way.

Lynn Hendricks is an aspiring picture book writer, the mother of two amazing daughters, the grandmother of a fabulous grandson, and an accredited elementary school teacher.

Sheila Hollihan-Elliot was previously a documentary film writer and nonfiction book author and since 2003 has been senior editor of Hudson River Valley's lifestyle *Hook* magazine. She believes in social change and loves cats! She is writing a book about the strays she rescues and helps.

Jeffree Wyn Itrich has been writing since she was a little girl. Eventually, she attended the graduate school of journalism at UC Berkeley, which prepared her for a career in communications. In addition to writing hundreds of articles, she is also the author of three novels, a children's book, and a cookbook.

S.R. Karfelt is married with children and spent a lifetime scribbling stories on random bits of paper while working in the technology field by day. She loves learning, reading, and making art with glue sticks. Writing memoir and magical realism stories are her passion. She lives in the Finger Lakes area of New York State.

Judy Kellersberger has written several hundred stories and songs in addition to being published in the *Chicken Soup for the Soul* series. Pete Seeger featured her poem/song "Tribute to the Hudson River" for the Quadricentennial. "Tribute to a Firefighter" hit #1 on Cash Box. Judy is completing a book of short stories and adventures.

Jon M. Ketcham is a two-time cancer survivor who offers hope to the hopeless and helps the broken re-kindle their dreams through his writing and speaking. He maintains a YouTube channel (@jonketcham) where his video series "3 Tatts and a Tale" makes art from his pain so that others won't feel so alone and unloved. He's also written five books.

Chip Kirkpatrick retired from AT&T and lives in NE Florida with Grace, his wife of forty-eight years, two cats and a flock of chickens. He has published several books and writes articles on metal detecting for *American Digger* magazine.

Pamela K. Knudsen is the author of the children's book, *Two Cats, a Mermaid and the Disappearing Moon*. Her short stories have been featured in several publications. She's a volunteer for a cat sanctuary and a community-radio volunteer DJ. Pamela lives in Laguna Beach, CA. Learn more at pamelakknudsen.com.

Helen Krasner is a retired helicopter pilot who now writes regularly for various magazines and websites, and has also published several books. She has had six stories published previously in the *Chicken Soup for the Soul* series. She lives in Derbyshire, in the middle of England, with her partner David and their three cats.

This is **T. Jensen Lacey's** twentieth story to appear in the *Chicken Soup for the Soul* series. Lacey has twenty-four-plus books and book contributions published and, as a freelance journalist, has more than 900 articles in newspapers and magazines. Lacey's work has appeared in *Southern Living*, *Alabama Magazine*, *Vanderbilt Magazine* and more. Learn more at TJensenLacey.com.

Monica Lawson spent her motherly, grandmotherly, great grandmotherly years writing short stories for the children in the family. Though never published, stories included escapades of the animals that came and went throughout the family. Monica includes her animal "kids" in paintings and stories for twenty-one great-grandkids.

Brenda Leppington lives in Saskatchewan, Canada and is retired from a career in health information management. Brenda enjoys writing, travelling, riding horses, and enjoying the freedom that comes with retirement.

Alexes Lester lives and works in Toronto, Ontario, Canada. She enjoys writing horror, dark fantasy and science fiction short stories but has also published nonfiction. She finds inspiration from studying old myths and legends, classic gothic horror and dystopian works, as well as women's history.

Laird Long is a big guy with a sense of humor. Laird has made friends with many cats, and believes the feeling was mutual.

Victoria Lorrekovich-Miller is a writer, teacher, and MFA Candidate at Saint Mary's College. Her stories and creative nonfiction have been featured in *Pithead Chapel Journal*, *Kveller*, *Piker Press*, *Chicken Soup for the Soul*, *The Bark*, *Dog and Kennel*, *WOW*, *YourTeen*, and more. She and her uber supportive husband have four cool kids who are making our world kinder.

Stephanie Luevano-Powell has been in love with writing since she was handed a copy of *The Black Stallion* in her fourth-grade class. She loves reading, writing, crafting, playing *Dungeons and Dragons*, and spending time with her spouse and two cats, Castiel and Jarlaxle.

Carissa Ann Lynch is the *USA Today* and *Wall Street Journal* bestselling author of *The Bachelorette Party*, *The Traitors*, *The Summer She Disappeared*, and more. She lives in southern Indiana, where she spends time with her partner, children, cats, and books. Carissa also works as a crisis intervention counselor.

Leeann Lynton enjoys writing fiction and an occasional true story. Her house is currently shared with two rescued cats.

Irene Maran is a retired high school administrator residing at the Jersey Shore with her four cats and six box turtles. She runs a weekly prompt writing group and is a professional storyteller. Her humorous stories about animals, family and friends are enjoyed by many in her community. "Laughing keeps you young."

Joan Friday McKechnie has several books published under the name Joan Friday which you can find on Amazon. She has also had stories and poems in children's magazines and a story about another cat in the *Chicken Soup for the Soul* series. Joan lives in southeastern Pennsylvania.

Laura McKenzie is a retired kindergarten teacher living in the heart of Texas with her husband Doug. She enjoys traveling and spending time with her children and grandchildren. Laura loves to read, write and volunteer at her church's food pantry. Laura is very grateful to be part of the Chicken Soup for the Soul family.

Barb Miller is a former K–12 teacher, receiving a B.A. in English/Journalism and a Master's in Curriculum and Instruction. She currently pursues a writing career, creating short fiction, personal narratives, and children's stories. She enjoys hiking, swimming, and spending time with grandchildren.

Timothy Nipko is a retired U.S. Coast Guard chief petty officer living with his wife in Colorado Springs, CO. He caught the author bug when a short article he had submitted was published in 2009. His hope now is that others will enjoy reading his works as much as he loves writing them.

Charlotte Louise Nystrom is a writer and poet from the rocky coast of Maine. When she isn't writing, Charlotte enjoys quiet pastimes — painting, yoga, hiking with her son, and drinking too much coffee. Charlotte strives to capture words that bridge connections and make the world a little softer.

Mary F. Oves is a retired teacher, avid traveler and freelance writer who resides in New Jersey. And while Mimi the Cat now lives too far away for visits, a handsome neighbor cat visits her on occasion for yummy snacks and warm hugs. Mary has nicknamed him "George" due to his striking resemblance to George Clooney.

Liz Palmer received her MBA from the University of Colorado in 1983. Splitting her time between Southern California and Las Vegas, Liz was an accountant and now does volunteer work and coaches track and field. She was crowned Ms. Senior Nevada 2022 and Ms. Senior California 2024 and was third runner up at the national level both years.

Wendy Joyce Patterson is a huge nerd and certified crazy cat lady.

Meet Our Contributors

Originally from Canada's East Coast, she now lives in Ottawa, Ontario with her two cats.

Kendra Phillips is a stay-at-home mom of two young daughters. In her spare time, she enjoys blogging and has worked as an editor for several online publications. Kendra loves writing stories that are filled with heart and humor. She is currently working on her first novel.

As a frequent recipient of her grade school's punishment du jour, the 500-word essay, **Marsha Porter** took up the pen at an early age. She came to love turn of phrase wordplay that might stir a reaction in the teachers who assigned what should have been, but wasn't, a dreaded task.

Rachel Remick lives in Tampa, FL where she writes and cares for dogs. A multiple contributor to the *Chicken Soup for the Soul* series, her stories have also appeared in *Rosebud*, *ellipsis...*, and *Bluestem*.

Donna L. Roberts is a native of upstate New York who lives and works in Europe. She is a tenured university professor who holds a Ph.D. in Psychology. Donna is an animal and human rights advocate, and when she is not teaching, researching, or writing, she can be found at her computer buried in rescue pets.

Rebecca Ruballos is a language professor and learning specialist at Berkeley College. She received her Bachelor's in Education from Nyack College and her Master's in Instruction and Curriculum from Kean University. She enjoys writing, traveling, and spending time with her grandchildren.

Candace Sams graduated from Texas A&M University and worked as a police officer with many agencies around the USA. She and her husband now live in a rural area with many fur babies by their sides.

Ramona Scarborough has given birth to ten books and one-hundred and sixty of her articles have been adopted by magazines, anthologies, and online venues. She writes a weekly article for her local newspaper. Ramona lives in Sacramento, CA with her husband Chris and their latest rescue cat, Muffin.

Leslie C. Schneider lives in Montana with Bill, her husband of fifty-five years. Multi-published in the *Chicken Soup for the Soul* series, she taught herself to write while raising her children on the Montana prairie. Besides writing, Leslie enjoys doing Ukrainian Eggs, quilting, crochet and bobbin lace.

Laurel L. Shannon is the pseudonym of this Ohio author. She lives with her Australian Terrier rescue, her appointed head of security who's never met an enemy but is always on guard against Bigfoot, aliens and ax murderers. Laurel also has two rescue cats who consider the dog to be an idiot and aren't sure about Laurel either.

Mandy Shunnarah (they/them) is an Appalachian and Palestinian-American writer in Columbus, OH. Mandy's first book, *Midwest Shreds*, was released in 2024 from Belt Publishing, and their second book, a poetry collection titled *We Had Mansions*, is forthcoming from Diode Editions in 2025. Learn more at mandyshunnarah.com.

Billie Holladay Skelley received her bachelor's and master's degrees from the University of Wisconsin. A retired clinical nurse specialist, she is the mother of four and grandmother of three. Billie enjoys writing, and her work crosses several genres. She spends her non-writing time reading, gardening, and traveling.

Rosie Sorenson, MA, MFT, is a former healthcare administrator and psychotherapist. Her work appears in *The Magic of Memoir: Inspiration for the Writing Journey* as well as numerous publications. Her book, *If You'd Only Listen: A Medical Memoir of Gaslighting, Grit & Grace* is available at all retailers. Learn more at RosieSorenson.com.

Deb Stark lives in rural Canada with her husband, a foster cat that refused to leave, and too many raccoons to count. Her stories have been published in places such as *The New Quarterly*, *GRAIN*, and *Fiddlehead*. In 2023, she was shortlisted for *MilkHouse* magazine's Best in Rural Writing contest.

Diane Stark is a wife, mother of five, and freelance writer. She is a frequent contributor to the *Chicken Soup for the Soul* series. She loves to write about the important things in life: her family and her faith.

Karen Storey is an award-winning fiction writer featured on the acclaimed *Bestseller Experiment*. Her stories have been published and placed in several international competitions and anthologies. Originally from New York, she lives in Warwickshire, England with her husband, whose surname Storey was the perfect wedding gift.

Gwen Swick writes poems and short stories and has a musical career. She is a songwriter, arranger, lyricist, and vocalist. Most of her career has been spent writing, recording, and performing across Canada with the groups Quartette and The Marigolds, and as a solo artist.

In addition to her stories for the *Chicken Soup for the Soul* series, award-winning author **Susan Traugh** writes curricula for teens with special needs. Her daughter, Annie, has accepted her mental illness and embraced healing. She just graduated college, with honors, and will pursue a career in social work. Learn more at susantraugh.com.

Dorenda Crager Watson is a writer of humorous essays, whimsical children's poetry, and simple living anecdotes. In addition to the *Chicken Soup for the Soul* series, her work has appeared in the children's magazine *Root & Star*, the *Minimalism Life Journal*, and the "Sunny Skyz" blog. Email her at

Meet Our Contributors

dcwatzworld@gmail.com.

As an escapee from the 9 to 5 office life, **Jodi M. Webb** writes from the Pennsylvania mountains about everything from treehouses to pretzels to jackhammers. She's working on a novel about the World War II home front and a children's book about foxes. Peek at the life of a writer (and reader) on her blog at www.jodiwebbwrites.

Over the years **Janet Wells** and her husband have raised nine cats—never more than three at once. They currently share their Western Pennsylvanian log house with their son and three tabbies. Mother of two and retired teacher of children with learning differences, Janet revels in retirement. She quilts, photographs nature, and writes.

Audrey Wick loves cats, books, and happily-ever-afters. She's an author with Harlequin and a full-time English professor at Blinn College (Texas). Her work has appeared in *Woman's World*, *Writer's Digest*, and through college textbook content with Cengage. Connect with her at audreywick.com and on Instagram and X @WickWrites.

Having retired as Supervisor of the NYS Research Library in 2010, **Roger A. Wilber** began writing in earnest, stories ranging from factual Civil War info to a series of fantasy books called *Jack & Jackson*. Wilber's loving, feline companion, Shadow, has always been his buddy and muse, sleeping on his lap or next to the keyboard as he types.

Jessica Lorin Wood lives in Connecticut with her husband and daughter. She received her Bachelor of Arts from Franklin Pierce University. Jessica enjoys painting, crocheting, and being outdoors with her family. She is currently working on a book about funny relationship experiences.

Originally from Syracuse, NY, **Sandy Wright** earned a B.A. from University of Miami. Now retired and living in the Rochester, NY area, she worked as a secretary, paralegal and musician, playing guitar and singing. She has a 45 record and music video of her originals, and performed in Daytona Beach, San Francisco, and Tokyo.

Meet Amy Newmark

Amy Newmark is the bestselling author, editor-in-chief, and publisher of the *Chicken Soup for the Soul* book series. Since 2008, she has published more than 200 new books, most of them national bestsellers in the U.S. and Canada, more than doubling the number of *Chicken Soup for the Soul* titles in print today. She is also the author of *Simply Happy*, a crash course in Chicken Soup for the Soul advice and wisdom that is filled with easy-to-implement, practical tips for enjoying a better life.

Amy is credited with revitalizing the Chicken Soup for the Soul brand, which has been a publishing industry phenomenon since the first book came out in 1993. By compiling inspirational and aspirational true stories curated from ordinary people who have had extraordinary experiences, Amy has kept the thirty-two-year-old Chicken Soup for the Soul brand fresh and relevant.

Amy graduated *magna cum laude* from Harvard University where she majored in Portuguese and minored in French. She then embarked on a three-decade career as a Wall Street analyst, a hedge fund manager, and a corporate executive in the technology field.

Her return to literary pursuits was inevitable, as her honors thesis in college involved traveling throughout Brazil's impoverished northeast region, collecting stories from regular people. She is delighted to have come full circle in her writing career — from collecting stories "from the people" in Brazil as a twenty-year-old to, three decades later, collecting stories "from the people" for Chicken Soup for the Soul.

When Amy and her husband Bill, the CEO of Chicken Soup for the Soul, are not working, they are visiting their four grown children and their spouses, and their six grandchildren.

Follow Amy on X and Instagram @amynewmark. Listen to her free podcast — Chicken Soup for the Soul with Amy Newmark — on Apple, Google, or by using your favorite podcast app on your phone. You can also find a selection of her stories on Medium.

Thank You

We owe huge thanks to all our contributors and fans. We received thousands of submissions for this popular topic, and we spent months reading all of them. Laura Dean and Crescent LoMonaco read all of them and narrowed down the selection for Publisher and Editor-in-Chief, Amy Newmark. Susan Heim did the first round of editing, and then Associate Publisher D'ette Corona chose the perfect quotations to put at the beginning of each story, and Amy edited the stories and shaped the final manuscript.

As we finished our work, D'ette continued to be Amy's right-hand woman in working with all our wonderful writers. Barbara LoMonaco, Kristiana Pastir, and Elaine Kimbler jumped in to proof, proof, proof. And, yes, there will always be typos anyway, so please feel free to let us know about them at webmaster@chickensoupforthesoul.com, and we will correct them in future printings.

The whole publishing team deserves a hand, including our Vice President of Production & COO, Victor Cataldo, and our graphic designer, Daniel Zaccari, who turned our manuscript into this beautiful, entertaining book.